Friedrich Hasselquist, Carolus Linnaeus

**Voyages and travels in the Levant, in the years 1749, 50, 51, 52**

Friedrich Hasselquist, Carolus Linnaeus

**Voyages and travels in the Levant, in the years 1749, 50, 51, 52**

ISBN/EAN: 9783742891655

Manufactured in Europe, USA, Canada, Australia, Japa

Cover: Foto ©Andreas Hilbeck / pixelio.de

Manufactured and distributed by brebook publishing software (www.brebook.com)

Friedrich Hasselquist, Carolus Linnaeus

**Voyages and travels in the Levant, in the years 1749, 50, 51, 52**

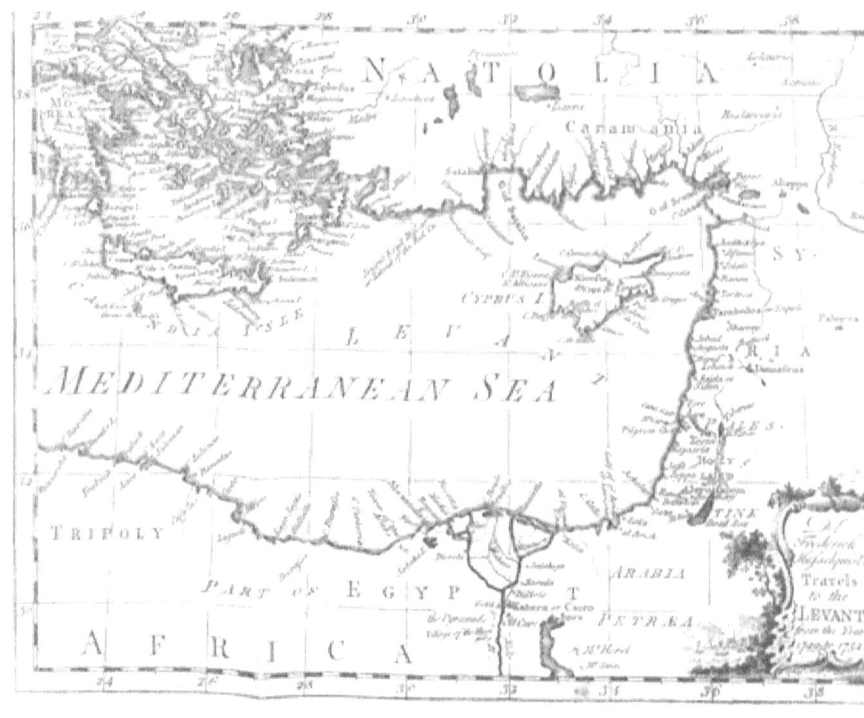

# VOYAGES
## AND
# TRAVELS
### In the LEVANT;

In the YEARS 1749, 50, 51, 52.

CONTAINING

Obfervations in **Natural Hiſtory, Phyſick, Agriculture, and Commerce:**

PARTICULARLY

On the Holy Land, and the Natural Hiſtory of the SCRIPTURES.

Written originally in the Swediſh Language, By the late FREDERICK HASSELQUIST, M. D. Fellow of the Royal Societies of UPSAL and STOCKHOLM.

Publiſhed, by Order of her preſent Majeſty the Queen of *Sweden*, By CHARLES LINNÆUS, Phyſician to the King of Sweden, Profeſſor of Botany at Upſal, and Member of all the Learned Societies in Europe.

---

LONDON,

Printed for L. DAVIS and C. REYMERS, oppoſite Gray's-Inn-Gate, Holborn, Printers to the ROYAL SOCIETY.

MDCCLXVI.

# ADVERTISEMENT.

A Few Copies of Dr. Hasselquist's Travels into the Holy Land, &c. in the Swedish Language, having found their Way into this Kingdom, Application was made to an ingenious Gentleman, who had lived some Time in Sweden, to translate them into *English*. An Opportunity of furnishing the Learned of this Country with so curious a Work, was not displeasing to One, who had been well acquainted with the Merits and Abilities of the Author, being himself a Pupil of the celebrated Dr. Linnæus. He accordingly undertook, and before his Departure from London finished, the following Translation; which indeed suffers in point of Stile, from the Translator's not being a Native of England, and from his adhering too closely to the Idiom of the Swedish Language: but it is hoped that when the candid Reader considers the great Difficulty of finding a Person sufficiently versed in Natural History, and the Swedish Language, and at the same time willing to undertake such a Task, he will rather forgive Imperfections, than wish to have deprived the Republic of Letters of so agreeable an Acquisition.

# ERRATA.

| Page | line | For | Read |
|---|---|---|---|
| 17, &c. | | naturalia, | natural Curiosities, |
| 29 | line 19 | not, | now. |
| 32 | 18 | was, | as. |
| 77 | 5 | February, | September. |
| 78 | 35 | Officers, | Officers Slaves. |
| 109 | 4 | even, | ever. |
| 110 | 21 | unfit, | only fit. |
| 132 | 1 | 12th of April, | 9th of April. |
| 157 | 2 | | here against the Bashaw. |
| 183 | 2 | **Mahhalia,** | Mammalia. |
| 193 | 10 | **Pirus,** | Picus. |
| 194 | 8 | Nuonida, | Numida. |
| 200 | 8 | Pirus, | Picus. |
| 222 | 17 | scolubrina, | colubrina. |
| 223 | 4 | Echencis | Echeneis. |
| 251 | 20 | veticum, | creticum. |
| 274 | 27 | Aga-onyx | Agat-onyx. |
| 437 | | Ichneumon | Ichneumon. |
| 444 | 7 | Crab-Treee, | Carob-Tree. |
| 450 | 20 | Moses, | Mosses. |
| 452 | 17 | a fruit, | a fruitful. |

# VOYAGES

## AND

# TRAVELS

In the LEVANT;

In the Years 1749, 50, 51, 52.

# CONTENTS.

| | Page |
|---|---|
| VOYAGE to Smyrna. | 1 |
| Travels in Natolia to Magnesia. | 33 |
| Alexandria. | 52 |
| Rosetta. *serpents acco.t of 63....* | 54 |
| From Cairo to the Pyramids. | 66 |
| Description of the Mecca Caravan. | 77 |
| The Sepulchres of the Mummies. | 84 |
| Damiata. | 108 |
| The Holy Land. | 116 |
| Jerusalem. | 120 |
| Jericho. | 125 |
| Bethlehem. | 143 |
| Palestine, Syria, Nazareth, Tyre, Sidon, &c. | 151 |
| Voyage to Cyprus. | 169 |
| Voyage to Rhodes, Chio and Smyrna. | 173 |

### Natural Curiosities.

| | |
|---|---|
| Quadrupeds. | 183 |
| Birds. | 193 |
| Amphibia. | 214 |
| Fish. | 223 |
| Insects. | 228 |
| Worms. | 239 |
| Plants. | 240 |
| Stones. | 273 |
| Natural History of Palestine. | 276 |
| Plants, Animals, &c. mentioned in the Scriptures. | 286 |
| Materia Medica. | 293 |
| Diseases and their Remedies. | 380 |
| Observations on Commerce. | 395 |
| The Author's Letters to Dr. Linnæus. | 403 |

The Map to face the Title.

Books printed for L. DAVIS and C. REYMERS.

THE Antiquities of EGYPT and NUBIA; engraved by the famous Mark Tufcher, of Nurenburg, from near 200 Defigns, accurately taken on the Spot, by Capt. Norden, F. R. S. elegantly printed on a Writing Royal Paper, 2 vol. Folio, Price bound 4l. 4s.

Capt. Norden's Travels in Egypt and Nubia, printed in one Volume Octavo, with Plates, 6s.

The Natural History of Norway, by the Right Rev. E. Pontoppidan, Bishop of Bergen; with 28 Copper-plates, Folio, Price bound, 1l. 1s.

Mr. Bingham's Antiquities of the Christian Church, in Twenty-three Books; together with his other Pieces. In 2 vols. Folio, illustrated with Maps, &c. Price 18s. bound.

The History of England; as it relates to Religion and the Church. By F. Warner, D. D. Rector of Queen Hithe, London, and of Barnes in Surry. 2 vols. Folio, pr. 2l. 2s.

An Ecclesiastical History; from the Birth of Christ, to the present Time. Written originally in French, by Mr Formey, Secretary to the Accademy of Sciences at Berlin. To which is added, an Appendix, giving an Account of the People called Methodists. 2 vols. price bound, 10s.

A Key to the New Testament; giving an Account of the several Books, their Contents, their Authors, and the Times, Places, and Occasions, on which they were respectively written. With an Introduction, concerning the Jewish Sects or Parties alluded to in the Gospels. Price 2s. 6d. bound.

The Beauties of England, comprehended in a pocket volume: Giving a succinct Description of the Antiquities of this Kingdom; the Seats of the Nobility and Gentry; the Remains of Palaces, Monasteries, Camps, and Castles; the Market towns, Cities, &c. the two Universities; London and Westminster. Intended as a Travelling Pocket Companion, pointing out whatever is curious in Art and Nature. Price bound 3s.

A Voyage to South America, describing at large the Spanish Cities, Towns, and Provinces on that Continent, with their History, natural, commercial, &c. by George Juan and Ant. de Ulloa, F. R. S. &c. 2 vol. 8vo. with Plates, price bound 12s.

Travels through part of Europe, Asia Minor, Syria, Palestine, Mount Sinai, &c. by the Hon. Mr. Van Egmond and Professor Heyman, 2 vol. 8vo. with Plates, price bound 10s.

Dr. Kampfer's History of Japan and Siam, natural and civil, with 45 Copper-plates, 2 vols. Folio, price bound 1l. 10s.

Antiquitates Asiaticæ, per Edm. Chishull, Folio, Royal Paper, price bound 1l. 1s.

Mr Chishul's Travels in Turkey, with a Preface by Dr. Mead, Folio, price bound 15s.

# SOME ACCOUNT

OF

## Dr. HASSELQUIST,

Written by

## CHARLES LINNÆUS, M.D.

FREDERICK Hasselquist was born the third of January 1722, at Tœrnvalla in East Gothia. His father Andrew Hasselquist, was curate there, and had the least income of any clergyman in the diocese. He died during the minority of his son, in indigent circumstances; his mother Maria Helena Pontin, being weak both in body and mind, was put into the infirmary at Vadstena. This Frederick therefore would have been unnoticed in life, if his uncle, the Rev. Mr. Pontin, had not taken compassion on him, and kept him with his children at the school in Linkœping; but he was soon deprived of this Benefactor, and obliged to support himself by teaching young children, until he was of age to go to the University.

In the year 1741, he came to the University of Upsala, where he was obliged to content himself with instructing others for trifling gratifications, but by this had the advantage of living constantly at the University, and daily hearing the lectures of the Professors. His inclination was immediately bent for Physic, and Natural History soon became his favourite study; he had also some talents for Poetry. The Faculty perceived the fervour with which our youth studied those Sciences his inclination led him to, and therefore in 1746 gave him a royal stipend. In 1747, he gave the first proof of the proficiency he had made in his studies, in his Dissertation on the Virtues of Plants, which he wrote well, and defended strenuously. In one of my botanical lectures in the same year, I enumerated the countries of which we knew the Natural History, and those of which we are ignorant. Amongst the latter was Palestine; with this we were less acquainted than with the remotest parts of India; and though the Natural History of this remarkable country was the most necessary for Divines, and Writers on the Scriptures, who have used their greatest endeavours to know the animals therein mentioned, yet they could not, with any degree of certainty, determine which they were, before some one had been there, and informed himself of the Natural History of the place. This is the more surprizing, as Botany is much indebted to several industrious Divines, who have strictly examined the plants of other countries; but though many of the Romish clergy travel to Palestine every year, not one has ever troubled himself upon this subject. Hasselquist was very desirous of being the first who should inform the Public of the Natural History of Palestine, and was determined to accomplish it. He imparted his design to me soon after, but, surprized at his enterprising spirit, I represented to him the length of the way, the great difficulties, the many dangers, and the very considerable expences which would attend such an undertaking, and lastly, his indifferent state of health, in particular his weak lungs, as he was subject

ject to spitting of blood: but he urged it the more, as weak lungs can only be cured by travelling and change of climate, and was enough determined in his resolution, to say, he would rarather walk all the way, than have his purposes crossed. His mind was fixed on the voyage; he therefore sollicited for some of the legacies left by persons of distinction for those who intend to travel, but fortune did not favour him in this attempt. He prevailed on his countrymen to contribute something towards this journey; when he had got this, he sollicited the Faculty of Physicians and they gave him two of the King's stipends, the Faculty of Civilians gave one, soon after the Philosophic, and at length the Theologic, gave him each a stipend. But how little was this proportioned to such an expensive undertaking Hasselquist in the mean time was preparing: he began to study the Arabian and other eastern languages; and that this enterprize might not obstruct his academical studies and designs, he gave the usual specimens of his abilities, viz. he was examined, he wrote, and defended his Dissertation, for the Degree, read Lectures, &c. that he might, though absent, receive those honours in Physic, which a youth of his merit and learning had a right to claim; therefore the degree of Doctor of Physic was conferred on him on the 8th of March 1751, at which time he was in Cairo. The Faculty was well acquainted with his industry and narrow circumstances, and therefore gave him gratis all Lectures, Examinations, Præsidia and the Promotion.

In the spring 1749, Hasselquist already a licentiate went to Stockholm, having first finished his academical studies, where he read Lectures on Botany

tany during the summer, and got the good graces of every lover and patron of this Science. He prepared himself every day for his Voyage, and the Levant Company offered him a free passage to Smyrna.

THE 7th of August he went on board, and arrived at Smyrna on the 26th of November. It was his good fortune to find Mr. Andrew Rydelius, Consul General from Sweden, at Smyrna, who was his countryman and relation, and received him with paternal kindness, and forwarded his undertaking by every means in his power. He staid in Smyrna all the winter, and beheld all the productions of nature in that temperate climate. In March 1750, he travelled to *Magnesia* in *Natolia*, viewed mount *Sipylus*, and returned again to the worthy Rydelius in Smyrna.

IN the beginning of May 1750 he left Smyrna, travelled by way of Alexandria and Rosetta, arrived, in July, at Cairo, the capital of Egypt; here he remained near a year, and had the best opportunities of informing himself of the singularity of the climate for which it has always been famous. Here he viewed the *Pyramids*, one of the seven wonders of the world; descended into the sepulchres of the *Mummies*; observed the strange rising and falling of the *Nile*; collected the scarcest productions of Nature; and this he did with more attention, than any one had done before him. During this time he corresponded diligently with his friends in Sweden, and filled his letters with curious Experiments and Observations, which were inserted in the papers printed twice a week in Stockholm under the title of *Literary News*, and all who read them, were prepossessed in favour of this attentive traveller. Our Hasselquist therefore was not forgot

in

# Dr. HASSELQUIST.

in his own country. The Faculty of Physicians proposed him as Professor extraordinary of Physic to the vacant place, and the Royal Academies at Upsala and Stockholm chose him a *Member* of their Societies; he made himself worthy of these honours, by the excellent Observations, which he sent to both Societies, which are printed in their Transactions. In those of Upsala for the year 1750, are inserted his Observations and Treatises on the *Egyptian Acacia*, which affords the Gum Arabic, page 9. The *Camel-Deer*, p. 15. The *Jumping Mouse*, p. 17. The *Oriental Thrush*, p. 21. The *Coote*, p. 22. The *Viper* of the Shops, p. 24. The horned *Viper*, p. 27. The horned *Snake*, p. 28. The *Scinc*, p. 30, and in the transactions of Stockholm for 1750. The *Endemical Disease of Aleppo*, p. 136. 1751. The *Hawk*, p. 196. The preparation of *Sal Ammoniac*, p. 259. 1752. The *Locusts*, being used for food in Arabia, p. 76. The mountain *Rat*, p. 123. It was surprising to see how anxious the nation was to support Dr. Hasselquist, when he lived in an expensive place, where he could not advance a step without considerable charges, and wanted money to accomplish his design. The lovers of Science contributed several times, and raised in a very short time about one hundred and ninety pounds; an instance, scarcely to be met with amongst the most opulent nations.

Dr. Hasselquist at length left Cairo in March 1751, and went over *Damiata*, *Jaffa*, and the *Holy Land*. Hence he travelled to *Jerusalem* with the Pilgrims who intended to celebrate their Easter there; and thence he went to *Jericho*, *Jordan*, *Bethlehem*, *Acra*, *Nazareth*, *Tiberias*, *Cana*, *Galilee*, *Tyre*, *Sidon*; thence he sailed over to *Cyprus*, *Rhodes*, *Chio*, and arrived safe at Smyrna, laden with an
incre-

incredible quantity of curiosities collected in the three kingdoms of Nature, being the productions of the East, Egypt and Palestine.

NOTHING now remained but to wait for a proper opportunity of returning home with his riches; but his strength was spent by the difficulties he had undergone in his travels, as well as by the violent heat of the climate in Palestine; and whilst he intended to recover it by tarrying in Smyrna, the serpent which he had long harboured in his bosom awoke, and a consuming hectic fever with weakness, restlessness, spitting of blood and shortness of breath, confined him to his bed, but he still possessed that hope, which is peculiar to those in his condition. He desired to be removed out of the city into the country, to enjoy the free air, and use milk as his only resource, which was accordingly done; but notwithstanding all this, our beloved Dr. Hasselquist wasted away daily like a lamp whose oil is spent, and *departed this life*, the 9th of February 1752, to the inexpressible grief of all who knew him.

WE were immediately informed of his death by Mr. Rydelius, whose love for Hasselquist was not to be extinguished by his departure; this gentleman also added to our sorrow by giving us to understand, that the late Dr. Hasselquist, had contracted a debt of 350*l.* on his travels, and that his creditors had at the time of his death taken possession of all his collections of natural curiosities, observations and manuscripts, which they would not part with, until their demands were satisfied. Thus did we lose our worthy and dear countryman; his name was in the like danger; and his labours were threatened with destruction by the hands of Barbarians. We knew no means of collecting

lecting on a sudden such a sum of money, but the worthy Dr. Bæck, first Physician to the Queen of Sweden, who has always loved the Sciences, and patronized learned men, undertook to present these unhappy circumstances to her Majesty Queen LOUISA ULRICA, who graciously protects Science, and is possessed of a most refined taste for the productions of Nature. Her Majesty immediately resolved to pay the debt out of her own purse, and redeem the Collection, without which the Public would very late, if ever, have enjoyed this Work. The next year all these treasures arrived safe and well preserved at her Majesty's palace of *Drottningholm*, at which time I was ordered to attend, and was astonished at the sight of so many unheard of curiosities. The collections of dried plants from Natolia, Egypt, Palestine, Cyprus, &c. all the *Stones* and sorts of earth from so many remarkable places in Egypt and the Holy Land; the many rare *Fishes* out of the Nile, and poisonous *Serpents* from Egypt, the rare *Insects*, the extensive collections of Oriental *Drugs*, Arabian *Manuscripts*, Egyptian *Mummies*, &c. could not but excite the admiration of the beholder.

LAST year Dr. Hasselquist's own original Manuscripts arrived, with the principal Observations he had made. Her Majesty was most graciously pleased to order me to arrange and publish them for the satisfaction and advantage of mankind. I have accordingly digested the Work in the best manner I could, ranged every thing under its proper *Tribe*; added *Names* to plants and animals, altered the *Technical terms* and manner of writing, without changing in the least the Author's meaning: I had the work corrected at the press, and myself inspected

spected its publication. I imagined it needless to add *Synonyms*, which would have swelled the book; especially as they may easily be found in the tenth edition of my System of Nature, in which I have introduced these names.

THERE is an incredible number of curiosities from the three kingdoms of Nature in the Collection of our late Author, which have been incorporated with the cabinets of their Majesties, and are already described, and may soon be published with other wonderful productions of Nature*.

HER Majesty has been pleased to give me a specimen of every plant, in which there were above two, these I have described in another Treatise, under the title of *Flora Palæstina*; and therefore think it needless to enumerate them here, as I would not insert any thing, which did not come from the Author's pen. I shall think myself happy, if I have fulfilled her Majesty's command, and answered the expectations of the Public.

* These have been since published in Octavo, under the title of Musæum Reginæ.

# TRAVELS

## TO

## THE EAST.

AUGUST the 7th, 1749, I went on board the ship Ulrica, belonging to the Swedish Levant company, which was now about making the 8th voyage to Smyrna, under the command of Captain Ekeroth. We sailed from Stockholm at ten o'clock, and came to Skaggehamn in the evening, where we lay that night.

THE next day we came to Diurhamn. The wind was southerly, which obliged us to tack frequently; but the weather was very fine. Here we lay wind-bound to the 13th.

I HAVE always had a great inclination to botanize on the sea coast of Sweden, and now a fine opportunity offered; but this opportunity proved ineffectual, as the husbandmen had already cut down the flowers of this summer. I was nevertheless in hopes that the shore would in some measure gratify my curiosity, and therefore on the 12th went on an island; but found nothing there except the Glaux maritima, or Sea Milk Wort, and Arenaria Peploides, or Sea Chick Weed, which was already in seed.

The rocks here seemed to be split by the waves in large perpendicular clefts, which were filled up with clear quartz, or cryftalline matter, by which one might plainly difcover traces of the generation of this ftone. The 13th, at two o'clock in the morning, we came to Daleroen, where we anchored, in order to fhew our pafs at the fort, and get cuftomhoufe officers on board to vifit us. Both fides of the harbour were built with fmall wooden-houfes, which gave the place the appearance of a little town. Thofe on one fide are called Iutholmen and the other Dalereon. The inhabitants of both places are chiefly pilots and fifhermen. They catch here, fometimes in large quantities, a kind of fifh, called by Linnæus, Cottus quadricornis (Four-horned Bull's head). The fituation of the place was very difagreeable, being furrounded with barren mountains and fandy hills. I could not learn that they had any other fign here of the change of the wind; but when the fea fwells towards the fhore they are fure of a northerly wind, which our pilots faid they knew from long experience.

The 14th, we failed by a gentleman's feat called Sandmar: here there is an elegant garden and a fine view of the fea. On the 16th, we left the harbour of Daleroe, and weighed anchor at five o'clock in the morning, in hopes not to anchor again in the Baltic, which happened luckily according to our wifhes.

Landsort was the laft land we faw on the Stockholm coaft; there is a light-houfe here for the fervice of feamen. Our pilots left us here, and our feamen took charge of the fhip. The Captain, among other accounts he gave us of his travels, as we

were

were walking the deck on the 17th, acquainted us, that he had carried the famous King Theodore to Holland. He was delivered to him near Corsica by Captain Blix, a commander of a Swedish man of war, who had taken him under his protection, when he fled from Corsica. Captain Ekeroth put him in a Dutch fishing boat in the Texel. His retinue consisted then of a footman and a cook. I relate this circumstance for the sake of some future Biographer, to whom it may happen to be unknown.

The high sandy mountains of the island of Gothland appeared to-day on our left, looking like so many great columns at a distance. We could discover nothing from hence through our glasses, but the steeple of a church[a].

Charles's islands were in sight on the 18th, in the forenoon. The mountains of limestone on the shore stood like high broken walls towards the sea. Both islands were so barren, that we could only see two shrubs on one of them.

The 19th, we had Œland on our right.

About one o'clock on the 20th, a little grey bird, of the sparrow tribe, came flying close after our ship. The Captain said immediately, that it signified a storm. Half an hour had scarcely passed, before we had so strong a gale, that the sea beat over our gunnel. I have afterwards observed several times, both in the Baltick, the North and Spanish seas, that as often as birds came on board, we had hard weather, which induces me to believe that the Peteril (Procellaria) is not the only forerunner of bad weather.

The island Bornholm was the first Danish land we saw on the 21st. We had Scania on our star-board, and were in sight of both the whole day.

The 22d, we came near the shore of Scania, and in the evening were within a cannot shot of Trælle-

[a] Linnæi Iter Gothland. 282.

borg. The fields of Scania were covered with sheaves of corn, and afforded the agreeable sight of a fertile country.

We lay to all the night of the 23d within sight of Scania, for fear of running a-ground near the Sound in the night, and at day-break had two fine views: one on shore, of the white chalk mountains of Seeland: the other at sea, of some ships which had come up with us whilst we lay by in the night. Drakoe is a handsome village, with a church to the left. We hoisted our flag here, and got three Danish pilots on board, who carried us past Copenhagen for six rixdollars. We saw that the road was dangerous; for a Dutch ship had yesterday run a-ground here in fine weather, and was now surrounded with a number of small craft from Drakoe, which were employed in getting her off. We saw a fine forest of oak between this village and Copenhagen, where there is penalty on any one who attempts to cut the timber. About noon, we were within cannon shot of Copenhagen, and could see the palace, fleet, arsenal, and some fine churches. Here the Danish pilots left us, after they had truly foretold us fine weather. We could see the city of Malma, with its churches, and large houses from the starboard, opposite Copenhagen. A handsome beach wood came in our view, in which were some fine houses; this was said to be the royal Danish deer park. The whole coast from Drakoe is very beautiful from the sea, and seems contrived by nature to refresh and give pleasure to seamen, long used to the melancholy prospect of nothing but sea and sky. We saw Landskrona from the starboard at two o'clock, and went quite near under Hven, which was entirely uninhabited towards this side. In the afternoon, we came to an anchor in the road between Helfingborg and Helfingneur, to pay toll to the Danes.

Helfing-

Helsingneur is a little town, the walls of the houses are framed with timber, and the void spaces filled up with either brick or clay, and near it lies the fortress Cronenburg, which, from its outward appearance, seems sufficient for what it is intended, a key to the Baltick.

I went up to town the 24th, where every thing that can accommodate seafaring people is sold in such plenty, that the town really merits the name of a Mart for seamen.

We went early under sail the 26th, and steered for Gottenburgh, where we were to take in some East-India goods and carry them for the Levant company's account to Smyrna. Kullen was the last land of Scania, about thirty English miles from the Sound, consisting of high hills, upon which there is a light-house.

The 27th, I saw animals and vegetables, the like of which I had never before seen. The former were Sea-nettles (Medusæ), which, yesterday and to-day, shone by thousands in the sea, and in calm weather and a serene sky afford an agreeable appearance from their shining green colour. The latter were sea weeds, called Fuci Vesiculosus, Fastigiatus, Saccharinus, to which hung a vast number of the smallest shells. We could see the coast of Halland before us. The 28th, early, we sailed past the town and fortress of Warberg and Nidingen, which is the first island on the Gottenburgh coast, where there is a light-house.

On the 29th, we knew we were not far from Gottenburgh, by discovering the island of Vinga and its light-house, soon after which a pilot came on board us.

We sailed past the fortress of Elffborg about noon, and there came to an anchor. This fort appeared to be in a good state, and well situated to command

command the harbour of Gottenburgh. The road, without Gottenburgh, hath many little rocks lying close to one another; some of them being under water, makes the navigation dangerous. The Swedish East-India company's ship Gottenburgh, was lost three years ago in her voyage home, on one of them, within the fort, which confirms this account of them. We saw Gottenburgh the 30th, which is known to be a strong and famous trading town, and the best in Sweden next to Stockholm. We had six miles to row from the fort to the town. The first objects that presented themselves to our view in the harbour, which is large and safe, surrounded with high mountains, were some small men of war and frigates; farther up five East-India ships; then three or four dock yards.

The saw mill is built on a rising ground, close by the harbour; it is furnished with many saws, which are worked by the wind; and is so contrived, as to raise the timber out of the sea. We came out of the large harbour, through a flood-gate, into a ditch or walled canal, which runs through the town. In this lay small craft, especially Dutch smacks that were employed in exporting East-India goods. The town is of middling extent. The houses are generally of wood, some few of stone. The buildings are very neat; they are covered with deals, which are painted yellow or red: there are small narrow yards to each house, which make the place dangerous in case of fire. The court-house, state-house, and East-India house, are the largest and handsomest buildings in the town.

Here I fortunately met with my relation Mr. Gustavus Tollander, who had returned this summer from the East-Indies: he was so kind as to shew me many curious observations, which he had made during his stay there, especially among the Chinese. I viewed attentively the Chinese weight, and was informed, that the

the weight China was divided in 1 catche, which contains 16 teel; 1 teel 10 mees; 1 mees 10 candrin; 1 candrin 10 caas. A catche is equal to $1\frac{1}{4}$ lb. A hundred catche make 142 lb. The common money weight contains 50 teel in China, which make 3 catche and 2 teel. A Spanish piece of eight contains 7 mees and 4 candrin. On comparing it with the medical weights, I find that 1 ounce is equal to 8 mees.

I was not a little glad to meet two more persons from the East-Indies the 1st of September. They were clergymen, and had returned this year; Mr. Thoren in the ship Freden, and Mr. Hiortberg in the ship Hoppet. They had both, besides the duty of their office, pursued the study of natural history, agreeable to their instructions from the directors of the East-India company, which they performed with honour and applause. Mr. Hiortberg was now busy in finishing his journal; he could draw, which made it an easy matter for him to adorn his book with the figures of what he had seen in natural history. He had in particular chosen fishes, and hath made some fine observations and figures of them, but especially on the Hound-fish (Squalus Acanthis) Scomber Ductor, and Remora (Echeneis). He had likewise collected some insects and vermes. He promised to present the whole to the Royal Swedish Academy of Sciences. Mr. Thoren has shewn himself in botany a worthy disciple of his master Dr. Linnæus. His collection of plants was said to be very considerable, which he had already delivered to Mr. Lagerstrœm, who sent it to Dr. Linnæus, by him to be made public, to the honour of the collector and pleasure of the lovers of nature.

The 2d of September I saw several natural curiosities from East-India and China, at Mr. Lagerstrœm's, one of the Directors of the East-India company,

pany. This gentleman has for several years been making collections of natural curiosities. Haste would not permit me to see more than a large collection of shells **and handsome corals,** especially one that **had** a large piece of the basis left, which was clay. This gentleman had got home, **in the last** ships, four gold fish in fresh water; they were **from** Canton, and quite lively. They eat wafers: **the** manner of bringing this fish to Europe is described by Dr. Linnæus, in the royal Swedish academy of Sciences for 1746. A heifer, nine months **old,** from China, which differed in nothing from our **cows** but that she seemed more lively and sprightly, as if she had been bred up in the fields and in the open air, and not confined in **a** narrow hut or a dark stable, which always give creatures a **sad and poor** appearance. She was of a red brown, fat and merry, and the voyage seemed to have had no bad effect on her. **A** live plant of the **Bamboo** reed, so much used by the Chinese; the stem was an inch **thick,** articulated, a span's length between the joints; the l**eaves sword**-shaped, the whole plant was two feet high. Mr. Arvidson, the librarian, shewed me the library of the college. Seba's excellent book was the dearest and best they had. They had already made a handsome collection of natural curiosities, amongst which were **the** Flying-fish, an Eel of an enormous size, the **teeth** of a Sea-horse, a very handsome Lithodendron, a Hair **Ball** (Ægagropila) of a Cow, the bigness **of** one's fist, a Parcel of Petrefactions given by the late Dr. Stobæus.

The cloaths which women here use in bad weather appear strange to travellers. They throw a piece of black stuff, **four feet long, over t**heir heads and half their bodies, so as likewise to cover their faces. It is used by all people of middling fortunes, and hath without doubt been introduced by the foreigners,

that

that first built the town, nor has it yet undergone the change, to which the dress of women is liable.

The 7th inftant, I went to a peafant's houfe in the country, where the window was in the roof, which made the rooms dark, but much warmer: In Scania, Smoland and Bohus, they ufe the fame method. Cabbages were planted here in large quantities by every farmer; and I am told that this ufeful plant is more ufed here than in any other place.

Early in the morning of the 8th, we hove up our anchor and fet fail from Elfborg fort. We faw Marftrand in the afternoon, and at night Skagens light-houfe.

The 9th, we had Jutland on our larboard.

On the 10th, we took the Efox Roftro Cufpidato, Artedi fpec. 2. (Garfifh). The defcription comes very near the common Pike; but is eafily diftinguifhed by its long roftrum. The fcales were green, the whole body was of a green colour, and its back and fide bones were green, which I have not obferved in any other fifh.

The 13th, we had a Wefterly wind and hard weather.

On the 15th, fome little birds, fuch as the Redftart, common Swallow, and a Sea Swallow, were driven by bad weather on board us, before we perceived it; not long after we had a violent ftorm from the N. W. which lafted for three days.

The 20th, fome Chaffinches and a Sea Swallow, the common forerunners of bad weather, came on board us. In the evening it blew a ftrong cold wind from the Weft, which was foon over.

The 21ft, in the morning, a failor, at the maft head, faid, he faw the Dutch coaft; our Captain believed us not fo far in our way, and therefore regarded it not: before three in the afternoon, we

faw

saw the English coast about Yarmonth, from the mast-head, by which we knew where we were, and that it was **neceſſary to** be upon our guard, as we were between the **Engliſh banks.** The founding lead is in ſuch a caſe a ſailor's **right hand**; and it was now much uſed between fear and **hope.** We founded, and found **twenty** fathom, and immediately after five, which **continued for** ſeveral hours, **and was a** ſign of **the uncertain ground on** which we were. The ſailors **believed us to be out of our** true courſe, and upon ſome bank not put down in **their chart.** We were ſo lucky as to have excellent weather, **and** the wind proving favourable, which brought us before night in our true **courſe.**

**The** Dutch have **here** their gold mines, for ſo **we may juſtly call their herring** fiſhery; **nor can it be denied** that they keep nearer **their** neighbours **than their own** properties. We ſailed by numbers **of** their boats **on the 22d,** and could once count **above** thirty on a little ſpot.

**On** the 23d, we entered the **narroweſt part** of **the channel,** between France and England, and **could ſee the coaſts of both** theſe powerful kingdoms **at the ſame time. We** were very near the latter, and could without a glaſs ſee its chalky hills, covered with flints, and Dover fort ſituated on the ſummit of them. **A good wind and** excellent weather drove us over **thoſe dangerous** ſhoals, that have been ſo fatal **to** ſailors. The 25th, about **noon, we came** into the Spaniſh ſea, having in **two days and a half ſailed 540** miles, being the whole **length of the** channel.

**Our** Swediſh flag hath nothing **to** fear from the rovers of **the** coaſt of Barbary, as long as the Swediſh crown, to the great advantage of our trade, **keeps at** peace with the moſt powerful of them. **A few** ſmall rovers, from the ports of Salee and Tangier,

Tangier, that sometimes infest these seas, are the only pirates against whom the Swedes should be particularly cautioned: and as an enemy ought never to be despised, we put our cannon in order, and the 26th gave arms to as many as were on board. In this posture our vessels commonly sail until they have passed Gibraltar.

The 28th, at noon, we were in sight of the famous head, beyond which the ancients thought there was no land, and were so near the shore that some Linnets (Fringilla) reached us, and wearied out, sought a night's rest in the shelter of our sails.

The 30th, as we were sailing in the Spanish seas, the weather was so fine, that it seemed as if the sky and sea strove to excel each other in beauty. The little knowledge I had, was confined to the three kingdoms of nature, and therefore I found myself in the same situation, as a person who walks in a park filled with the finest animals and plants, without understanding natural history. Such a one can say no more, but that it is very handsome. I doubt not but many fine opportunities passed unobserved by me, which might have given hints for useful observations to a person who had any knowledge in astronomy and natural philosophy. We had now passed by St. Vincents head, which is a head-land well known to sailors, when we, the 9th of October in the morning, overtook a Dutch frigate of war, which was carrying home a Tripoline Ali Effendi, who returned from his embassy to the Dutch republic, and was the same that some years before had been in Stockholm on the same errand. It seemed very suspicious, considering the place we were in, to see Turks on board a ship, and a number of armed men, who hoisted no flag when we did; this occasioned our seamen to arm themselves for their defence;

fence; but our fufpicions ended, when the lieutenant, with a fubaltern and eight men, came on board to enquire whence we came, and whither we were bound.

Here we obferved large droves of Porpuffes coming from the W. towards the S. E. which were the firft we had feen fince we left the North fea. The failors fay they foretell bad weather, when they appear on the furface of the water, efpecially in thofe places to which they direct their courfe. But they were miftaken this time; for the fine weather, which we had through the Spanifh feas, continued with violent heat for fome days.

The 11th, we were the whole day in fight of the African coaft, and towards evening had the Spanifh coaft on our right as before. We were now very near going into the Mediterranean fea; but were obliged to be content, and cruize for two days between the Spanifh and African coaft, on account of a brifk Eafterly wind.

The 14th, in the afternoon, we went through the ftrait that divides Africa from Europe. High limeftone mountains were to be feen on both fides of the channel, out of which there came the fmoak of many fires, which are lime-kilns, that they have in the clefts of the rocks of both coafts. Befides thefe lime-ftone mountains, we could fee others of loofe fand, which were not fo fteep, but more gradually declining to the fea. They were quite green, covered with fome fhrubs, and had fome vineyards. The profpect of thefe mountains was far from being agreeable. The ornament of the Northern mountains, Ever-green Pines and Junipers, are not to be feen here.

We faw the town and fortrefs of Gibraltar the 15th; they are fituated on a high rock, that terminates

nates the Spanish mountains towards the sea. Ceuta lies almost facing it on the African coast. When these are out of sight, the Straights are passed, and another sea is entered.

WE saw the Mediterranean by sun-rise, and sailed along the Spanish coast, to which seamen always keep nearer than the African. A beautiful little bird (Motacilla Hispanica) came on board us from the Spanish coast. It was the forerunner of hard weather, which happened to us a few hours after, with a strong N. E. wind, which lasted all night. We had violent thunder and lightning, with hail and rain, in the night of the 18th, which was an uncommon sight for Swedes. We were yet in sight of the high Spanish mountains, which by day we saw covered with snow, and at night shining with fires, which are partly those of the guards, and partly those of the lime-kilns. We caught a Lark and a Wagtail (Motacilla corpore e fusco viridescente, pectore ferrugineo) on board. Many of the former were drowned; only this one came in a miserable weak condition on board.

THE 25th, in the forenoon, we had Formentera on our left. This is an island in the Mediterranean, over-against the Spanish coast, upon which we could only see a few bushes; its shores rise perpendicular from the sea.

WE experienced for some days the autumn of this climate: storm, cold weather, rain, and at night terrible lightenings; but at nine o'clock, in the night between the 28th and 29th, twelve miles to the Westward of Sardinia, we had the most terrible and severe weather that we had yet suffered in our voyage. The wind from the North, attended with violent hurricanes and lightening from all parts of the sky, with some thunder: then a shower of rain, with

with hail; but this did not laſt above half an hour. The hail ſtones which fell, were partly of an oval form, ſome round, ſome elliptical, others angulated. The largeſt were bigger than walnuts, the leſſer like nutmegs. The outſide was white and clear, with a kernel in the inſide, which was blueiſh, and the bigneſs of a pea. I found ſome of them that weighed an ounce.

The 1ſt of November we could ſee the African coaſt from the maſt-head; from thence a bird called Emberiza africana came on board us.

The 2d, we ſailed by Sicily, with a ſtrong North wind: juſt before this we had ſeen ſome Porpuſſes.

An innumerable flock of Sparrows (Emberiza melitenſis) ſurrounded our veſſel on the 3d, and immediately after we had a hard gale that laſted all the following day.

The 7th, we were in ſight of the coaſt of Morea, when a Levant, i. e. a N. E. wind met us, and obliged us to cruize to the 11th, without gaining the leaſt.

Early on the 12th, we had Candia and Cerigo on our left.

The 13th, we ſaw Morea to the left, and Milo to the right, when we were in hopes ſoon to end our voyage, and the fine weather we now had, made ſome amends for the diſagreeable neceſſity of being ſo long at ſea. But our happineſs was at an end in the afternoon. The nearer a ſailor comes to the ſhore, the ſurer he may be of inconſtant weather. A North wind met us with a moſt dreadful ſtorm, and obliged us to drive about for two days.

It was lucky for us, that on the 15th we were ſo near Milo, that we could run in during ſuch a furious ſtorm. The harbour of Milo is one of the beſt in the Archipelago, ſurrounded with mountains on all ſides, of which one hath a ruined caſtle and a village at the entrance, which without doubt hath one of the highest situations, and most extensive horizons of any in the universe. We came to an anchor in full twenty fathom water. The depth of the water in this harbour, makes it of much more consequence in bad weather.

The 16th, in the forenoon, we rowed a shore, and went up to the town of Milo. I was glad to find some plants in blossom at this time of the year, though autumn had already taken hold of the greater part, and of those the withered remains were only now to be seen. The first I saw was the autumnal Dandelion, which grows in Sweden, and flowers about the same time. The Anemone Coronaria was in full blossom, some of which were white, others blue. Nerium (Oleander) stood in two places in large bushes beside the road, and adorned the place with its stiff green leaves and long pods, but had not yet ripened seeds. A Fig-marigold, half a foot high (Mesembryanthemum Nodiflorum) grew in all the fields, with little obtuse and succulent leaves, without flowers. In the wall, grew two shrubs or bushes four feet high; one of them had little oval green leaves, without flowers (Rhamni Species); the other had hoary leaves, which I likewise described. The road was full of pebble stones and clear quartz in small pieces, red and white spar, besides sand-stone and hard lime-stone. On both sides, the walls round the gardens were built with a rough sand-stone, with which was mixt with some coarse light yellow clay in large pieces; this was in some places turned quite red by the heat of the sun.

After walking near a mile from the shore, we came into the town. The sight of it could not but excite the compassion of the beholder, as nothing
was

was to be seen but the remains of ruined houses formerly stately, built of square lime-stone. Within these poor walls, lived miserable inhabitants, whose dwellings differ from the worst of prisons, only as these receive light through the door, instead of the windows, and have the liberty of going in and out of them. We went immediately to the Dutch Consul, and after dinner with the Venetian Consul, to see the principal church. On the shore I found the Nerium (Oleander), Erigeri Species, Fig-marigold, &c. In the gardens, which are bad, are very large Palm-trees, some Fig-trees, some large old bushes of Rosemary, Narcissus, Marjoram, which was there reckoned a rare plant, and was almost the only one kept in pots. Wild fowl they have in plenty. Amongst them they had a black game, larger than the Swedish; this was a rare bird, so far to the Southward. The town, though poor, is full of people. Children come out of every corner, but all miserable. The better sort dwell in the first floor, but their dwellings were alike bad. Here are two Greek churches; but no Romish chapel or missionary. I went into one of the above churches, which made a tolerable appearance. They shewed me a curiosity, which deserved attention. It was a piece of a ship's plank, bored through by a fishbone, which was part of the tooth of the Monodon (Unicorn fish). A French Captain had found it in the keel of his ship, as she was careening in Morea. He cut out the piece and took it to this place, to be hung up in the church. It was curious, but not miraculous, as these good people imagined. The French have here a Consul of their nation; the Duch and Venetians have each one from among the Greek inhabitants. There is no Turk in this island. The

Captain

captain Pascha sends a galley here while he cruizes in the Archipelago to fetch the Turkish emperor's yearly tax, which is high enough considering the poverty of the country and the scarcity of money. It is governed by primates, who collect and account for the taxes, and compound differences. The people in general are very friendly and polite. The women's dress is one of the oddest and least becoming of any of the islanders in the Archipelago. They were naked from the neck to the waist, and had a short petticoat reaching to the middle of the thigh, a loose garment covered the head, and their plaited hair hung down to the small of the back. The island produces some cotton, which the French and Venetians buy. They also have bad wine.

The 18th, after taking a pilot, who was to conduct us through the Archipelago, we set sail.

The 19th, we saw the island Parso. The 20th, Tius, Negropont; and the 21st, we anchored on the coast of Karaburno, which is on the continent of Natolia; we had Natolia on the one side and Scio on the other. I went on shore the same day, but found nothing to reward my labour, except the common wild Thyme. Haliotis (Scar Ear) and Pumex (Pumice stone) were the other naturalia found here.

The 25th, we sailed under Scio, and had an opportunity of seeing its handsome town, which makes a fine appearance; but the plantations and gardens are a more material ornament, as they produce the famous **Mastix**.

The 26th, we came in the Gulph of Smyrna, and had Natolia on both sides.

The 27th, we had like to have made an unfortunate end of our voyage, at a time we thought our misfortunes

fortunes were all over. We had the wind constantly a-head, which obliged us to beat up between two shores; this is dangerous in a narrow channel. By sailing too near the land, at day break, we run aground. A Greek and a Turk, who were fishing on the shore, came immediately on board, and offered us their assistance in procuring small vessels to lighten ours; but a land breeze filled our sails and help'd us off. At noon, we anchored without the Castle of Smyrna, which commands the entrance, when Messieurs Palm and Hebbe, our Swedish merchants, came on board. We went into the harbour, and were saluted, according to custom, by the guns of all the vessels, except the French, who never honour any nation with a salute, nor receive it from them.

We went on shore in the afternoon with the captain, and were, by our consul Mr. Rydelius, received with a politeness to be expected from a gentleman of his noble qualifications.

The 29th, I waited on Mr. Peysonel, the French consul, and member of the Academy of inscriptions and belles lettres. To his great knowledge I am indebted for the following observation relating to natural history. Corals have in our age been esteemed a proper subject for the pens of the greatest naturalists. Nature hath so contrived this part of her works, that Corals have had a contrary lot from other naturalia, and have been classed under the different kingdoms of nature. And it is yet uncertain, to which they properly belong. In Mr. Peysonel's company, the learned Count Marsigli had the good fortune to overcome all the doubts he had entertained about these naturalia, when in his invaluable Historia Maris he laid before the world what he took to be the flowers of the

the Corals. At that time they were thought to be vegetables. We know of none who immediately diffented from this opinion. Mr. Peyfonel, by fome obfervations he made on the French coaft, before Marfigli printed his book, had reafon to think otherwife, experience convincing him that Corals were inhabited by worms. Mr. Peyfonel did not make natural hiftory his chief ftudy; he did not fet much value on thefe obfervations, yet communicated them to his brother, a learned phyfician, who intended to publifh them.

At length, Count Marfigli anticipated Mr. Peyfonel, who fuppreffed his and his brother's obfervations; but afterwards informed Mr. Reaumur of them, who knew how to make ufe of fuch a confiderable fpeculation. Mr. Reaumur gave it in to the Royal Parifian Academy of Sciences augmented with his own obfervations; nor omitted to attribute the honour to the real difcoverer. This was the rife of an opinion about Corals, that fince hath been thought worth the enquiry of the learned, and has received an almoft univerfal applaufe, which the inventor never expected.

A TRAVELLER, who, either for his pleafure or fome ufeful purpofe, would chufe to be acquainted with the ceremonies of thofe religions which have claimed the attention of mankind, fhould vifit fome city in the Levant, where he will fee them all, except idolatry. Many Chriftians imagine that the Greek church comes neareft with refpect of ceremonies, to that, which was predominant at the beginning of chriftianity. I faw thofe of the church of Smyrna fo remarkable for her antiquity, and yet more for having preferved herfelf in the tolerable fituation the now is in, though perfecuted by the Pope and Turk, while her fifters are fcarcely known here.

The church of Smyrna hath a bishop, successor to him who received this remarkable title from the supreme Shepherd. His power is limited to those who live in this city, of whom, by contributions and money for ceremonies, he hath his revenue, which is one of the most considerable among the Greek clergy.

Few of those, who have published travels, have given us any account of the state of physick out of Europe. Few physicians have travelled out of the circle of the learned world; though others have been attentive to what regards their respective professions. I have thought it my duty to make myself acquainted with what regards medicine in those places through which I went. Smyrna, in the time the Grecians made physick a part of heavenly doctrine, was adorned with temples, sacred to the God of Health and Medicine. They struck medals in honour of those who practised this sacred science, and with judgement administered those remedies, which Providence had revealed to them[a]. Time hath greatly changed the state of this Science here. The Greeks have yet remaining some sparks of that fire, which shone in their fore-fathers; but which would, without doubt, be extinguished, if a few, more encouraged by the hope of getting a living than out of love for the science, had not determined to acquire knowledge in our learned Europe. There are some Greeks to be found in Constantinople and Smyrna, who have studied physick, chiefly in Padua: most of them born on some island in the Archipelago. Scio, in particular, has a number of tolerable physicians, and also supplies other places with them; I know not what pretentions islands have to furnish good

---

[a] See Mead, Orat. de Honor. Med.

phy-

physicians: Stanchio (Cous) and England afford us remarkable examples. I had an opportunity of making these observations, on the 9th of December, when I was called to a consultation, to enquire into the disease of their chief brother physician, a Greek from Scio, who died within a few days of an Asthma convulsivum. He observed strictly the rule he had followed in his practice, to leave all to nature, without using any drugs, unless diætetical. These are almost the only drugs prescribed by the physicians in Smyrna, and the diet consists in a sort of fasting. They give for reason, that the air is nourishing, and sufficient to keep the sick in life; but this convinced me of my former experience, that the most salutary rules may prove detrimental, when carried too far, and not applied to circumstances. The physicians here, in my time, were Doctor Demetri, who was above 80 years old, was born in Scio, had travelled through England and Germany, practised nine years in St. Esprit, the chief hospital in Rome, and in his youth had acquired some knowledge in botany, which he did not neglect, as he at this age had a complete knowledge of Ray's and Tournefort's systems. I gave him some idea of Dr. Linnæus's famous system. He received my informations in the same manner, as an aged soldier, incapable of attending battles and sieges, is yet rejoiced to hear of new expeditions. Dr. Zani was the other of the faculty in Smyrna; he appeared to be a young, handsome, and naturally-ingenious man, provided with such learning as is required for knowing common diseases: he had great hopes to gain the peoples confidence, towards which he was already pretty well advanced.

The 16th, I made my first jaunt on horseback, which gave me no favourable opinion of the inhabitants of the East. The miserable roads, over hills and dales, full of stones and mud, put me in mind of the incomparable roads in Sweden, and gave me a much worse opinion of the celebrated Southern countries, than I before had. But what on this journey caused a woeful remembrance to a Swede, was the place, where five years ago, Mr. Kierman, merchant in Smyrna, and son to Mr. Alderman Kierman in Stockholm, was shot dead by some highwaymen. The loss our trade suffered by the death of this young man, was not to be repaired by the lamentations of the Turks or the punishment of the murderers. The former however shews that, amongst those we esteem barbarians, there are lovers of virtue, and the latter confirms to us, that the Turks have learn'd the wise rule, that justice is due to all men. Budgia, an agreeable country-seat of the Dutch Consul Hochpied, to which we came, expelled these melancholy reflexions. Its Cypress park, filled with Gazellas, Peacocks, Pheasants, Partridges and Nightingales, is incomparable.

The diversions of the Carnaval began amongst the Franks, the beginning of the year, with balls and genteel suppers. I was present, the 5th of January, at the entertainment the Dutch Consul Hochpied gave to all the Europeans. Every thing was well conducted, after the European manner. Musick is the only thing, we must put up with, after the manner of the country, which is bad enough. It consisted of two miserable violins, and two lutes, neither of which was well played. This noble art is now no more to be found, in a country where it once had arrived to the highest perfection. In vain may we now look for an Orpheus among the Greeks; but a dance, a remain of the Grecian age, performed by the

the Greek women, afforded me infinite pleasure. They were about fifteen in number, the foremost of which conducted the dance, by making signs with a garment she held in her hand. The art consisted in keeping an equal half-circle, to be observed under all their different turnings. They likewise several times made a labyrinth, but immediately reassumed their former station. There was something particular in this dance, which at first sight, convinced me it was ancient. My conjectures were confirmed by Mr. Peysonell, the French Consul, who hath much knowledge in what relates to Grecian antiquities. He told me, that some monuments of marble had been found, on which this dance was sculptured. It is so agreeable when danced by Greeks, dressed in the ancient manner and conformable to the dance, that no modern invention of this kind seems to equal it. The musick used on this occasion did not appear to me to have been designed for it by the antients. What I afterwards heard them sing, seemed to me better applied.

The hard frost, which had lasted a whole week, (the like was not remembered by the oldest men living) was now so far broke, that I in the afternoon of the 2d of February could venture myself in the gardens, without the town, to see what havock winter had made amongst my flowers, which I a short time before had seen in their glory. They had withstood the cold pretty well, so that Chrysanthemum and Calendula, with several others, yet adorned the fields; but some of the Syngenesists had suffered a little. Art has been but of small assistance to the gardens here, except in planting a few Orange-trees, which do not grow wild. Nature in this place is amiable; but, if a little art was used, the gardens here would soon possess much greater

beauties

beauties, than those in our Northern Europe, which require so much cost and labour; Orange-trees grow here in abundance, nor does any body care to pluck the fruit, which remains on the trees the whole year, until the flowering season, when it falls off. Some Fig, Olive, and Pomegranate-trees, stand here and there, without order. Poplar-trees are common enough few Dates and Palm-trees are to be seen, and those seem to be very old. Cypress trees grow in some places, and mount towards the sky, like tall Pyramids. Such are the greatest ornaments nature has given to these countries. Hedera Helix (Ivy) grows in such abundance about and within all the gardens of Smyrna, that it can scarcely be more common in any place. It makes the greatest part of their hedges, and creeps about every where in their gardens, to which it is an ornament but of little service. I saw some of nature's master-pieces, of this plant, which confirm'd me in my former opinion, how useful it is to adorn gardens, especially if art leads it to proper places, where it is most wanted. I saw an Ivy and a Vine together, cover a Pome-granate tree, which made a noble appearance. In another place, four Vines had crept up a Fig-tree, and with their fibrous roots fastened to the bark, which was not less agreeable; but the handsomest of all was a gateway, nature had made of Ivy, which had twisted itself together, over a miserable garden gate, to the thickness of three feet, and the length of eight. The gate consisted of some unplaned and rough deals nailed together, ordinary enough for a common stable door; but the covering might have been an ornament to the entrance of a royal garden. The fences round gardens are mostly such as the want of wood taught them to make. They are chiefly hedges, and therefore perma-

permanent. They make them of Willows, which are planted at the sides of a ditch, at four feet distance; or of Caprificus, which is yet handsomer, and peculiar almost to this country, planted in the same manner. I believe, that our Swedish husbandmen will not dare to plant such fences; but I know the former hath been under consideration, and I wish it was done in the same manner it is here, as I am persuaded it may.

BANKS are more common here. Ivy, and a parcel of other bushes grow on them, with common Reed, Arundo Phragmites, (Donax) much larger than the Swedish, and make them durable and a good defence. I was curious to know how this Reed came to grow in such quantities on these banks, and enquired of the inhabitants whether it had been sown or planted there? They answered in the negative. I asked whether they had carried the earth from the sea shore, and the roots in it, which afterwards grew up? This they likewise denied. The earth for the banks is dug on the spot, and thrown out of the ditches on both sides. It was not however very difficult to discover whence this plant came. It is not long since the sea went up to these gardens, which runs now a cannon-shot from them, and then, as now, Reed grew on the shore. The sea decreased, and its bottom became dry land, whereby the roots of this Reed remained with its former shores, which, after the ground was dug up for banks, were at liberty to spread, grow up and seed, like the largest wood; but this was not so easy, whilst they lay hid in the ground under a highway. Clay walls are the worst kind of fences used here. The spring began already, on the 12th of February, to bring forth the beauties of the Southern regions, owing to the mild climate. The Almond-tree mond-tree flowered around Smyrna on bare boughs. Anemones and Tulips adorned the fields, and grew spontaneously in valleys, and at the foot of mountains. The former are pretty, of different colours, purple and deep red, cochineal red, with a white ring at the basis of the petals. I described to day a Solitaire, a bird kept in a cage in our Swedish house. It is a kind of Thrush (Turdus solitarius), highly esteemed by the Eastern nations for its song; and they have told me, that it sells to the Turks at Constantinople, for 200 Piasters. It whistles, and can learn to sing entire airs, if it be kept to it, and exercised. They are found in the Grecian islands. Whence they are brought over and sold by the Greeks, who in their language, call it Μεγαλα. If kept in a cage, it is fed with fresh meat, insects and currants.

I was desirous to see Opobalsamum or Balsam of Mecca in a place where I was certain to find it good and genuine. This is seldom found genuine in Europe, and perhaps never entered an Apothecary's shop in Sweden, unadulterated. It is a drug that is seldom to be had genuine, even in Turkey; for the bushes from which it is taken are scarce in Arabia, and the quantity they yearly afford is barely sufficient for the court of the Turkish Emperor, and the grandees of the empire. A few of the common Turks, who make pilgrimages to Mecca, may chance to get a small quantity not mixed, but scarcely one in a thousand that yearly go there return without some mixture, which they sell for the true Balsam, though they have made it of Turpentine, &c. Of this kind I take the greatest part to be, which the Druggists and Apothecaries in Europe have; as I saw their merchants in Smyrna buy such mixtures, and send them to Europe, there to be disposed of under the name

name of the true Balsam of Mecca. I saw some the 13th of February, which I am sure was of the true kind; as it agreed with the descriptions the best authors have given us, and what I myself have learn'd concerning its transportation. I had frequently opportunities to see, what was called Balsam of Mecca, but I never believed any to be the true, except this, which I have described.

SPRING was now advancing apace; and as the heat encreased, I went without the town on the 14th, to see what effect this fine weather had on nature, and what sort of plants the spring afforded. I went to the burying-places of the Turks, to see whether they contained any thing worth notice. They bury most of their dead without the town, they have however near some of their churches, and even private houses places fill'd with graves. But the largest and most numerous are without the town. They occupy a large terrace around the town, and therefore make an incredible quantity of earth useless, which they encrease daily, by digging new graves and searching for other places, when they bury their dead. They have their burying-places surrounded with fine walls, and handsomer than those about their gardens and vineyards. At each grave they had raised up a stone of coarse marble, for the most part grey, but some brown. On these they had bestowed more or less art, according to the estate and esteem the deceased enjoyed while living. I concluded those were grandest, over whom was built a triangular monument of stones. Next were those with oblong stones, on the farther end of which was engraved a turban or Turkish headdress; if this is green, it signifies that an Emir or relation of Mahomet lies here. The poorest had plain stones without any art and labour,

bour, except cutting them out of a rock and smoothing. There were some that had inscriptions. The burying-places of the Turks are handsome and agreeable, which is owing chiefly to the many fine plants that grow in them and which they carefully place over their dead: Cypresses of remarkable height, and an innumerable quantity of Rosemary, were the plants chiefly found here. The latter were now in full blossom and afforded a delicious odour. The former, which the Turks esteem mourning trees, were in fruit, and are agreeable both summer and winter to the sight and smell. The Turks act much more consistent than the Christians, when they bury their dead without the town, and plant over them such vegetables, as by their aromatick and balsamick smell can drive away the fatal odours, with which the air is filled in such places. I am persuaded, that they by this escape many misfortunes, which affect Christians, from their wandering and dwelling constantly among the dead. A large and fine variety of Ranunculus Ficaria; the Androsace of Linnæus were new flowers of this year, which I saw, and the Almond-tree which was snow-white with blossoms. Why does the Almond-tree, which hath white flowers, blossom on bare boughs? not for the same reason as the hazel; perhaps the fruit, having a stone, requires a longer time to grow? They adorn the rising grounds, and according to nature's order ought to afford much fruit, as they bloom at a time of the year when the sky is constantly serene, and it neither rains nor is there any kind of bad weather, which in many countries prevent a fine blossom from giving the wished-for fruit.

THE 17th, I found Hyacinthus Muscari grow in common round the town, and in full blossom. The Turks

Turks call it Muscharumi, and it serves them in their love affairs in this manner: A young man sends this flower to a girl he loves; When she sees it is Muscharumi, she must remember a word in rhime to answer this, which is Ydskerumi, and puts her in mind by implication what her lover expects from her. This is properly called an allegorical manner of speaking. This evening I learned an ingenious method of giving wine a good and pleasant taste, from the French consul Mr. Peysonell, who had lately got it from the Greek bishop in Smyrna. I have described it in my collections, and took care of the thing with which it is to be done: this Mr. Peysonell likewise gave me.

The 24th in the afternoon, I had an opportunity of seeing the Jews synagogue. I went there with Mr. De Costa, the principal Jew merchant in Smyrna, and a man of knowledge acquired both by observation and reading. There are now about six synagogues in Smyrna; there were more formerly, which were destroyed by fire, and not since rebuilt. Those remaining are small, but handsome. In the middle of the synagogue was an elevated place surrounded with a closet, within which were benches. I took those, who sat there, for holy men. Round the walls were likewise benches, upon which the men sat, and on the sides on the floor and in galleries were separate closets, in which the women performed their devotions. From the cieling hung a quantity of glass lamps and some metal candlesticks. In one of these synagogues I was shewed the books of Moses, wrote in a fine Hebrew letter on parchment, covered with silk, rolled up and tied round with ribbands. They had about four closets filled with such volumes: these closets stood in the wall; and on the pannels of the doors the

Law

Law of Moses, the ten commandments, and other parts of the Pentateuch, were worked with letters cut out of black cloth, and sewed on cloth of different colours. In each synagogue sat a man on one side of the door, dressed in black or white, reading in the books of Moses; and several people that sat on the benches likewise had them and read after him. Coming home, I got an Iris (tuberosa) imberbis, corollis apice purpureis.

BARNABA is one of the prettiest villages round Smyrna, being about two hours journey from the town, whither we went on horseback the 2d of March. An Aga had the command of this, as well as some other villages hereabout; but the last possessor of this office having several times furnished the Franks with occasion of complaint, at the beginning of this month they petitioned the Porte to dismiss him. He was accordingly discharged, by which means, the Franks became more at liberty to enjoy the pleasures the country might afford. The husbandman was now ploughing the land that had been fallow last year. The soil is here quite loose and easy to till, and therefore requires little labour in cultivation. It consists chiefly of a loose clay mixt with sand and covered with rich mould. They always use oxen to plough the field; the construction of the plough I have described in another place. It is amusing to see them take off the plough-share when they have done their work, and put in on again when they have occasion. We passed by the burying-ground of this place, than which many of our country parishes in Sweden have not larger. It should therefore seem, that it was more than sufficient for a village, which contains not above 20 or 30 families; but, to bury after the

Turkish

Turkish manner, who never lay a corpse where another before hath been buried, such a place must been larged every year; and probably, all the land belonging to the village will in time be filled with grave-stones and bones of the dead. The largeness of the place, and the number of monuments shew, that the village must have been a considerable time inhabited, as people live to a great age, and few die in a year. We alighted at the house of Mr. Begler, the chief Grecian merchant in Smyrna, a man whom I ought to mention with respect; he had good sense, had lived long in Holland, and now had an extensive trade to that country in company with a Dutch merchant. His house was built in the Dutch taste, and surrounded with a small garden, where no other plants grew than those of the country. Marjoram (Origanum Majorana) which almost every farmer in Sweden has growing in his garden, was reckoned the scarcest plant, and kept in a pot near the entrance of the house, with Cheiranthus Incanus over against it, on the other side were Fig-trees, Almond-trees, Orange-trees, Oriental Plane-tree, (Platanus orientalis) &c. which with us are kept in hot-houses and pots, but here in the open air left to nature; I took however notice, that the hard frost towards the latter end of February had ravaged the Orange-trees, whose leaves and fruit were entirely destroyed. This had likewise happened in the town, amongst the trees that were there. On our return we saw Storks, that were travelling from the Southward to the Northward, who took up their lodgings in a wheat-field, where they walk as gentle and fearless as if they were tame. These birds are most favoured in Turkey. The Turks are their

greatest

greatest defenders; and if a Christian should happen to kill one of them, he would endanger his safety. Those who own a house where Storks have nested, are supposed to receive great blessings from heaven, and to be free from all misfortunes. A nest of them is esteemed by a bigoted Turk, more than a field full of Sheep and Camels.

The 1st of March in the afternoon, I viewed the dock-yard in Smyrna, as they were about laying down a Swedish ship. This is a miserable place, built by the Turks, where ships can be laid over to clean them, but a middling vessel will not be hove down for less than 150 to 200 piasters. The place over which we went and returned took up my attention more than the dock: It consisted of a pretty spacious field, which, as well as I can guess, may contain little more than one acre. I beheld this field was a new world, or a new enlargement of the inhabited world; it may be difficult to find a place which so clearly proves the decrease of the sea, as this: Here I could plainly see a dried bottom of the sea, which consisted of clay fill'd with shells and all sorts of sea-insects; around its extremities, on the former shore, lay all sorts of pebble-stones, which the sea had thrown up. Here no plants had yet had time to root, and be changed into mould; but I am persuaded that within a few years one may walk here as in a garden, fetch fruit out of a vineyard, or mow a corn-field. Towards the latter a good beginning was already made by the Turks at the west-end of the place, where a little stripe was sown with barley, which grew freely. The place on which Smyrna is built hath had the like origin and appearance, with its gardens, vineyards and corn-land: I could never have found any thing more agreeable than our Swedish arrow-headed grass (Triglochin

(Triglochin palustre) which I found to the northward of this field. If I had not been able to discern with my eyes, and confirmed by the inhabitants that this place formerly stood under water, this plant had been sufficient to convince me and others, who know its nature, and that through the whole world it grows in such places, where it can receive nourishment from an earth that hath some remains of sea salt.

I HAD an inclination to see the inland situation of Natolia, before I left its coasts, and therefore set out on the 11th of March for Magnesia, which is 8 hours travelling from Smyrna. I set out at sun-rise, accompanied by a Drogman, an Arminian servant and a guide. We were all well armed, which is customary in this country, and frequently necessary in the shortest journey. We took horses from the caravan, which goes every Wednesday and Sunday from Smyrna to Magnesia. In one hour's travelling from the town we came to a large field, covered with Olive-trees, and in some places turned into corn land. Round these fields were several villages, under the command of an Aga, who had his seat in Barnaba, one of the largest and handsomest. After this we saw a quite different prospect, and this so odd, that I doubt whether any one who has not seen the Eastern countries can have any idea of it: a mixture of hills and vallies, like the high billows and gulphs in a boisterous sea. In no place was it more evident that the continent, we call earth, was in the beginning the bottom of the sea. The hills were in their form unequal, some being flat towards the top; others of a conick figure. At a distance they seemed composed of sand, gravel, clay, or some other earth, being covered with mould and plants. But at a

D  nearer

nearer view they are found to confist of a dark brown, coarfe, loofe flate, compofed of thin flates, and which may eafily be broke by the fingers. I found hills of flate at the road fide, with breaches cut through them to make paffages for travellers. The other hills of Natolia confifted of Lime-ftone, which was whitifh, and of a coarfe grain: in thefe I likewife faw fome large breaches; but an innumerable quantity of loofe ftones of this kind covered both hills and roads. Nor were there wanting loofe ftones of Quartz, Spart, reddifh Lime-ftone, Sand-ftone, Spars mixt with Quartz; yet unmixed Quartz was fomewhat fcarce, and always in fingle pieces. Such mountains as we moftly have in the North, are not to be feen here. Mould makes the upper furface of all hills, in which grow various plants, but none fo common as Arbutus Andrachne. This bufh covers the hill in every place, and grows in fuch quantities, that I have never feen any plain fo covered with Juniper-bufhes in Sweden. The latter were fo fcarce, that I fcarce faw ten on the whole road. The Spanifh Pine (Pinus Picea) was fomewhat more common, and occupied the moft barren places; but moft of thefe trees were young. All the hills lay uncultivated, a fign of a country badly till'd. If Natolia was well inhabited, good hufbandmen would certainly make the hills turn out to fome account. Here might be planted good vineyards of the fine vines that grow about Smyrna. Here a number of fheep might feed in places that agree well with them, where the fheep's Fefcue grafs (Feftuca ovina) grows fufficiently. Goats might feed here to a much greater number than are now found here, there being plenty of food for them. And if all other places, which here lie uncultivated, were to be turned into corn land,

a careful

a careful husbandman might raise the finest crops on these hills. The vales between the hills did not appear very remarkable to me. They rather consisted of small vales dividing one hill from another, than of large and level plains. I saw no more than two or three such plains, but they were not large, or else over-run with the Andrachne. The prospect of the country is rather strange than pleasing; and the roads are very bad, as travellers must ride amongst broken stones up and down the highest hills. In some places the roads were paved, which seem to be the remains of the ancients care for the conveniency of travellers. We met also with stone-bridges, which seemed too good to be built by the people who now inhabit the country. They were formerly of more use than at present, as the river must have been larger; for we could now conveniently cross it without passing the bridge. Taverns were frequent on the road. We came to three or four, but they have nothing to give travellers but coffee, and water, which every one might fetch from the well. The coffee-house consisted of a heap of stones piled, covered with boughs. Here a Turk made a fire for the coffee-pot, and to light pipes; these, with a cup, were all we could get for our bodily wants. Wine and brandy are strange things for a Turk to give or sell to a traveller; but if he be treated with a glass by a traveller, he will forget the rigour of his religion during the time he drinks it. A Turk of the better sort commonly makes it a matter of conscience not to transgress the law that forbids them the use of spirituous liquors. There are however more to be found that regard this as a commandment not rigorously enforced; and when the number of Turks who believe drunkenness no sin, comes to equal that of the Christians, life will be

much

much more miserable both for them and strangers. We alighted to rest at one of these places, and I seized the opportunity to see what plants the spring had brought forth. Saffron (Crocus sativus Linn.) was the first, and the most remarkable I found. I should have been well satisfied with seeing this plant grow in its native country, if I had found nothing else in this journey. The oriental Saffron is not a distinct species from the European; but its goodness and virtue in physic hath always been more esteemed than the latter, therefore the dose of it is less as it is stronger. It grew here, but in no considerable quantity, amongst the **Arbutus Andrachne**; not at the top, but towards the decline of the hills; nor exposed to the heat of the sun, but in shady places. The colour was a pale yellow; but I saw some near Smyrna of a more dark and almost deep yellow. Natolia is well stored with this precious plant, without culture; and in certain places, as round Magnesia, towards the confines of Brussa, large quantities are gathered and exported to different places in Asia and Europe; I have however good reason to suspect that all our apothecary shops have not the sort to sell that is gathered here, when oriental Saffron is prescribed. The physician as well as the apothecary cannot but suspect its genuineness, after having gone through the hands of so many druggists, who, as I myself have seen, understand the art of encreasing a drug they cannot gain by when sold genuine. Therefore, if any one is desirous of having the true oriental Saffron, which is such a noble medicine, he must endeavour to get it from the first hand, which can best be done by ordering it from any of the above-mentioned towns, and some islands in the Archipelago, where it grows in yet larger quantities. A physician, who is not

certain

certain of this drug, will find it confistent with prudence, rather to prescribe English Saffron in a larger dose, than to prescribe one thing and get another. The Hyacinth (Hyacinthus) and Star-flower (Ornithogalum) were the other spring flowers I found here. We came to Magnesia at 3 o'clock in the afternoon, and got lodgings in the first Khan or Caravanserai place, which for its use answers to an inn in Europe; and where a traveller hath the same kind of accommodations, according to the customs of the country. The house was well built, but kept in bad repair, covered with lead, and over the whole roof were raised arches at the distance of 12 feet from each other. The building was two stories high. The upper were lodging rooms, and the lower magazines for goods and standing for horses. It consisted of a quadrangle which enclosed a fine large yard, in the middle of which was a good fountain, affording excellent water. This the Eastern nations are always follicitous to keep in order, for themselves and travellers. I here first experienced how a traveller is lodged in Turkey. We were led to a chamber, the passage to which was more difficult than the high hills I afterwards ascended; as on the latter I had firm ground to stand on, but here loose stones. The inward appearance was such as might be expected in a place which has not been cleaned for 1000 years, viz. from its beginning, and perhaps some thousands of people have lodged in it. A rush matt was laid on the floor for each of us, on which we put the bed-clothes we had taken with us; and this was all our furniture, table, chairs and bed. They make no great preparations here to accommodate travellers, and yet they live tolerably well, though not very agreeably, in the beginning, to those who are not accustomed to it. Muselem (thus

the

the chief commander of a town in Turkey is called) was the firſt I had to wait on, to deliver him my letters of recommendation from his friends in Smyrna, and to let him know my intention of ſeeing the town and places adjacent. I went immediately to him, and made him ſome preſents I had brought with me. No traveller approaches a Turkiſh officer, eſpecially if he has any buſineſs with him, without bringing him ſome preſents. This is the cuſtom of the country, and was the ſame in ancient times, as may be ſeen by the travels in the Old Teſtament. Sweetmeats, tea, or ſome ſuch matters, are what a traveller had beſt offer, as they are acceptable. When I firſt came in, he was engaged in more important buſineſs than to be at leiſure for me. He was at his prayers, which were thoſe, that after the Mahometan religion are performed an hour before ſun ſet, and no Muſulman will on any account omit or poſtpone them. I therefore went away, and was by his ſervant brought into a houſe where a Turkiſh wedding was celebrating. I was politely received here, as well as in every place I went to in the town. I could not ſee the marriage performed, nor the married couple. Very few Turks, much leſs a Chriſtian, are allowed to be preſent. But I was at liberty to behold the diverſions of the gueſts, who were in a large room, which always is before the Turks chamber. They conſiſted here, as in other places, in muſic and dancing, tho' quite foreign to our taſte. The muſic were two ſmall kettle drums of copper, and a kind of rough and ill-ſounding dulcimer. The muſicians beat both ſo hard, that in a very large room, open on all ſides, none could hear what another ſaid, tho' he ſpoke loud; but there was nothing like order or time kept. The dance was performed by one perſon,

person, who might justly be said to dance for all. He was dressed in a short jacket, was bare footed, and looked like a Turkish soldier. He held in each hand two wooden spoons. Thus accoutred, he skipped about the middle of the room, and moved his head and arms as much as his feet, at the same time often bending his body backwards, forwards, and sideways. He held the spoons, two in each hand, in such a manner between his fingers, that he could frequently strike them together, which with the rough music made a noise no ways agreeable to our ears. As far as I could comprehend, the chief pleasure consisted in seeing a person for full three quarters of an hour persist in a motion so strong, as to put the body and every limb at once in full action. By this we may see that something of the customs of the ancient inhabitants of these places, whose greatest diversions consisted in feats of activity, still remains. I went back to Muselem, and being now admitted to a hearing, was received with much politeness. He was so young that his whiskers had but just begun to grow, and was therefore early enough appointed to such a considerable employment. The road to preferment is the same amongst the Turks as amongst other nations. Merit is sometimes of service, but connections, riches and power best avail. Kara Osman Oglou, one of the most remarkable persons at this time under the Turkish government, was his father. He had found means to get the command over all this part of Natolia, which reaches from Smyrna to Bursa, and had, at the change the Turkish Emperor made this year amongst his officers, prevailed so far as to be appointed Muselem in Magnesia, where he put his son in his room, and sent his son-in-law, who had hitherto been in Magnesia, to Smyrna. Himself lived in Kyragatch, a village two days journey from Magnesia, where are the richest and finest Cotton plantations in Natolia. He could immediately raise 20,000 men, which were under his command; and it was rumoured that his revenue were 1200 piasters a day. It was now about sun set, when the Turks eat supper; I therefore took my leave, after being desired to call again after supper. I had scarcely time to go from the sopha to the door, before the cloth was laid and two dishes cleared. The Turks eat extremely fast. I have known a dinner of above twenty dishes to have been finished in a quarter of an hour.

I could not undertake any thing before I had made another visit to the Muselem. Being a physician, I was much regarded by him; and his example was not only followed by his servants, but through the whole town wherever I went: so far from pointing at me or my servant, and calling Jaur (unbeliever) which is otherwise customary amongst the Turks when they see a Christian, especially a stranger, I saw and heard myself called and taken notice of as Hekim Packi: however, I had not this complaisance for nothing. Muselem, as the chief of the town, began very carefully to think about his health; which was not only followed by his servants, but by all in the town whom I had occasion to converse with. It is common enough amongst the Turks, and even Greeks, to be sick as often as they have an opportunity of speaking to a physician. Most of them are subject to the hypochondriac disorders; and as this disease always occasions persons to be suspicious of their health, especially in the country, and in little towns, where they seldom have an opportunity of conversing with them who

can

can give them any satisfaction, it is no wonder they should be curious, and that a physician should be both welcome and employed. There is no occasion to desire to feel the pulse. The first thing the person does who consults a doctor, is to put forward his naked arm. I know not where they learned this, as perhaps neither they, nor their fathers before them, ever appeared before a physician capable of judging by the pulse. If I may guess, I should think it transmitted by the parents to their offspring, and to have been first introduced by that great physician who lived here, and put such great and just confidence in the pulse. It is not difficult to imagine that the great doctor from Stanchio (Cous) to acquire perfect experience, on which he built his science, here introduced the custom, that, when any diseased person consulted him he felt his pulse, which he taught his disciples; of whom the people learned it, and have retained it to this day without knowing the reason; in the same manner as hath happened with religious ceremonies amongst some nations, who now, tho' they still use them, know not whence or why they were introduced, those who introduced and propagated them having through the change of times been extirpated. I gave my Muselem some medicines I had taken with me from Sweden in order to strengthen his stomach. A Seraglio of fifteen women, which at so early an age he kept, was enough to hurt it; but I would not advise any physician, who may chance to be in my situation, and is consulted by a Turkish grandee, to tell him this, as he might perhaps become a martyr to truth. It is best to think and do what appears to be of service, and talk as little as possible. By way of recompence he gave me, as Lord of the

Town,

Town, liberty to go whither I pleased, and promised to take care that the mountains and places where I intended to botanize should be clear, which I esteemed the best reward I could desire.

The Greek and Armenian churches kept this week (April 12) holy. They use the Old Style as we do in Sweden; but our Celsian amendment of the Swedish almanack brings our Easter and Lent at the same time with the Roman Catholics and others that follow the New Style. The ceremonies, which certainly make the greatest part of the divine worship amongst the Christians here, were better to be seen this week than at any other time, because now they were to be more devout. They all tend, and were by the ancients evidently instituted, to shew and represent all which the Scriptures historically tell us of Christ's sufferings, resurrection and his great works. On Thursday preceding Good Friday, was celebrated a commemoration of Christ's washing the disciples feet, in both churches. On Good Friday, they represented the burial according the Scriptures. On Easter, was personally shewn the Resurrection of Christ; however, the person of our Saviour was not represented by any body, but painted on a table with an ensign in his hand, which was carried by priests. The Greeks have likewise processions, but dare not go farther than round the church, though the Roman Catholics go through all French-Street, from the Capuchins to the Jesuits Convent. They have this liberty as subjects of European powers; but the Grecians are not allowed, as they are subjects of the Turkish Emperor. I saw the ceremony of washing the feet performed by the Greek Bishop at 11 o'clock in the forenoon, in their largest church St. Pholini, which was done in this manner: After mass had been read in the vestry, where the priests and Bishop

Bishop alone had taken the Lord's Supper, there came forth twelve priests dressed in habits of ceremony; they had mitres on their heads covered with crape, which is the head dress of the Greek priests. These took their places on a square stage raised three steps from the ground, and seated themselves on two benches, six on each side. The Bishop soon followed dressed in his episcopal habit, with two, if not three, palls and small bells hanging to them, and a Bishop's mitre of gilt silver and richly set with precious stones. He mounted the theatre and took a a front place, so as to have his Abbots before him on each side. At the same time an aged man that had been Bishop in another place, but deposed by the Turks, ascended the pulpit which was opposite to the stage, dressed in a pall, accompanied by four priests, and had with him the writings of the Evangelists wrote in folio in literal Greek, and bound magnificently in silver. So soon as he had left his episcopal chair, I was permitted to seat myself in it by some of the chief of the Greeks, whence I could plainly see all the ceremonies. Any one that will represent to himself the Bishop as Christ, and the twelve priests as the twelve Apostles, and then read the account the Evangelists give us of this act, may easily conceive how all was conducted. The priest in the pulpit read the history of Christ's washing the disciples feet; and as fast as he read what Christ did, the other imitated. There was even occasion for Judas to be present to make up the number; but no priest will voluntarily take upon him to act his person if he is not paid for his trouble; wherefore he that takes upon him to represent the person of Judas for a little while, receives fifteen piastres. It would be but of small consequence, if he had only the name of Judas during the time his feet are washed, but he commonly retains

it

it for life. Peter politely refused when that part of the text was read which concerned him, wherefore eleven only were washed. The Bishop again put on his pall, and finished with a blessing, after he had washed, dried, and kissed the feet of his meanest brethren; and they in return had the honour to kiss his head or rather mitre, with which the scene concluded. During the whole scene, many large and small wax candles, and a prodigious number of lamps were burning. The Bishop held three small wax candles, and each priest held one. The congregation sung in choruses their hymns, but in their Greek method, which is the most pitiful that can be heard. Noise and riot, which proceeded even to blows on the head, were not wanting whilst this scene lasted. In a Greek church the people cannot sleep, which often happens in the churches of other persuasions, as these are obliged to stand up, and be in a constant motion by crossing and bowing; but they fall into the other extreme, and are too much awake going out of church. I saw the Greeks receive the Lord's Supper. Married priests only receive with their own hands the bread and wine, which is given them by the Bishop. This was also done, as I have already noticed, before the washing of the feet. The bread was of wheat, thick, hard, in small cakes of three inches diameter, and seemed to be of the kind the European masters of vessels have baked in Smyrna for ship-bread, which otherwise never is used by the inhabitants of the country. The cake was by the Bishop broke into smaller bits, which were taken by the priests that stood round the altar, who bit off a piece and took the wine, which was likewise given them by the Bishop. The people received the communion from a priest after the washing of the feet. He stood in a little chapel beside the vestry, and through

a window

a window reached out to them the Sacrament. He had bread and wine mixt together in a silver cup, of which he gave a tea spoonful to every body that advanced. This was done as the people were pressing out of the church. The confession had been before made, which is done here as in the Latin church, each confessing by himself (Confessio Auricularis). The Greek church enjoins children to be confessed as soon as they can speak, and they even give them the Lord's Supper. The Armenians performed this act in the afternoon; but it was far from making the appearance which that of the Grecians did. It was done before the altar in the church by one of their chief priests, as they have no Bishop living here, but are subordinate to the Bishops of other congregations who now and then visit them. Mass was first read; the priest was dressed in a pall, and had an episcopal mitre of silver; he seated himself on a carpet; before him stood a chair, in which such as were to be washed seated themselves one by one. The first that were washed were twelve priests, but the humility was carried farther than with the Greeks; for here the whole congregation had this liberty, without distinguishing the richest merchant from the lowest servant of the stable, of which two conditions this congregation chiefly consists. The priests washed and dried the feet, and anointed them with fresh butter, which they said was made out of the first milk of a young cow. The person washed and anointed kissed the priest's head, went chearfully away, and made room for another, which they told me would last a good part of the night. On each side of the priest was a number of people, old and young, who sung in the same disagreeable tone as the Greeks had done; but in the literal Armenian tongue,

tongue, which is likewife ufed in their public worfhip, and differs as much from the Armenian they commonly fpeak as the literal Greek does from the modern Greek. They had lefs regard to order and decency here than amongft the Greeks. He that came firft began to fing; and if any thing was to be done, as dreffing and undreffing the prieft, lighting the candles, &c. they ran to and fro without order. They had not fo many lights in proportion to the fize of the church, which is large, handfome and magnificent, and by far furpaffes the Greek church. The fair fex never fhew themfelves openly in any of the Chriftian churches in the Eaft, or mix amongft the men; but are always prefent in the church, where they have galleries for themfelves, before which are fixed lattices through which they may fee all that paffes in the church, but cannot be feen.

THE burial of our Saviour was celebrated by the Greeks in the afternoon of the 13th. The daughters of Eve have, by virtue of the Evangelic Hiftory, referved this ceremony to themfelves, which is but right, as nature has made them propereft for what is here required, namely, to weep. I know not how many there were that fulfilled their duty, as I dared not to go there. Their howlings were difagreable enough at a diftance, and nothing amiable could be feen, as they were veiled.

THE Armenians had a large and magnificent mafs on the afternoon of the 14th, Eafter eve, at which I was prefent. In the choir beneath the altar was placed a defk, on which were laid the books of the Evangelifts, wrote in literal Armenian, bound in folio in red and gold tiffue. On one fide of the defk was placed an armed chair, which was occupied by the chief prieft (who was to direct the act inftead of the Bifhop) dreffed in his black prieftly habit, and a cowl.

cowl. On each side of him sat a priest on the floor, dressed in the same habit. Six married priests went forward to the pulpit, one after the other, some of which read, others chanted, something out of a book. They were dressed in their black priestly habits, and when they began their office, a handsome pall was put on them. On each side of the pulpit stood a priest, having a pall and mitre, who held some wax candles, near whom were some boys dressed in white surplices adorned with crosses. When these had made the round, twelve handsome young men came up to the same place dressed in white surplices, which reached to the ground, adorned on the back and sleeves with red crosses. They were bare-headed, shaved to the ears, and the crown bald like the Romish Monks. As far as I could learn, some of these were disciples to the clergy, the others common servants, but who had the advantage to have been at the hallowed places near Jerusalem, and acquired the name of Hadgi. They were all handsome and well-made youths, and seemed to be fitter to be under the command of a Colonel than a Bishop. They kissed the Vice-Bishop's arm as they went forward, and observed the same at their return. Each of them chanted or read something out of a book, in the same manner as the former; and betwixt each of their chanting, one of the priests who sat on the floor rose up, and repeated some words thrice over. I understood not what they were, but was told they were Gloria. Their song ended, one of them that had before chanted mounted one of the steps, and stood before the altar, which was hid by a curtain. After he had chanted a piece out of the same book, the vocal and instrumental music began below the altar. The latter consisted of small iron pipes, not unlike a kind

of

of dulcimer, which were ſtruck againſt one another; and two round braſs plates, which were, according to true time, ſtruck together. This is Turkiſh muſic, and does not ſound very bad in a ſong. At certain times ſmall bells might be heard. After the muſic had laſted awhile, the curtain which hid the niche of the altar was opened, when an old venerable prieſt was to be ſeen, having on a gilt epiſcopal mitre adorned with precious ſtones, ſtanding a ſmall diſtance from the altar. On each ſide of him ſtood a prieſt in black habit, and nearer to him ſtood the prieſts who had before been at the pulpit with the incenſe pot and candles in his hands. The prieſt began to chant and give benedictions, which were anſwered with ſinging and muſic by the congregation. A little while after the Sacrament was brought forth from a little cloſet behind the altar. It was borne by one of the above-mentioned diſciples, who carried it as high as his head, and placed it on the altar. At the ſame time came another, who took the mitre off the prieſt, who was now to pronounce a benediction over the Sacrament and exhibit it to the congregation. Every one lighted the candles, which were before diſtributed through the whole church for money, and were large and numerous. Two were lighted at a time, as faſt as the ceremony advanced. The largeſt, which ſtood on the front of the altar, and were about ſix inches diameter, were ſeemingly lighted when the Sacrament was bleſſed. It was however not they that burned, but ſmaller candles fixed to the top were lighted in their ſtead. The prieſts chanted and the congregation ſung, until the ſcene was concluded. The prieſts on each ſide had a plate faſtened to a long ſtaff, with which they made a tinkling when any thing of conſequence was performing; nor did the

the priest with the incense pot omit his duty, for he often waved and distributed his odours both towards the altar and choir. The curtain at length was let down, to signify that all was ended, and for every one to return home. On each side of the principal altar were two smaller, on which no ceremonies were performed; but in a handsome large chapel without the church, there was mass read by other priests, for those who had not room in the church.

The 15th, Easter-day, the festival of the Armenians and Greeks began. The manner in which it was celebrated by the latter was worth notice, as it testified how much this nation retains of its former inclinations for dissolute diversions at festivals. He that knows what is related about Bachanals, &c. of their ancestors, may here see the remains of them in their offspring. They purchase from their masters the Turks, the liberty of pursuing their pleasures uncontrouled; for which they pay to their Muselem in Smyrna one purse (500 pieces of eight); but in Constantinople they give five or six purses. In consideration of this, they are at liberty, in their houses and in the streets, to get drunk, fight, dance, play, and do every thing their hearts desire. An Easter seldom passes in Constantinople, without some persons being murdered. There was a high mass in both churches on the night before Easter. This concluded about midnight; and scarce was it ended, before the whole congregation cried Χριςὸς ἀνέςη, because then their great and long fast had ended, wherefore they in that very moment began to eat of what they had taken to church with them; and having begun their joy in church, they rushed out, in order to return with pleasure to their ordinary food; and this so violently, that I am persuaded many received miserable Easter marks, who were

E just

just beginning their joy. A high mass and magnificent procession was performed by the Bishop of St Trinity church about noon on Easter day, to the honour of our Saviour's resurrection. There was nothing wanting in point of magnificence and shew, which could attract the attention of the audience.

The 16th and 17th, nothing was to be heard but the Greeks Easter frolicks, in the streets and alleys, houses and yards. They strove, especially the mob, who should eat and drink most. They danced their Greek dances through Frank-street, after bagpipes, drums, and instruments unknown to us, but neither so tuneful or agreeable as to merit much attention. They had a sort made of the peritonæum of oxen, spread on a circle of wood, which they beat with their fingers. They invent several tricks to get money from those that chuse to look on, to defray the expences for liquors. Amongst the rest, I saw one who could ballance so well with his head, as to set a large bottle of wine on it, on which he laid a roll, upon this a glass of water, in which he put a rose bush, and with these he danced through the whole street, hopp'd and kept good time. In their songs they often cried Χρίςὸς ἀνίϛη. No murder was heard of, this festival, as the Bishop had on Easter-eve used the precaution to declare him excommunicated, who should, during the holidays, carry a knife or pistol about him. The Armenians are a more sedate and wise people, and don't celebrate their holidays with such superfluities. I never saw them dance, drink, or make a noise in the streets; but if they divert themselves, it is done in some house or chan, where the Armenian servants assemble and enjoy innocent diversions, or a company ride out on horseback, in which they

greatly

greatly delight, and shew that they inherit of their forefathers the art of good horsemanship.

SEDEKIO near Smyrna, is a remarkable place, because the great Sherard, who in his time was Regent of the Botanic world, here gave Flora a seat, wherefore it cannot but be viewed with pleasure by a Botanist. I determined to visit this place on the 20th. This great lover and patron of Botany spent his time agreeably here every summer, during his stay in Smyrna as Consul from England. I have seen the house where he hath enjoyed the greatest pleasure of perhaps any European that ever was in this country, when he employed his time in making the great Botanical collections, by which he rendered himself immortal. Near the house is a little garden laid out by him, in which he introduced no foreign plants, nor was at great pains in adorning it. He knew it was better to spend his time and money on such matters in his native country, than in a barbarous place, in which his stay was so uncertain.

# ALEXANDRIA.

MAY the 15th, I rode out to see the gardens of Alexandria, which were the first places I saw after my arrival. I procured an equipage which I had never used before. It was an ass with an Arabian saddle, which consisted only of a cushion on which I could sit, and a handsome bridle. On each side of the ass walked an Arab, and another followed, who took care to help me along. The beast was one of the handsomest to be seen of the kind, lively and well kept. I here missed the advantage I had a fortnight before of riding on horseback. The great opinion Turks have of themselves, and contempt for Christians, Jews, and Moors, are in Egypt very evident; of which this is a proof, that they never permit any of the above-mentioned people to ride on a horse, which they esteem too noble a creature to bear such despicable wretches, and which ought only to serve a Muselman. A few Arabs or Moors, who are in some esteem, lawyers or the like, are permitted to ride on a mule. The Christians laugh at this foolish behaviour, which is only the height of stupidity. Since custom has introduced the use of these creatures, they can scarcely be deemed despicable: but on the contrary, one may in some measure be well satisfied with this institution. No town has better conveniencies of

going

going from place to place than Cairo or Alexandria. The ſtreets are almoſt all full of aſſes. A perſon who chuſes not to walk, mounts the aſs he likes beſt, and gets on apace. For one, two, at the moſt three para, he may ride through the whole town. The Moors own theſe beaſts, and value them high enough. Few would imagine that they pay more for ſuch a miſerable beaſt, than a fine horſe coſts in Europe or here. The perſon who owned that I rode on, ſaid it coſt him 20 ducats, and that he would not take double the money for it, as it ſupported him. In the place I had hitherto reſided, I had walked in gardens of Lemon, Orange, Fig and Mulberry trees. I had ſeen whole fields filled with the fineſt vines. I had travelled through foreſts of Olive-trees, and reſted myſelf in the agreeable groves of Cypreſſes; but I ſaw not one of theſe Eaſtern glories in Egypt. Here I met a garden filled with other ſorts of plants, which the Creator hath given to the Southern countries. Palm or Date trees now defended us with their agreeable ſhade. I began immediately to enquire of the inhabitants what they knew concerning the qualities of this vegetable, in order to encreaſe the hiſtory of them, which is yet ſo defective amongſt Botaniſts: As whether they knew any thing about a male and female of the Dates, and their fecundation? But the French interpreter interrupted my enquiries by changing the diſcourſe.

The 30th, at two o'clock in the morning, I left Alexandria in a little boat. At 12 o'clock I came into the opening of the Nile that leads to Roſetta, where it is about a cannon ſhot over. The ſhores were at firſt dry and covered with ſand; but farther up the country, which is level, they were full of fine Palm-trees. The ſhores afterwards became narrower,

rower, and were elegantly adorned with Rushes and the finest Rice-fields; yet farther in were close Palm-woods. We sailed by two small castles. Some villages lay on our left hand, situated on Delta. Dolphins and Porpoisses tumbled about in the water. I came at two o'clock to Rosetta, and was well received by the French Consul Du Salauze. Towards evening I went out in the fields, which had been sown with Rice eight days before. The Rice was three inches high; the water stood four fingers high on the ground, and was raised by wheels worked by oxen, and conducted on the fields in channels. This is done during the time the Rice grows and ripens. I heard a sound which seemed artificial; for example, as if somebody had knocked together hard wooden sticks. I asked what it was, and was told that myriads of little frogs which kept under water emitted this sound. We were on the road persecuted by two kinds of creatures of different nature, tho' both intended to hurt us; they were Gnats and Buffaloes. The latter especially seemed to be angry with me and the interpreter I had with me, as we were dressed in red. Our Janissary was obliged to drive the animals from us with his cudgel. Under the Turkish Government one must always be ready for attack and fence. The people in Rosetta are tolerably civil; therefore a person is in no danger of being attacked by them. Our other enemies, the Gnats, tho' they were much weaker, yet could not be subdued by this guard. Their number made them intolerable and invincible. The Rice-fields, because they are constantly under water, occasion a swampy ground, fit for the support of these vermin, and in these they lay their eggs. They were a different sort from those we have in Europe, being less; but bit worse, and left great boils in the skin, with an intolerable

tolerable itching in the place they bit. They are quite different from those I saw at Alexandria, which were as large as we have them in Sweden, but of a different colour, namely, ash-coloured with white spots on the joints of the legs.

The 11th of June, I saw at Mr. Barton's, the English Consul, Tamarinds which closed their leaves every evening towards sun-set. A variety of a Cat head, something more oblong than in the common Cats. She was of a considerable size, being the length of five spans, three and a half high, and two and a quarter broad. This sort is found in Egypt. I got some information concerning Sal Armoniac, and how it is made in Egypt in large quantities. It is made of Soot, which is gathered of the burnt dung of Oxen and Camels, and is carried hence in great quantities by the Venetians. The manner and place of making it is kept secret. The Scinc, a medicine which is used in Europe, but its history scarce known, is a Lizard, found on the shores of the Nile in Egypt, and even in the houses up in the country. It is dried and sold to the Venetians and Genoese, who powder it, because then more convenient for transportation; wherefore it was difficult to know whence this drug came. The inhabitants of Egypt in general fear this animal, and few are to be found that for the sake of gain catch and sell them to the Europeans. The Egyptians use this drug to excite venery, and of them the Europeans have without doubt learned to make the same use of it.

I should mention something concerning the hatching of Chicken in Egypt. The method the women use is extremely odd. They put the eggs under the arm pits, and have the patience to keep them there until they are hatched by the natural heat

heat of the body. I got some corals that were taken in the Red sea.

A WHOLE company of us rode out on asses on the 12th of June, to take an airing with the Consul. We saw an incredible number of peasants on the road driving asses laden with dung, and some with Saf-flower (Carthamus) which had already been reaped. Both were designed for firing, to supply which article every thing is taken in Egypt. Cassia fistula, Oily grain, Bammia, were now in blossom. On our return, we saw a number of women, who went about inviting people to a banquet, in a singular, and, without doubt, very ancient manner. They were about ten or twelve, covered with black veils, as is customary in this country. They were preceded by four eunuchs: after them, and on the sides, were Moors with their usual walking staffs. As they were walking they all joined in making a noise, which I was told signified their joy; but I could not find it to resemble a joyful or pleasing song. The sound was so singular, that I am at a loss to give those an idea that have not heard it. It was shrill, as womens voices commonly are; but it had a quavering which was much distinguished, and which they had learned by long practice. It was much like the sound I heard the frogs make near Rosetta.

At six o'clock in the evening, we went with the French Consul to see a festival, which was celebrated by a rich Turk, whose son was to be circumcised. The father was one of the richest private persons in Egypt; he therefore spared no cost to celebrate this festival, which is by the Turks done with all imaginable grandeur. The festival lasted 30 days before the circumcision of the child, and this was the last day. The preparations had been

alike

alike each day with open table for every body, fireworks, illuminations, mufic and dancing, &c. We went to fee the illuminations, which were made in a large plain before the father's houfe. They were not like thofe made in Europe; but were pretty enough confidering they were made by the inhabitants of this country. They were three: To the right in a corner of the place was reprefented a Rhombus, which was terminated by a fquare, the corners of which were cut off. To the left in the other corner was reprefented the machine, in which the Coran every year is carried to Mecha, when the caravan with the pilgrims travels thither. Here were prettily reprefented the carpets raifed and divided into pinnacles, with the Camel that bore them. In the middle or near the houfe of the Turk, at whofe expence this feftival was celebrated, was a large portico; the whole was conftructed of lamps hung on cords, without any other building. The fireworks confifted chiefly in a great number of rockets, which mounted well; fome wheels and fountains, with two boys who had faftened round their waifts two machines refembling horfes, out of which poured forth fire on all fides. It was pleafant to fee the people who had affembled in great numbers, fit ftill on the field in a ring, without making the leaft noife, quite contrary to what is done in Europe on the like occafions. The mufic was to the tafte of the country, with hautboys and kettle-drums. They brought us Coffee, which was of the beft kind, and Carpets in cafe we would fit down. It was believed that the expences of this circumcifion amounted to 8000 ducats. Thefe expences are in a great meafure paid by the large prefents he receives from all his friends. It was rumoured that this man had received twenty or thirty

I

thirty camels laden with prefents. On fuch occafions, all thofe that depend on him muft fhew their duty with fome prefents, which confift in camels, fheep, oxen, or fomething of the kind that belongs to their eftate.

About noon on the 22d of June, appeared fome Egyptian dancers under the windows of the French houfe, where I had an opportunity of feeing them. Each country hath its peculiar pleafures, which from times immemorial have been adapted to the people's difpofitions. The Egyptians, inclined to a loofe life, are pleafed with the tricks and inventions of thefe common dancers, as they are entirely adapted to excite fenfual defires. It is furprifing, that in a country where all other women are locked up and guarded, thefe fhould be permitted by the government, not only to fhew themfelves to the people, but even to appear in the commoneft, and, as we Europeans fhould think, moft unbecoming habits and geftures. Thofe that follow this practice, and by it acquire money, are young country laffes, and fometimes married women, all dark-brown, and little better than naked, being dreffed in a blue linnen garment adorned with different kinds of bells, together with a parcel of hollow filver machines which ring when they move themfelves, and make part of the mufic that ferves them in their folly. They were veiled according to the cuftom of the country, with a covering which only left an opening for the eyes, and hang loofe over the face, which they adorned with all forts of tinkling pieces of brafs, filver, and even gold if they could afford it. They feldom appeared barefaced, but made no fcruple to difclofe thofe parts which our European ladies never expofe to public view, though they fhew their faces without blufhing. It is a cuftom introduced in later times, which

which the greatest part of the old men imagine as unbecoming as we think it ridiculous when we see it, but retained to this day by their offspring in the East. The music they used on this occasion, beside their rattling-stuff, was a kind of drum with one head, or parchment extended on a wooden circle, which a woman beat with her fingers; and a kind of violin with two strings to it, which sounded more like a wind instrument than a violin.

About noon on the 23d, I saw a burial, which was one of the most remarkable processions in the country. It was a Scheik, for so they call the Lawyers of the Moors and Arabs. This man was upwards of eighty years of age; who by a pious and honest life had acquired much love whilst living, and was greatly lamented when he died. It was thought that he had acquired so much respect by a virtuous life, as to be pronounced a Saint at his burial, which is customary amongst the Mahometans as well as Christians. He had been warden of a Mosque situated in the Christian quarter; wherefore he had an opportunity of making himself known and esteemed by the Christians, to whom he did good services on those occasions wherein they needed his assistance, which is very necessary in a tyrannical country. These Scheiks constantly endeavour to gain the confidence of the populace, by which they make themselves necessary and even dangerous to the Turkish Regency, as being capable of raising a mob.

The procession was as follows: An old worthy Dervice marched foremost, bearing an ensign, such as they have on the Minarits of their Mosques at festivals. On each side of him walked a considerable Moor: An innumerable croud of people followed, all men, without any order, some lining the streets.

streets. Amongst these were some Scheiks who carried ensigns. Then came the corpse laid in a miserable coffin without a lid, covered with a piece of coarse linnen. After which followed a pretty large number of women, all veil'd with their customary black garments. Some men carrying ensigns and walking in ranks closed the procession. All the men cried with a loud voice, and called to God in behalf of the deceased and themselves, which occasioned a terrible and disagreeable noise; but the women made the same noise I heard when they invited to a banquet. It is singular enough that they should not rather sing mournful tunes: I asked the reason, and was answered, they imagined that joy agreed better than sadness when a righteous man died, at whose happy state every body ought to be well pleased. At other burials in Cairo I saw women lamenting. It was extremely odd to see how anxious every one was to touch the corpse. It was with much trouble the bearers advanced, on account of the number of people that thronged upon them to enjoy this benefit. After they had touched the corpse, they raised their hands to their forehead, at the same time lifting up their eyes very devoutly. The procession went through the street where the French have their house, as the deceased was to be carried to a Mosque at the end of the street. This was very disagreeable to the Muselmen who attended, on account of the Christians beholding their devotion; and for every blessing they bestowed upon the dead, they uttered a curse against the enemies of their faith. Conjurers are common in Egypt. They are peasants from the country, who come to Cairo to earn money this way. I saw one the 24th, who was expert enough, and in dexterity equalled those we have in Europe; but

but the Egyptians can do one thing the Europeans are not able to imitate; namely, fascinate serpents. They take the most poisonous vipers with their bare hands, play with them, put them in their bosoms, and use a great many more tricks with them, as I have often seen. The person I saw on the above day, had only a small viper; but I have frequently seen them handle those that were three or four feet long, and of the most horrid sort. I enquired and examined whether they had cut out the vipers poisonous teeth; but I have with my own eyes seen they do not; we may therefore conclude that there are to this day Psylli in Egypt; but what art they use is not easily known. Some people are very superstitious; and the generality believe this to be done by some supernatural art, which they obtain from invisible Beings. I do not know whether their power is to be ascribed to good or evil; but I am persuaded that those who undertake it use many superstitions. I shall hereafter give a plainer description, with some observations on this subject.

The 2d of July, I waited on the Greek Patriarch, who hath his seat here instead of Alexandria, and is the successor of St. Athanasius. He was a pious man, of about sixty years of age, seemed to understand the principles of his religion well, and was greatly inclined to the Evangelical doctrine. He spoke no language but the Greek, and was dressed in the habit of the Greek clergy. I went afterwards to the Coptite Patriarch, an Egyptian of the Cophtite nation, about forty years old. He was not to be distinguished by his habit, which was such as are worn by an Arab or Turk. He was very polite, and was employed at my arrival in adjusting differences between his followers; being in matters of small consequence a Judge, or, in virtue of his office, a Mediator.

a Mediator. He ordered some persons to shew me his Patriarchal church: the entrance to it was in a narrow dark street, through a miserable little gate, which indeed was only a hole cut through a brick wall. The church consisted of two stories; the under story being pretty large divided into five rooms, with closets that went across, one joining the other. In the foremost stood the altar in a niche under an arch, on which lay a manuscript Ritual in the Cophtite language. The closet without this room was elegant enough, and well constructed after the taste of the country, with costly woods from India in all parts inlaid with large crosses and other ornaments of ivory. On the altar stood a few candlesticks, which partook of the simplicity of the first church. The feet of them were of Sycamore; and a small bough of the same tree served for an arm or pipe, to the side of which the candle was fastened: from the cieling hung several lamps, the cords of which were adorned with Ostriches eggs: on the walls were a parcel of painted pannels; the Virgin Mary with the infant Jesus; St. George on horseback, fighting with the dragon; St. Antony, with a great many more of their Saints, were represented in the ancient manner of painting. Among the rest of the pannels some naked women were painted; which they said were in remembrance of some Indians, by their church regarded as Saints. There were no carved images. It was remarkable to see amongst other things in their church, a number of crutches, made of unbarked boughs of Sycamore and other trees, about three feet long, and of moderate thickness, with a cross at the upper end about a foot long. A parcel of them stood in the choir or foremost room, and in every other place in the church; but in the room

nearest

nearest the door, lay thousands of these staffs. I enquired for what use they were designed; and was answered by a Cophti, that in former times, in the beginning of the church, the Christians had used them for arms, to defend themselves from their enemies when they came upon them during divine service; and from that time it has been customary for every one to have such a staff during the time mass is read; which now serve only to lean on with the arms, for which they are commodious and necessary in a church where no benches are to be seen.

The 3d. Now was the time to catch all sorts of Snakes to be met with in Egypt, the great heats bringing forth these vermin: I therefore made preparation to get as many as I could, and at once received four different sorts, which I have described and preserved in Aqua Vitæ. These were the common Viper, the Cerastes of Alpin, Jaculus, and an Anguis marinus. They were brought me by a Psilli, who put me, together with the French Consul Lironcourt and all the French nation present, in consternation. They gathered about us to see how she handled the most poisonous and dreadful creatures alive and brisk, without their doing or even offering to do her the least harm. When she put them into the bottle where they were to be preserved, she took them with her bare hands, and handled them as our ladies do their laces. She had no difficulty with any but the Viperæ Officinales, which were not fond of their lodging. They found means to creep out before the bottle could be corked. They crept over the hands and bare arms of the woman, without occasioning the least fear in her: she with great calmness took the snakes from her body, and put them into the place destined for their grave. She had taken these Serpents in the field

field with the same ease she handled them before us; this we were told by the Arab who brought her to us. Doubtless this woman had some unknown art which enabled her to handle those creatures. It was impossible to get any information from her; for on this subject she would not open her lips. The art of fascinating Serpents is a secret amongst the Egyptians. It is worthy the endeavours of all naturalists, and the attention of every traveller, to learn something decisive relative to this affair. How ancient this art is amongst the Africans, may be concluded from the ancient Marii and Psylli, who were from Africa, and daily shewed proofs of it at Rome. It is very remarkable that this should be kept a secret for more than 2000 years, being known only to a few, when we have seen how many other secrets have within that time been revealed. The circumstances relating to the fascination of Serpents in Egypt related to me, were principally, 1. That the art is only known to certain families, who propagate it to their offspring. 2. The person who knows how to fascinate Serpents, never meddles with other poisonous animals; such as Scorpions, Lizards, &c. There are different persons who know how to fascinate these animals; and they again never meddle with Serpents. 3. Those that fascinate Serpents eat them both raw and boiled, and even make broth of them, which they eat very commonly amongst them; but in particular, they eat such a dish when they go out to catch them. I have even been told that Serpents fried or boiled, are frequently eat by the Arabians, both in Egypt and Arabia, though they know not how to fascinate them, but catch them either alive or dead. 4. After they have eat their soup, they procure a blessing from their Sckeik (Priest or Lawyer) who uses some superstitious ceremonies,

monies, and amongst others, spits on them several times with certain gestures. This matter of getting a blessing from the Priest is pure superstition, and certainly cannot in the least help to fascinate Serpents; but they believe, or will at least persuade others, that the power of fascinating Serpents depends upon this circumstance. We see by this, that they know how to make use of the same means used by other nations; namely, to hide under the superstitious cloak of religion, what may be easily and naturally explained, especially when they cannot or will not explain the natural reason. I am inclined to think that all which was formerly, and is yet reckoned witchcraft, might come under the same article with the fascination of Serpents. The discovery of a small matter may in time teach every body to fascinate Serpents; and then this power may be exercised by those who have not got it from the hands of a holy Scheik, just as the heat would naturally hatch chicken in an Egyptian oven; whether a Scheik did or did not lay himself naked on it, when the eggs are just put in; yet to this ceremony do the superstitious Egyptians ascribe the happy event of the chicken being hatched, when they are asked the reason. I have been told of a plant with which they anoint or rub themselves before they touch the Serpents; but I have not hitherto received the least description of it, therefore I regard it as fabulous *.

* Mr. Jacquin, in a letter to Sir Charles Linnæus, says, that the Indians in the West-Indies charm Serpents with the Aristolochia Anguiceda; and the late Mr. Forskohl on his travels to the East, likewise informed Dr. Linnæus, that the Egyptians use a species of Aristolochia (Birthwort) but does not determine which species it is.

# From Cairo to the Egyptian Pyramids.

I left Cairo at four o'clock in the afternoon of the 17th, accompanied by a Janiffary and my servant. I had befides for companions a traveller, born in Aleppo, and bred at the court of the German Emperor, who was entitled a Baron, furnamed Burkana, and had lately arrived from Rome; a Georgian Chriftian, who was a phyfician here, and a Jew Rabbi from Nuremberg. We all rid on affes. After we had rid through the miferable, narrow, foggy, and unpaved ftreets of Cairo, we came into a pretty fpacious and uninhabited plain, which refembled a little defart; but with this difference, that fome Sycomore and Tamarifks adorned this dry and fandy plain with their green leaves.

We afterwards came to Old Cairo, which is a fuburb to Cairo. We faw fome large, and according to the tafte of this country, handfome houfes, as we paffed by, which are the fummer habitations of the Turkifh grandees. Adjoining to each was a large, handfome, and fpacious garden, with fine trees of Caffia, Acacia, Plaintain, Dates, Tamarifk, Senfitive plants, and many others, but all in diforder, being entirely left to nature. Thefe feats were fituated on the Nile, and were such as might certainly please the possessors of them.

The most remarkable thing at Old Cairo, was the place where the depth of the water is taken, when the Nile encreases. This is a pretty large house, built in a square near the river. Its roof terminates in a white pyramid: in the foundation wall are holes, through which the water has a free entrance: in the middle of the building is erected a marble obelisk, on which is a scale of inches. Here they daily see whether the river decreases or increases, till the water is let into the town and over the country. The Regency sends somebody hither to take the mark every hour; and at this time their superstition will not permit any but Mahometans to enter it. It was therefore impossible for us now to see the inside of this holy place, but I had an opportunity of seeing it another time. We went in a flat-bottom boat over the Nile, with our asses and all our equipage, and landed on the other side at Gisa, one of the handsomest villages round Cairo, where they make Sal-armoniac. We continued our journey to another village some distance from this, where we lay that night. It gave me singular pleasure to see the perfect husbandry practised here, in a level country, with villages, peasants, women, fields, cattle, husbandry, utensils, &c. in them. Egypt resembles entirely our flat country in Europe. At this time every thing was like our autumn: the fields were dry and bare, and in the plains was scarce a green leaf to be seen, except in some places where the fields were sown with Cucumbers and Sesamum (oily grain). It is in our winter and spring, from December to the month of March, that Egypt is in its glory; for then the Nile is confined within its banks, and the fields are sown. Then a person

F 2

can

can see from a little hill a striking resemblance of a green sea, I mean the verdant earth, without being able to see the end. We came to our quarters, and were politely received by the Sheick, who was the principal man in the village. He ordered us to be conducted to a large room of a stone house, which was the property of a Turk in Cairo. After some time we got our supper, which, after the manner of the country, was sparing. Our Sheick had killed two kids. In the same water they were cooked, was also boiled a quantity of wheat-bread to a pudding: of this they filled two vessels, each as large as two men could carry. In the middle, and upon the bread, was boiled rice; round the edges the meat was laid, cut into small pieces; the floor served for a table; a rush mat for a table cloth; the palm of the hand for a spoon, and the fingers for knives and forks. A person that cannot be satisfied with this treatment from Arabs, will fare but indifferently amongst them: but if he takes in good part the well-meaning manner in which they treat strangers, I doubt whether more good will, frankness, and hospitality, is to be met with amongst any nation than amongst them. This hath been the manner of their fathers, whose history we have in the Scriptures; and such it is to this day, and will remain so for ever. We set out at break of day for the place of our destination. After we had travelled an hour and a half over plains, and near several villages, we came to the Arabian tents, who have their camp round the Pyramids. Their chief is a Scheick, and without his permission none can approach the Pyramids. He sent his eldest son out on foot to meet and welcome us, and he conducted us to a little house, built for travellers, at some distance from their tents. I there ordered him the presents I had

brought

brought with me; and after he had given us coffee, we mounted our asses. The Scheck came then himself from his quarters, accompanied by his youngest son, both mounted on excellent horses, and conducted us to the Pyramids. There I learned the difference between a real and imaginary idea, between seeing a thing with one's own eyes, or those of others. I had read all the descriptions travellers have given of these Pyramids; I had seen drawings of them; I had heard them described by those who had been here: and more than that, I had myself seen them at various distances since I came to Egypt; but with all this, I knew not what the Egyptian Pyramids were until I came within twenty yards of them; and less yet did I know of their inward appearance until I had been in them. We first went round the largest and handsomest Pyramid, to contemplate its height, breadth, form and construction. After the entrance had been opened, and we had lighted our flambeaus, and discharged some pistols at the entrance, we went in. The Scheck and his son faithfully kept close to my side through all the vaults, walks, and rooms. We went in at seven, and came out half an hour before nine o'clock. After we had come out, I began alone, whilst the others were taking some refreshment, to climb up on the out-side, and gather what naturalia I there found of stones and petrifactions. I chose the West side, and kept nearest the left corner, because it was easiest there to ascend. I had already got to the middle of the Pyramid, and between each step found something worth notice; when the stones, heated by the sun, began to burn through my boots, and therefore were much less to be touched with the hands, which prevented me for this time from reaching the top, and obliged me to content myself with gathering at the foot of it whatever I could find worth notice. We afterwards went to the smaller Pyramids, round which I rid, and beheld attentively their appearance. I was determined to know whether stones alone must satisfy my curiosity, and if a burning sand had excluded every thing that had life from this place. If I had not searched attentively, I should certainly have been of the opinion, and confirmed what I was told in Cairo, that no living creature, much less a plant, was to be found near the Pyramids. The earth is of such a nature here, that it would appear to many a miracle, if any animal or plant could here find nourishment and sustenance. I found however both; namely, one single plant, which was Gum Succoury (Chondrilla juncea). Of animals, I found the little Lizard, which I had every where seen running on the walls in the Levant, running here in numbers on the sand. But what most pleased me was a Lion Ant (Hemerobius Formicaleo) which insects have their own republic. These run by hundreds in the sand, in the same manner as Pismires. Each held stone, sand, or rotten bits of wood between their curious jaws or maxillæ, and hastened with them to the dwellings they had made in the sand. I saw numbers of this insect's nests. They were thrown up in tufts in the sand, about the bigness of the two fists, and a little depressed at the top. In the middle of this depression was a little hole, about the bigness of a small pipe stem, through which they went in and out. I attacked them within their intrenchments, in hopes of seeing the inward construction of their nests, but I was deceived, and only demolished their outworks; from which went a private passage, so artfully conducted, that it was in vain to endeavour to come to their innermost dwelling. All the architecture, magnificence,

cence, and expence that shine in the excellent Pyramids, cannot give a contemplator of nature such high ideas, as the art of these little creatures can excite.

BETWEEN the tents of the Arabs and the Pyramids, I saw the dreadful large image, mentioned by every author. It was now so much abused that nothing like a face was to be seen. The Arabs, who as Mahometans suffer no images, have entirely ruined the face, by casting their lances at it. It must have been an excellent piece formerly, as the whole image was cut out of one part of a limestone mountain.

WE returned to the Arabian tents. I was curious to see in person their manner of living, of which I will give a short description. The Arabians assemble in certain families, who occupy a place where they erect their tents. These chuse a Scheck or Leader. His office is to compromise quarrels between them, and lead them on when they are attacked. Their œconomy is compendious, but quite sufficient to make life agreeable: they dwell in tents, which commonly are made of camels hair: they are divided in such a manner, that the women live in different rooms from the men; as both sexes, according to the custom of the East, are not permitted to live constantly in the same room; nor are women permitted, by the Mahometan religion, to shew themselves to other men. The furniture of the rich consists of a mat, which they spread over the ground in their tent; upon which they place a sofa which serves them for table, chairs, and bed. They have some copper vessels in which they boil their victuals, and some wooden dishes in which they serve them up. Their estate consists in cattle, as horses, asses, camels, oxen, cows, sheep and goats, of which each family hath their own before the tent.

tent. For this reason they keep a number of dogs. At this time the Arabs had all their cattle at home, and fed them with cuttings of straw and dried trefoil, but the horses with barley. At the time of the year when Egypt is verdant, they search for such places as will afford food for their cattle. The greatest property of the Arabians consists in horses. They have reason to set a great value on them, as they are certainly the finest and best in their kind that can be seen. An Arabian horse is slender, has a long neck, clean legs, fine skin, is full of fire, and runs very fast. They are mostly sorrel or brown bay, but some are white and iron grey mixt. A black horse is very rare to be seen. If they get one of this colour, without spots, they reckon him unlucky, and part with him. The Arabs are excellent horsemen; they sit fast and well on a horse, being used from their youth to it. Their saddles are almost made in the same manner as ours; but the hindmost tree is so high, that it covers more than half-way up the rider's back. The stirrups are flat in the Turkish manner, and hide the whole foot. They never use a girt, which makes it so much the more difficult to ride and mount. The Arabian youths often stand straight in the saddle, whilst the horse runs in full career, and keep themselves in a just ballance, throw their lances, and turn backwards and forwards; some of them whilst the horse runs in full speed, throw themselves over and stand on their heads in the saddle. Their cloaths are not very elegant. Over the body they have a piece of white woollen cloth, which they cast several times up and down from the feet over the shoulders, so that they always have their arms at liberty: they likewise use linnen. Those with whom I was, had red gampaches round their legs, and a turban

round

round the head. Their arms are a lance, commonly twelve feet long, with a point at one end, which they use in battle, and when they take a long ride; a battle-ax faſtened to a ſtick of three feet length, with a little edged oblong iron club faſtened to ſuch another ſtick; theſe they conſtantly carry with them. They uſe no fire arms, nor ſabres, nor knives.

The Arabs are of a middling ſize, full of fleſh, but not fat; they have ſtrong muſcles and a rough ſkin; their countenance is dark brown; and after they are married they let their beards grow, which are always black.

With the new moon at ſeven o'clock in the morning on the 27th, began the time when all the Mahometans invert the order of nature, turning night into day, and day into night. This is their famous *Ramazan* or *Ramadan*, which laſts for thirty days, or the whole courſe of the moon. Under all this time every Muſelman refrains from meat, drink, tobacco and coffee. In a word, none can without puniſhment take a drop of water from ſun-riſe to ſun-ſet; but no ſooner is the ſun gone down than they begin to eat, drink, and be merry until ſun-riſe. All minarets, or ſteeples of their Moſques, are at this time adorned with burning lamps all the night long, as likewiſe are the principal ſtreets. I went on a balcony at ſeven o'clock of an evening, to ſee Cairo's innumerable minarets illuminated, which afforded a fine ſight.

On the 27th was celebrated a feſtival, to which nature gives Cairo alone a right, and therefore cannot be celebrated at any other place in the world. It was on this day that the water of the Nile was let into the town, and therefore a beginning was made to Egypt's fertility for the enſuing year. As the good

good or bad fortune of the country depends on this day, in respect to the plenty of the water, it is justly one of the most solemn in the whole year. The Nile is entirely under the direction of man: it overflows the country, but wanders not at will: it is conducted to all parts of the countries which may want it, with prudence and circumspection; but the art of man cannot contribute to its encrease. This is the work of nature. When the Nile begins to encrease, a dam of earth is cast up at the opening of the ditch, which the Emperor Trajan made from the river, and goes through the city, which formerly ended in the sea at Rosette, after having watered the whole country through which the ditch was made. When the water hath risen to a sufficient height, which can be seen by the famous Nilometre, this dam is opened and the ditch filled with water, which is afterwards encreased and led over the whole country. The day this is done is a festival, and was now celebrated. The festival was not so remarkable this year as in others, because the Turks had now begun their Ramadan, when every body is silent and devout. The scene was commonly performed in this manner: the Bashaw in Cairo, accompanied by a detachment of 1000 or more Janissaries, with his Kiaja and other officers, goes to the dam on horseback at seven o'clock in the morning, where he enters a Tchiosk (an open summer-house) and orders those that are to open the dam to hold themselves in readiness. The honour of opening the dam is divided between the Turks, Cophti, and Jews, and is opened by them in their turn. When every thing is ready for opening, the Bashaw throws with his own hands a spade upon the dam. This done, it is removed by those who are
appointed

appointed for the purpose, with the loudest acclamations of numbers of people.

THE Turkish Emperor had sent a new Bashaw into Egypt, which happens almost every year. Ali Bashaw, who six months before was grand Vizir, was now appointed Bashaw. He came on the evening of the 16th, to Bulack, after a voyage of ten days on the Nile. He had been long coming a short voyage; but these vessels have neither sails nor oars, being drawn with ropes by a number of people on the shore. At the arrival of a Bashaw, the Beys and other officers in Cairo, make handsome preparations to receive him. With these, the English Consul Mr. Barton and I rid out to see the procession. After we had come out of the city and Bulack, we alighted and went along the shore on foot. We had the Nile on our left hand, which now had risen to a tolerable height, smooth, and agreeable to behold; and on the right, magnificent grand tents of the Beys and other grandees; before each was a fine illumination of lamps in different figures, hung upon cords. I went into the tent of a young Bey, in which was a room capable of containing two hundred persons; the whole of the inside covered with fine cloth of gold, with sofas of the same kind, and fine Indian carpeting on the earth: a magnificence much more becoming a Prince, than a person who some years ago was bought for fifty or sixty piasters, whose business was to sit on his knees, pour out coffee, and light the tobacco pipe for one who had risen in the same manner to honour. This is the rise of the Egyptian Regents. The Bashaw had landed with his vessels on the other side of the river, opposite the tents, where he lay over night in his vessel. The next morning he came over, and was received on the shore

shore by all the Beys, with much magnificence. He mounted a horse, and they accompanied him on foot to a house hard by, where the Bashaw commonly remains for some days before he makes his entry into the city. He forms a wrong idea of the Turks, who imagines them to be rough, unpolite, and ignorant of what we term complaisance. They are far from wanting it. I received on this occasion, as I had often done before, several proofs of it. Several who knew us not, desired us to walk in, and we were politely treated by them.

## A Description of the MECCA CARAVAN from CAIRO.

THE Caravan goes every year from Cairo to Mecca, about this time. The Bey's march from the city, is one of the most remarkable ceremonies of any to be seen in the East. I had an opportunity of beholding it on the 10th of February. It began at eight o'clock in the morning, and went from a place below the palace, where all those assemble who are to go to a place without the city, where the Caravan hath its encampment. They observed the following order on this occasion: 1. A number of spare camels saddled. 2. Six field pieces on their carriages, drawn by six horses. 3. Six Palanguins constructed of grand silk hangings, which covered a sofa, each carried by two camels, the one behind the other. They are for the use of the Bey, and the principal officers on the journey. All the others must ride on camels. 4. About forty camels with provisions, and as many with ammunition. 5. A number of camels carrying water in leather bags, for whose support handsome legacies have been left by the former Sarracenian Sultans of Egypt, which still continue to be paid. 6. Beds for the sick, carried by camels, one on each side. 7. Field music of drums, kettle-drums and hautboys. 8. A number

ber of spare camels with empty saddles, in no order, followed by a number of Scheks. 9. Six fine large led horses, excellently saddled, out of the Turkish Emperor's stable, which he keeps in Cairo, to serve at grand ceremonies. 10. The Bashaw's chief eunuch (Kiflar Aga) with his slaves, above twenty, on horseback. 11. A number of spare camels. 12. A number of fine well-saddled led horses. 13. The Commissary of the Turkish Emperor, whom he keeps here to buy slaves of both sexes, horses, jewels, curiosities, &c. 14. A number of spare camels, adorned with ostrich feathers on their heads, and with shells and pearls. On some of them rid black slaves. 15. A number of Scheks on foot. 16. The officers led horses. 17. The officer who hath the inspection over the water on the journey, and is one of the greatest, with his slaves in armour. 18. Two pair of kettle drums; a large one and a smaller together. 19. A number of spare camels, about sixty. 20. A troop of Pilgrims on foot, followed by some Scheks. 21. A troop of camels laden with water. 22. Two pair of kettle-drums, followed by a number of well-dressed camels in three troops, between each a pair of kettle-drums. 23. Two guides riding on camels; these were old men, each holding a red ensign, adorned with green Arabian letters, in his hand. 24. A Cadi, who is one of the principal officers of the Caravan, and manages whatever relates to religion and justice on the journey, followed by a number of ensigns of different colour: after which came a number of green ensigns carried by Scheks. 25. The Turkish cavalry (Spahi) in the same order as at the Bashaw's entry; but with this difference, that each troop was closed by a number of officers, slaves riding on camels, some dressed in black, others in white cloaks, and numbers of led

camels

camels with rich saddles, and covered with velvet housings. 26. The Janissaries on foot, intended to escort the Caravan on the journey, to the number of four hundred. 27. The Bey's two horse tails and two ensigns. 28. The Bey's Secretary, followed by some officers of the Janissaries. 29. The Aga of the Janissaries and Azapes, in his dress of ceremony, attended by his slaves and ordinary guard. 30. All the Beys in ceremonial habits, with their officers and attendants. 31. The corps of the Azapes, with their officers in the same order as before, with a number of Cuirassiers on foot, armed in the ancient manner. 32. The corpse of Janissaries with their officers, preceded by a number of young slaves on foot. 33. Some officers of the Bashaw's court, in white cloaths. 34. The Bey himself, who commands the Caravan, followed by Seven Kiaja, and his slave Cuirassiers. On his right was carried a green ensign, which is the one that is by the Bashaw, in the Emperor's name, delivered him, to be hallowed, by touching Mahomet's grave with it; and he is enjoined, at the peril of his life, to carry it safe backwards and forwards. It is afterwards sent over to Constantinople, and is a great encouragement to all faithful Muselmen, as they follow it without fear against their enemies. The Bey was a man of seventy years of age, rich and well esteemed, and was now a fourth time employed as conductor of the Caravan. 35. The treasurer of the Bey, with other officers of his court. 36. His music, consisting of a number of kettle-drums, trumpets and hautboys, closed by ten drums, all on camels. 37. I afterwards saw nothing, but an amazing number of Scheks (rulers of the church) divided into troops, and Dervices (who are the same amongst the Turks as Monks amongst the Papists) all

all on foot. There were enſigns of different colours to each troop, ſome green, others yellow, others red, and others white and red, &c. One troop carried long reeds, ſuch as grow near the Nile, inſtead of enſigns. I was told theſe were the fiſhermen of the Nile. The inventions theſe people had in their march were innumerable, and all ridiculous, giving them more the appearance of people that had loſt their ſenſes than of rational beings. All repeated in a high tone of voice, but without the leaſt harmony, the Mahometan confeſſion of faith. They all continually caſt their heads backwards and forwards. They muſt either have ſtronger heads than other people, or be well practiſed, to be able to continue this motion ſo long, without being affected with ſwimmings. With each troop were ſome that had diſguiſed themſelves in different manners. 38. The cavalcade was compleated by the camel that carried the pavillion, under which are ſuppoſed to be the carpets the Emperor ſends yearly to Mecca, to cover the magnificent moſque in which Mahomet's tomb is. The camel was moſt magnificently adorned with feathers, ribbands, lace, falſe pearls, &c. and conducted himſelf in ſuch a manner as to do honour to his office. The pavillion he bore was formed like a pyramid, about ſix feet high, and covered with green ſilk, emboſſed with gold and ſilver letters. Under this the carpets were ſuppoſed to be carried; they were not however there, but were packed up and loaded on other camels, ſo that this had only the honour, without bearing the load. A beaſt choſen for this occaſion may certainly be deemed happy in compariſon to others of his kind. After he has made this journey, he is kept in a ſtable during the remainder of his life, a penſion being allowed for his ſuſtenance, and is ſerved very carefully by

ſeveral

several persons appointed for the purpose, being free from all future labour. The tapestry sent to Mecca is made by Coptites in Cairo, who have a certain number of rooms allowed them in the palace. They are black stuff, woven only for this purpose, and embossed with letters of gold. They are changed every year; and those that are carried there one year, are taken back again the next, being then divided into several pieces, most of which are sent to the Turkish Emperor, who gives part of them to some Mosque for covering the doors, or to some of his greatest favourites, as valuable presents. The Bey of the Caravan reserves some for himself, and gives a piece to the principal officers. It was pleasant enough to see how the mob crouded towards the camel as he passed, in order to touch the pavillion, which they esteemed holy. Those that could not come so near as to touch it with their hands, threw their handkerchiefs or sashes on it, that they might at least possess something which had touched so holy a thing. I asked my companion, who knew the customs of the country, whether they did not make a superstitious use of those things; but he denied it, saying, that they only keep them in testimony of having seen a thing, for which they have so great a veneration. Some travellers say, that the Alcoran is carried under this pavillion; but I know not whence they have taken this relation. I have asked Turks that were well informed of every thing, but all answered, that no Coran is under it. The Turkish Emperor gives of his revenues from Egypt to the Bey 20,000 ducats, to defray the expences he is at in conducting the Caravan. A Bey, who only makes the journey once, gains nothing by it, but rather loses, on account of the many valuable equipages he muſt procure, and the preſents he is obliged to make the Arabian Princes through whoſe territories he marches, that may allow him a free paſſage, which he hath ſometimes difficulty to gain even with preſents. After the Bey has thus marched the Caravan with all its attendants through the city, he encamps at the diſtance of about half a day's journey, in a large plain, where he waits eight days. In this time all aſſemble, who either out of devotion, or on account of traffic, intend to go to Mecca. It was rumoured that the Caravan would this year conſiſt of 40,000 ſouls. A number of women alſo undertake this journey every year. The Caravan is divided into two troops; one conſiſts of thoſe which come from the whole African coaſt, from Tetuan and Morocco, to the three Republics of Barbary. Theſe make about 10,000 men, who in going bring up the rear of the Caravan; but returning, they are in the front. When one reflects on the long journey they take, who come from the remoteſt parts of Africa, and go to Arabia, and that the countries they paſs through over land are uninhabited deſarts of burning ſand, we cannot but conclude that they are induced to undergo theſe hardſhips by an inconceivable zeal and religious fervour. The other troop conſiſts of Turks, from all parts of the Turkiſh Empire, except Syria, and thoſe that border on Perſia, who form another Caravan at Damaſcus, which meets and joins this at an appointed place on the road. The Turks traffic conſiderably on this journey. They do not all go out of devotion, that travel to Mecca: a conſiderable number go for the ſake of gain. They buy from the Franks in Cairo, and carry to Arabia Cloths, Cochineal, Spices, Lead, Braſs, falſe Pearls, and other things, together with, what ſhould have been firſt mentioned,

mentioned, an immense quantity of Spanish or German Dollars. They bring back Coffee, Opobalsamum (Balsam of Mecca) Myrrh, Frankincense, Zedoary, with other drugs, China ware from India, fine Cotton Stuffs, Turbans, Indian Silks and Tissue, or Gold Stuffs, &c. By these merchants the Bey gains considerably: for the time is always fixed how long the Caravan is to be on the journey, and how long it may stay in Mecca. If the merchants cannot settle affairs within the limited time, which is very short, they desire the Bey to defer his march for some days, to which he complies, provided they pay him a certain sum every day, which they willingly do, as their profit can well afford it.

## From CAIRO to the burial Places of the MUMMIES.

IT was now a convenient time to visit the burial places of the ancient Egyptians, where embalmed bodies are yet to be found, under the name of Mummies, as the journey might be made in boats across the country, which was now under water. I set out on the 16th, accompanied by Mr. Roboly, a French interpreter in Alexandria, two Janissaries, and two French merchants. We came to Old Cairo towards evening, and lodged with some Syrian merchants from Damascus. Whilst we waited for supper, we sent for one of this country's musicians, who was a Christian Coptite, to amuse us with his music. His instrument was common in Egypt, and in many other places of the East, being without doubt of great antiquity, and probably resembled David's harp. The Christian Coptites, and even the Franks, who trade here, call it Psalterium. It is in the form of an oblique triangle, so large as to lay commodiously on the knees when they play on it. It has two bottoms, two inches from each other, with about twenty catguts of different sizes. Our musician, whilst he was playing, sang some Arabian songs on Providence, a contented mind, &c. which afforded an agreeable entertainment. It was perhaps with this simple, but ingenious, instrument, that David's Psalms were sung
and

and performed. We went the 17th at sun-rise, on board one of the vessels in the Nile, after we had encreased our company with our landlords. We sailed first for the large Pyramids, which I had a mind to see once more, as well for their being so much worth notice, as particularly for the pleasure I now had of coming to them on the water, the same way I some months before had gone by land. This voyage is the pleasantest that can be imagined. We sailed in from two to four feet water; and those places which the water hath not yet overflown, or where it had already begun to decrease, appeared clothed with a charming verdure, a great part sown with Turkey wheat, and some parts, tho' but few, with Lucern, the latter not being commonly sown before the water has entirely decreased. Innumerable flocks of different kinds of birds are to be seen on the places not under water. I particularly saw the Royston Crow, or common Crow (Corvus Cornix) Sand Piper (Tringa Hypoleucos) which had lately arrived, a kind of Dotteril (Charadrius) as large as a Dove, which I have described; the common field Lark (Alauda arvensis) a kind of Crane, Ardea virgo temporibus cristatis, the oriental Crane (Ardea orientalis) which I have described in Smyrna. The Pelecan (Pelicanus Onocratalus) which flew by us in large flocks: as this is the time of their migration, when they come to these Southern parts from the Black Sea and the coasts of Greece, the usual places of their summer's residence. All these excited my attention, but none so much as the Crane, call'd Ibis: I thought this most remarkable, as an incredible number covered the fields. A person that hath the least knowledge of Nature's œconomy, may easily find why the Creator hath ordered this bird to come in such numbers to the marshy Egyptian fields

fields at this time: here they find in great abundance their proper food, from the number of frogs that cover the country when the waters decrease, and multiply extremely during the time of the flood. The bird, by seeking its proper food, does the country a singular service, freeing it from vermin; which, were they to remain and rot, would certainly occasion a stench mortal to men and beasts. This bird never leaves Egypt. I have seen it all the time the country was dry, but never in such numbers as now in certain places, as they can then range over the whole country; but now the water obliges them to seek for dry places. When the frogs are not so numerous, it lives on little grasshoppers, and other insects which are never wanting in the burning fields of Egypt; and they would certainly be in much greater numbers, if they had not this enemy. I have shot it in both seasons of the year, but found a remarkable difference in its fatness, which proves that at this time it gets greater plenty of proper nourishment. The accounts of Bellonius concerning the birds that come to Egypt during the overflowing of the Nile, are very just. About noon we came to the large Pyramids. Those of my companions who had not seen the inward construction of the largest went in, and I took the opportunity of looking for natural curiosities. I found none but such as I had seen here before, except a fine black Jasper, which will bear a good polish. The remarkable Rat (Mus Jaculus) which the Egyptians call Gerbua, or Yerbua, and which I have already described (Act. Upsal. 1750, p. 17.) and the little thin Lizard, which I saw here for the first time (Lacerta Ægyptiaca). This was by the ancient Egyptians so far honoured, as to have its image engraved on an antique jacinth in my possession. I now determined to put in execution my

intention

intention of climbing to the top of the Pyramid, which the heat prevented me from doing before; but it seemed as if fortune had resolved that the weather should always hinder me from reaching above the middle of its height. When I had got to the middle, there came such a wind, that I and my servant were glad to find ourselves in a part of the Pyramid where we could lay ourselves down between the steps, until the violence of it had gone over us. I thought it therefore too much to venture to proceed farther, as in case of another such accident I might not perhaps find the same shelter. We continued our voyage, which through the carelesness of the master was not so agreeable as before. He carried us to places where the water was not deep enough, so that our boat stuck fast in the mud. It was not so dangerous to run a-ground here, as before Œland or Yarmouth. The watermen of the Nile knew a convenient method of helping the boat forward. Six of them went on each side, put their shoulders under the gunnel, and, as it were, carried the whole boat, in which were above twenty persons, with much baggage. In the evening we came to Abusir, a village, near which is one of the holes leading to the Sepulchres of the Mummies. Before we reached the land, the shore was full of people, old and young, women and children, who came out of the village to see and enquire what we wanted. Peasants are in every place curious and full of wonder, when they see strangers; and the Egyptians are moreover suspicious. The Scheck of the village came on board, accompanied by two of his neighbours, who had the appearance of Arabs, armed with sabres and pistols. They enquired our errand, and permitted sheep to be brought us for money, to be dressed for our supper. The old man went away immediately, and

left

left us his companions. He was scarce got on shore, when he made signs to our Janissaries, that they were permitted to fire on those who remained on the shore after him; which the boys, of whom the croud chiefly consisted, took in good earnest, and went home. These two men supped with us very moderately and rationally. My interpreter asked one of them, who was a large and strong man, why he eat so little? He answered, "A fool eats more than na-"ture requires, and afterwards sickens with it." Our guests wished us a good night, and we rested in our boat, where we were better off than if we had removed to some of the miserable huts of the peasants.

On the 18th, in the morning, the Scheck of Abusir sent us a cake of flower, honey, butter and water. The relish of it was heightened by the simple and well-meaning manner in which we knew it was given. The greatest virtue the Egyptians and Arabs have retained of those that were to be found amongst their forefathers, is hospitality. It would be a great error in the father of a family, to let a stranger go away without having treated him with something. A person who is hungry, and finds them eating, may boldly seat himself by them, and eat with them, without fear. This is a liberty they desire to have returned, as well by their equals as others. We walked to the cave of the Mummies. On the other side of the village we met with a wood of the Ægyptian Acacia, which in this dry sand was a mere shrub, whereas in good ground it grows to a large tree. It was yet in blossom, and at the same time bore ripe and unripe fruit. We met with hares (Lepus timidus) round this wood in such numbers, that without dogs we killed some of them as they run by us. This occasioned my interpreter to come hither again, after we had returned to Cairo, for the

sake

fake of hunting only, and he killed above twenty within two days.

The Arabs and Egyptian peasants are the only people that don't disturb these creatures, which are persecuted in all other parts of the world. Mr. Barton, the English Consul at Cairo, told me that Counsellor Carleson, during his stay in Egypt, had there shot the first hare that had been seen by the Franks in that country. Before that time it was scarcely known that this creature was to be found in Egypt, at least not to the Europeans, and yet less to the inhabitants of Cairo, who neither admire the meat, nor such a manner of hunting. On a little island near this place, the French have introduced hares for the pleasure of hunting; and I was informed, that they had increased remarkably; nor are the Rock Goats (Capra Cervicapra Linn.) scarce in this part of the country. We saw their tracks in the fine sand that covered the ground every where, as plainly as we can discern the tracks of different beasts in the new-fallen snow in Sweden. If we had now been furnished with a good long-barrel'd gun, a swift Arabian horse, and a staunch hound or a hawk, we might have diverted ourselves in a manner truly royal, and which is here chiefly practised by the Arabs of quality, who kill the Rock Goats with their lances whilst running, never making use of fire arms. We at length came to the pit, situated not above a cannon shot from the village of Abusir, on a sandy plain, and resembling the fox-holes in Sweden. We descended with much danger and difficulty on a rope ladder we had brought along with us from Cairo. At the bottom of this pit, on the side fronting the desart, was the entrance into the famous Sepulchres of the Mummies. This lime-stone rock, which I take to be the basis of all Egypt, has

with

with an infinite deal of labour been hollowed out, for the reception of the bodies and ashes of their dead. The first objects that presented themselves to us, were an amazing number of conic urns, or earthen vessels, fifteen inches long, and nine inches diameter at the bottom. They are made of a very coarse clay, burnt in the manner of our earthen ware, but not glazed. The opening is at the larger end, covered with a lid of the same workmanship, a little raised and cemented with mortar. In such urns as have been well preserved, is found a piece of middling coarse fleasy linnen, artfully wound in foldings, and kept together by twine, which is obliquely wound over from the upper to the lower part. Within this linnen is preserved a quantity of dark grey ashes, mixed sometimes with a beak or bone of a bird. These ashes, covered with the linnen, are in the same conic form as the urn, and are commonly found packed close within it. There is often found a lump of ashes without an urn, which seems to have been destroyed by time. It happens sometimes, tho' very seldom, that they find in the urns a bird, in which the feathers, head, legs and feet, and even the colours, are so well preserved, as that one may know what kind of a bird it is. The Crane, call'd Ibis, and Cranes (Ardea Grus) are the only kind, as I have been told, that could be known again. I had not the fortune to find one preserved, tho' I opened many score of these pots. I have been told by those who have found them, that their heads and legs have been laid under the wings, and thus prepared in the same manner as those whose ashes are to be seen. There are even found embalmed dogs, laid in linnen. I have seen one in the possession of the French Consul at Cairo, Mr. Livencourt, which was so well preserved, that I
could

could see, by its hair, colour and appearance, that the same common sort of dogs is yet in Egypt, that hath been there some thousand years ago; and that none of the many varieties we have in Europe have been transplanted here. Dogs had then a better lot in Egypt than now, as they are accounted unclean, unworthy to come under the roof of a Mahometan, killed if they touch his cloaths, and forced to live in the open air on the legacies left them by the charitable people and alms, or seek their food from what fortune throws in their way. I have been informed, that the French Jesuit Sicara, who for the sake of antiquities travelled with much attention some years ago in Upper Egypt, had there found an ox embalmed in the same manner, which he sent over to Paris. We left the burial place of irrational beasts, and proceeded farther to that of man. This is not done without some danger of losing the way, especially if one ventures too far in the passages. On both sides of this passage are niches, in which Mummies in their coffins are preserved, standing upright on their feet. The niche is closed up with a wall, so that nothing can be discerned on the outside.

At ten o'clock in the morning, we returned from these subterranean places, which afforded me less pleasure than the open plain I saw around them, where I searched for natural curiosities. The insects I found in the sand were the greatest advantage I reaped from this journey. I found some, which I am persuaded no naturalist had ever before seen. Some of those I found were known to me. Of these I collected within a short time six species of Libellulæ (Dragon fly) four Cicadæ, and some Grylli (Locusts and Grashoppers). Of what use is a wild desart, filled with burning sand? Can any living creature

creature subsist in it? Are not these deserts useless spots on the earth? Such are the questions of a person who casts a hasty eye on these wild plains. But if he remains there a little time, and is not frightened by the scorching heat of the sun, or the flying sand, bends himself down a little, and looks around him with attention, he will in this dry sandy wilderness find a confirmation of that truth, that the Creator hath not made any thing in vain: and that no place is to be found on our globe, which is not by nature destined for some living creature. In the afternoon we set out on our return, and came to a little fine wood of the Egyptian Acacia (Mimosa Nilotic,) which had on one side a large field planted with Turkey wheat. I here saw that Acacia, like most other trees, hath its gall (Galla) which is soft, white, consists of several coats, with many cells. This was now full of caterpillars, who without doubt bring forth a small fly (Cynips) which time would not permit to see. We saw the herb Purslain growing in the moist places, where the water that ran from the fields had stagnated. We came to a swampy desart, overgrowing with the thorny Rest Harrow, and covered with the Ibis. This plant, which occasions so much trouble to the husbandmen in Scania, is no less common in Egypt. I have seen it in many other places cover whole fields. If the Egyptians were desirous of tilling all the land fit for husbandry, they would certainly spare no pains to destroy this pernicious weed; but they follow, with the same religious zeal as other nations, the footsteps of their ancestors: the son lets the water run on those fields where the father and grandfather did the same; and the fields which then brought forth thorns and thistles, continue to produce the same weeds under the children and

grand

grand children. In many places in the scriptures, mention is made of Thorns, but none knows the plant meant by that word, it might be worth while for writers on the Scripture plants, to think of this Rest Harrow; which not only grows in large quantities all over Egypt, but even in the bordering countries of Asia. In this desart, not far from the water, a Mahometan hermit had his dwelling near a tomb erected over one of his saints. These are very common in Turky, but more so in Egypt. We continued our voyage, and sailed all the night the same course we had taken before. I had leisure to describe a bird in the voyage, which my Janissary had shot in a wood of Acacia, near the sand heath; it is by the Arabs called Kervan, and highly esteemed, if they get it alive to keep in a cage. It comes into the ordo of Picæ, and is of the genus of Corvus, tho' its beak hath no setæ at the basis. When I came home on the 19th, I met with two European travellers of condition, who had lately arrived in Egypt; one of them was a Popish prelate (Desiderio de Casa Basciana) who had been this three years guardian of the Popish convent in Jerusalem, and was now on his return to Italy: a man of merit, who received me with great politeness. I had letters of recommendation to him from the Dutch Consul Hochpied, and the Jesuits and Franciscans in Smyrna: it was therefore a favourable circumstance for me to meet him on his journey. He very kindly gave me other letters to the person who succeeded him in his office. The other was Commissary Lauder, a Scotchman. The Emperor of Germany, as Great Duke of Tuscany, had sent him to get necessary intelligence relating to the Levant and India, which might contribute to forward

the

the trade, which he had established in Trieste and Leghorn.

The water in the channel of Cairo had on the 24th of September so evidently decreased, that it could be seen by the marks near the houses on both sides of the channel, to be half a foot lower. This remarkable decrease is occasioned by **a channel about a day's** journey from Cairo being opened, which leads the water **on a spacious** country between Cairo and **Alexandria. The weather was** now remarkably altered. It had changed from **being** burning hot, to **moist and** cold, equal to what **we have** in Sweden in the months of September and October, accompanied with a strong wind and cloudy sky, but without rain; **for this** is a very uncommon thing at Cairo, **and is esteemed** a wonder if some drops fall in No**vember and December;** but **in some** years it rains in Alexandria **for** several whole days together. The Turks begin **now to dress in** furs. It is greatly conducive to preserving health, **to** change cloaths according to the different **seasons. Flies were** now **seen** in much greater numbers, and **more** brisk than before. This was without doubt owing to the excessive heat in **the summer** months, which robbed **them of a** great part of their vivacity, and forced them to keep in their retreats, where they had **shade;** but cool weather gives them air and liberty **to** try their fortunes every where. **Mi**grating birds **of** different kinds arrived at **this** time, Cranes, Pelicans, Sand-pipers, a kind of Petti-chaps.

On **the 29th, I went** to see the Well of Joseph, which is one of the curiosities visited by all strangers that come to Cairo. This Well is dug and cut in the lime-stone rock, on which the palace of Cairo is built. On the side of its opening is the famous labyrinth,

labyrinth, which is about three-quarters of a mile deep, and two fathoms wide, being square: it closes continually from the upper to the lower part, and at length answers to the depth of the Well: it is six feet wide in the narrowest places, but in some places wider. In several parts of the wall on the right-hand, are cut holes through which the light comes in. At the end of the labyrinth is the bottom of the Well, out of which water is taken up, by the usual manner of drawing up water in Egypt, and thence led to a large Mosque, and a large Bagnio at the Bashaw's palace. The water is brought to the Well from another reservoir which lies deeper, from whence the water is drawn by oxen. To the lowest of these reservoirs, the water is brought by aquæducts from the Nile, near Old Cairo. This is the remains of a work which testifies the magnificence of the ancient Sovereigns of Egypt. The inconceivable labour and incredible cost which have been bestowed on this labyrinth, certainly merit the attention of travellers. The rock is of the same kind with that on which the Egyptian Pyramids are built, viz. a whitish lime-stone, filled with different kinds of shells and sea insects, entire and not changed. The greatest part of the palace, formerly in a good state of defence, is now destroyed; some towers only being left, of which one hath been entirely preserved, but it is without a garrison or ammunition; the whole of it built of hewn stone, of the kind I have already mentioned. We beheld at last the ruined building, which was formerly the palace of the Sarracen Sultans. Here we saw magnificent Granite columns, above two fathoms or twelve feet in length, of one piece, with well wrought capitals and handsome foliages, cut in stone, and some obscure remains of painting in water colours, handsome

some enough for the time in which they were executed; some palm boughs were the most visible. The roof and columns of a very large hall were yet entire, in which was also to be seen a number of Arabian inscriptions, with Coptic letters round the cornish of the roof. From the ruins of this palace, almost the whole city of Cairo may be seen. As far as I can judge, I suppose Cairo to be twenty-four miles in circumference. The view is far from being agreeable: ill-built houses with flat roofs, grey, dusty and dirty walls, with a number of minarets of Mosques standing up amongst them, cannot, do not, make it more agreeable.

The 12th, the verdure began to appear in Egypt, the greatest part of the water having drained from the fields. At this time the country appeared in its full beauty, wherefore I went to Old Cairo, to have an opportunity of seeing what vegetables this season could afford worthy of observation. Bladder Ketmia or Venetian Mallow, is a plant eaten in Egypt, contrary to the custom of other countries. It was now in full growth, and had already finished its flowering, when the country people took it up, tied it in small bundles, and carried it to the city for sale.

The Turks, being fond of war, are not ignorant of military exercises. In Cairo they order their slaves, who are all young Christians, mostly bought from Circassia and Georgia, to be instructed in those exercises to which they are most accustomed, which consist in riding well, firing on foot, but mostly on horseback. The latter is not unworthy of attention. They hold their gun in one hand close to the thigh, and in the other they have the bridle and a match: they touch the fuse when the horse is in full speed, and if they are well trained, hit the mark, which is a jar set up at a certain distance. The person

son who beats down the jar, receives a reward from the officer who commands the troop. Their third exercise is to throw a lance. Instead of lances, whilst they are learning, they use branches of palm-tree, with which they ride after one another in full gallop. I saw all their revolutions as I was riding by the place of exercise, between Old and New Cairo, where they assemble three days in the week, under the inspection of an officer of distinction.

I spent the 13th, on an island directly opposite Old Cairo. I had here an opportunity of seeing the Reed of the Nile, of which frequent mention is made in the scriptures. There are two sorts of Reed growing near the Nile: one of them has scarce any branches, but numerous leaves, which are narrow, smooth, channeled on the upper surface, and the plant is about eleven feet high. The Egyptians make ropes of the leaves. They lay them in water like hemp, and then make good and strong cables of them, which with the bark (Integumentum) of the Date tree, are almost the only cable used in the Nile. They make floats of this Reed, which they use when they fish with nets. The other sort is of great consequence. It is a small Reed, about two or three feet high, full branched, with short, sharp, lancet-like leaves: the roots, which are as thick as the stem, creep and mat themselves together to a considerable distance. This plant seems useless in ordinary life; but to this is the very soil of Egypt owing, for the matted roots have stopped the earth which floated in the waters, and formed out of the sea a country that is habitable. Before I left this place, I observed attentively the shore of the Nile. It chiefly consists of sand, which is composed of a whitish Quartz, or Cristalline particles, united to some oblong laminæ of black Mica, and a very small proportion of rust-coloured Spar.

During my stay in Old Cairo, I ventured to do a thing, which I believe very few travellers before me have done; neither would I advise any one to follow my example, for it might not perhaps be attended with equal good fortune. It was my going on the 15th, into a Turkish Mosque. According to the laws of Turky, a Christian, who goes in one of their places of worship, must either turn Mahometan, or be burnt alive. Money will scarcely obtain a mitigation of the law in this case, tho' it helps in all other cases, even in the most notorious offences, except when any person hath been too free with their women; for this offence is as heinous in their eyes, as seeing their Mosques. The Mosque in which I went, is just beside the mark-house of the Nile: I chose a time when none of the Turks who live there were present; and entered it, accompanied by a French interpreter, Mr. le Grand, and a good honest Janissary, who was devoted to me, after I had given the door-keeper a handsome fee. Such things may have good and bad consequences, therefore a traveller should never undertake them, without great circumspection; and the more, as all the advantage he derives from his curiosity is, that he may say he has seen a place of this kind; for there is indeed nothing remarkable in them. The Mosques are almost all built in the same manner, consisting of four galleries, which form an open square; but the galleries are covered and supported by columns. If these are of marble, porphyry, or granite, in these consists the greatest beauty of the Mosque. In the middle of that side which points towards Mecca, is an oblong niche cut in the wall, in which the Coran lies, and directly opposite

posite to it, is a small gallery between two columns, pretty high from the ground; from which their Scheiks or Priests read to the people some part of the Coran, or something else which may excite them to observe their doctrine, and live accordingly. In some of the other galleries are the steps that lead to the minaret or steeple, from which the hours of prayer are proclaimed six times a day, viz. at sun-rise, at noon, three o'clock in the afternoon, at sun-set, half an hour after seven in the evening, and at midnight. If the minaret is well built, it makes the outward appearance of the Mosque agreeable, and contributes a little to the beauty of the city, if such a thing is to be found amongst a people who despise architecture, and glory more in destroying than erecting. Their steeples are cylindrical, with one or more balconies, and four doors, one from each quarter of the world. In Old Cairo is a grotto much esteemed by the Christians, as Christ and his mother were concealed in it when they fled to Egypt. Over this the Coptites have built a church, they keep in tolerable repair, and use the grotto for a chapel.

NEAR Mataree is a well of sweet water; all the others are salt. Here is likewise an obelisk, which is the handsomest in Egypt. I never believed natural history was so useful in the study of antiquities, as I experienced on the 25th. A person who is acquainted with birds, may see at first sight of what kind those are, which are carved on it. I could know a Strix (Owl) which stood uppermost on the top of the obelisk; a Scolopax (Snipe) much like the pluvialis. an Anas (Duck) and, what I think more remarkable, could plainly discern the Ardea Ibis alba in the position it is yet to be seen in all the fields of Egypt, carrying its head high and tail low.

The entrenchments of Selim's camp, who took Egypt from the Mahometans, were yet plainly to be seen. They were built of brick, dried in the sun, made of clay and straw, in the manner the Israelites were obliged to make them during their slavery in Egypt, in the time of Pharaoh; of these bricks, the remains are to be seen to this day in a Pyramid at Sacchara, which was built of them.

The Egyptian peasant now continues plowing and sowing the field, which he has begun with the month. Their utensils are of the most simple kind, but they are sufficient for tilling the lightest ground under the sun. Their principal instrument is a plow, which consists of a long handle, two uprights to which the reins are fastened, with a small ill-made share. They use oxen for their works of husbandry; their instruments are indifferent, when they cast up clods too large to be left entire, they break them with a kind of hoe, which they also use in preparing the beds in a garden, and to clean the small partitions in the fields. Before I left Matarée, I desired to see the Sycamore, which, as they relate, afforded our Saviour shade when he fled into Egypt. I regarded this tree as a lover of nature. It is only four fathoms thick, so that it is not so large as others I have seen in Egypt. It was a little hurt on the Eastern side, and less in that part. By comparing it with young trees of this kind, whose age I knew, I imagine this, and the other trees of its size, to be about three hundred years old; an age that will not warrant us in regarding it as a relique.

The Janissaries gate is on the left hand of the entrance to the palace of Cairo, where they have a guard room for officers and common soldiers. In the

the afternoon of the 26th, I went thither to see an edifice, which was erected by the usurping governor, to transmit his name to posterity. It consisted of a handsome hall for the Janissary Aga, closing at the top in a dome, and had the walls adorned with festoons, but the roof was supported by some fine marble columns from Italy. On each side of the hall was a gallery, with a flat roof and painted walls.

We must not expect to find any traces in the Turkish architecture, of the magnificence which is yet visible in that of the ancient Egyptians, Grecians, and Saracens. A Turk understands not how to lay a stone properly, much less how to raise a wall. The Armenians are their architects, who, by their natural inclination for the art, assisted by what they have seen on their travels in the East, build as well as can be expected from people who owe all their knowledge in a manner to nature. If these people were to travel to Europe, and there cultivate their parts, we might see in the East, masters in every useful science, who might probably vie with the ancients, and surpass many of the moderns. In the entrance to this place, are to be seen a number of various kinds of arms, used in the holy wars; being the remains of trophies which the Saracens and Turks took from the Christian forces after their victories: such as helmets, harnesses, battle axes, pikes, partizans, and some bows, one of which was of a prodigious size. These were the destructive instruments of those times, before an unlucky chemical invention taught men a shorter way to send one another to the other world. The Janissary Aga, the Kihaja, who should direct the police, and a Tchiauz, are the officers that are obliged to live constantly in their guard-room, which I saw. A number of Capigi, or subalterns, are constantly in their stations. There is no fixed number of Janissaries: they come and go as they think proper. The soldiers think themselves too good to be obliged to keep a strict guard. They find their account better by keeping in the city, where they have an opportunity of robbing and abusing whom they please. This is the employment of those who ought to protect people from violence and injustice.

On the 27th, I saw black slaves sold in the Aurel in Cairo; they were brought from Abyssinia, Æthiopia and Dongala. The greatest part were women, almost naked, having only their private parts concealed: they had their hair plaited in small locks, anointed with some kind of grease, and adorned with corals and coral beads, which hang in the nose and ears. Ornaments are necessary to all nations.

On the 6th of December, advice came to Cairo, that the German Emperor's Commissary, Mr. Lauder, had returned to Egypt, which he had left two months before to travel to Smyrna. In the Archipelago he met with three of the Emperor's ships of war, bound for Alexandria, and with them returned. The same day we heard that Captain Jacobson, of Stockholm, had arrived at Alexandria from Leghorn. He had sailed from Alexandria two months before, and now returned with 27,000 Spanish dollars, on account of the Jews in Leghorn, besides merchandize.

Some days after we perceived that Ismael Effendi, who commanded the castle of Alexandria, was determined to raise the mob against the Emperor's three ships of war. A strange flag, and especially a black bird (the Imperial Eagle) in it, was sufficient to give the Turks a suspicion. They had sent to Cairo from Alexandria, to give notice to the Regency

gency of their intention, and at the same time raise this city; but received a cold reception from the Pacha and Janiffary Aga, who knew on what account the ships were come.

The first of January 1751, Mr. le Grand took of me the credentials by which I was empowered to act as Conful in Egypt. I knew not what he intended to do with them, but believed he would, as he ought, deliver them to the Regency. I was informed to day by the Englifh Conful that he had delivered the power and letters with it to the Jews, who rent the cuftoms in Cairo; and defired them to do what they pleafed, as this matter concerned a foreign nation, and he would not give himfelf any trouble about it.

The Mecca Caravan made its entry this day, after it had been out fince the 10th of September of the laft year. Many of the people had perifhed on the road; many by the rainy, cold, and bad weather, which they could not bear; fome were killed by the Arabians, with whom the Caravan is obliged to fight every journey, when they come to plunder. It fhould feem that 100,000 fouls coming into a city on one day, would occafion a great change in the price of provifions; and I doubt whether there is a city in Europe, capable of receiving at once fo large a number of guefts without feeling it; but in Cairo no want of victuals was known, on account of this remarkable encreafe of inhabitants. This is not only a proof of a rich country, but likewife of a fparing people, who have not yet forgot that nature is content with a little. They loft the Bey of the Caravan and 480 camels on the road. It muft have been a tedious journey, when camels could not ftand it. One of the grandees of Cairo, who had been two years in Mecca, returned, and was received with particular honour. All thofe who

who had made this holy journey, had the first story of their houses painted, and hung over their doors the mitre-shaped Aloe, which grows in large quantities in the gardens of Cairo, to testify their hope by this ever-green. This was both a joyful and sorrowful day. Those who could embrace their relations and friends, after this dangerous, and by them greatly-esteemed journey, had reason to sing joyful tunes, and meet them with harps and drums; but they who had lost their friends, filled all the streets with the lamentations and cries of hired mourners. This is a trade practised of old, and retained to this day in Egypt, with another quite the contrary, and both to be bought. When joy and sorrow are to be sold, nothing will be found in the world which cannot be accomplished with money.

CAIRO celebrates every year on a certain day, viz. the 28th of January, the birth-day of Mahomet, in a more particular manner than any of those places who esteem the name and memory of the founder of this Eastern religion. I may say, that all who could stir were this day in motion at Cairo, all of the name of Muselmen celebrated the day, and people of other denominations went to be witnesses of their joy. The large handsome square Lesbikie, was the centre of the festival; it is not far from the Turks street, and exactly opposite one inhabited chiefly by Coptites, on the left hand of the road that leads to Bulac. This place, which some weeks ago stood under water, in the evening was bright with illuminations. A city must possess a Nile before it can have, in one and the same place, at one time a pleasant navigable river, at another a field covered with verdant plants, and then blaze with different kinds of bonfires. Festivals of this kind are

are to the women of Cairo, as holidays are to school-boys. The latter leap for joy, when they get out of the sight of a severe school-master, and have an hour to indulge the inclinations of childhood. This must likewise be the case with the former when they are allowed a day, on which they get an opportunity of enjoying those pleasures to which their sex, over the whole world, are naturally inclined, and most when they are kept under constraint. It is however a misfortune for this sex in Egypt, that the festival cannot procure them all the liberty to be wished for. The eunuchs, their sworn enemies, follow them constantly; but their schemes are spoiled if they can't outwit these wretches. The reason why this day is more celebrated here than in other places, is, because the eminent Abubekir's race live here, and can prove themselves descended in a direct line from the father-in-law of Mahomet. Of this family was in my time remaining a Scheck, the most respected of any in Egypt, who had once a brother (dead some time before); and on their children, which were numerous and always marry one with another, depends this family so much respected in Cairo, which, according to appearance, is not likely to be extinct for many years. A proof of the regard the people in Cairo have for the head of this family, was to be seen this day, when he received the visits of the principal men in the Regency, the Pacha excepted, who came to his house, and by kissing his hand, shewed the great esteem they have for him. Some time after they celebrated another festival, to the memory of two sons of prophets; but in another manner, and without illuminations on the above-mentioned place. The houses in the largest streets were adorned with hangings,

hangings, and lamps put up before thofe of the principal perfons.

On the third of February it rained in Cairo, which is worth remarking, as it happens fo feldom. The weather varied at this time in Egypt, as it does with us in April, but differed in regard to the climate.

The 22d it was quite cold with a ftrong North wind: all the trees lofe their leaves about this time, and put forth new. Salix Calaf, Sycomorus, Mimofa, had got young leaves, and the firft bloffomed on bare boughs, which about this time were brought to the apothecaries, who diftil from them the Calaf water, fo famous and fo much ufed in Egypt.

The 7th of March happened a revolt in Cairo, but it had not the defired effect. Some of the Beys, who were banifhed on the ufurpation of the reigning Abraham Kiahajas to the fupreme power, had found means to fteal into the city, with an intent to make an affault on their enemy; but they had the misfortune to be difcovered. The Governor fent men to furround the houfe, in which they were concealed. Their faithful hoft, and three of the confpirators, loft their heads in a moment; fire was put to the houfe, and all, even the women, who were in it, were burnt alive. The other Beys and their accomplices faved themfelves by flight, and the Governor avoided this blow, which ferved only to ftrengthen him in his power. The riot lafted no longer than from four to feven o'clock in the afternoon. The Turks difpatch their affairs quickly, well or ill.

I left Cairo on the 10th of March, juft as the Palms were ripe for copulation; all the bloffoms

were

were now in their beauty, the trees shot forth new leaves, and wheat and barley were now in ear; after I had been there for nine months, and had sufficient opportunities of knowing Egypt, a country without an equal, and Cairo, a city which is best described by the title its Lord the Turkish Emperor gives it, when he calls it *singular in its kind*.

TO

## TO DAMIATA.

THE 13th of March in the forenoon, we paſſed by Mauſora, a place which hath got an immortal name by the unlucky pilgrimage of the French King, Louis the Holy, to Egypt. It is now a little town, or rather a large village, about half way between Damiata and Cairo, well diſtinguiſhed from the other villages, by ſix Moſques, and its ſmall houſes, which however are tolerable handſome and built of ſtone; the others having mere clay huts, and ſome are without a Moſque. We came to Damiata after a voyage of three days on the Nile.

THE 16th early, I went out to botanize round the town, but this neighbourhood affords nothing different from the other parts of Egypt. Cichorium ſpinoſum[a], Centaurea calcitrapoides[b], Carduus ſyriacus[c], Tragopogun picroides[d], Medicago polymorpha[e], Trifolium reſupinatum[f], Scorpiurus ſulcata[g], Lathyrus hiſpanicus[h], Ranunculus ſceleratus[i], Euphorbia peplus[k], Poa annua[l], Hordeum murinum[m], Adiantum capillus[n], Trifolium procumbens[o], Poa bulboſa vivip.[p], Apium graveolens[q], Salix ægyptiaca[r], Chenopodium viride[s]. Much larger quantities of dew fall about this time in this part of Egypt, which is neareſt the ſea, than in others more di-

[a] Thorny ſuccory. [b] Knapweed. [c] Syrian thiſtle. [d] Goatsbeard. [e] Snail trefoil. [f] Reſupinated trefoil. [g] Caterpillars. [h] Spaniſh chichling vetch. [i] Crowfoot. [k] Spurge. [l] Annual poa. [m] Barley. [n] Maidenhair. [o] Procumbent trefoil. [p] Bulboſe poa. [q] Stinking parſley. [r] Ægyptian willow. [s] Gooſefoot.

tant, by which the fields are enriched, even where the Nile cannot overflow. The rain likewise contributes to it, falling here frequently during the winter and spring months, which scarcely even happens at Cairo. The Palm began now to open its male flowers, which however is not general before the ensuing month. In Damiata, which affords an incredible quantity of flax, they manufacture a kind of handsome napkins with white, blue, red, yellow, and more sorts of stripes, of which they sell large quantities to Turkey. I saw this manufacture, which is established in a little quarter separate from the town. On my return to my lodgings, I went into a house where they dressed Rice, the chief commodity and riches of Damiata. It is pounded by hollow iron pestles, of a cylindric form, an inch in diameter, lifted up by a wheel worked by oxen. A person sitting between the two pestles, pushes forward the rice when the pestles are rising. Another sifts, winnows, and lays it under the pestles. In this manner they continue working it, until it is entirely free from chaff and husks. When it is clean they add a 30th part of salt, and pound them together, by which the rice becomes white, which before was grey. After this fining, it is passed through a fine sieve, to part the salt from the rice, and then it is ready for sale. Damiata sells every year 60,000 sacks of rice, each sack of seventy-five oke, of which the greatest part goes to Turkey, and some to Leghorn, Marseilles, and Venice. Rice is one of the chief productions of Egypt, and of course therein consists in a great measure the riches of the inhabitants; it grows only in the rich fields round Damiata and Rosetta, which are easily watered by the Nile. The Egyptians undoubtedly learned the cultivation of rice under the reign of the Califs, at which

which time many useful plants were brought over the Red sea to Egypt, which now grow spontaneously there, and enrich the country. The Regency at this time would not give themselves the trouble of introducing any thing of the kind, and perhaps would not even cultivate what they already have, were it not for their slaves, the ancient inhabitants of Egypt, who are obliged to practice what their forefathers taught them, without reaping the least advantage from the sweat of their brows, being obliged to offer every thing to the luxury of their tyrants.

On the 19th in the afternoon, I sailed on the Nile, to view the situation and appearance of the town. Damiata is a little town, built on the shore of the Nile in the form of a half moon, situated on the right hand in coming from Cairo. The Nile makes a little turning to the East, before it falls in the sea. This reach, which is something broader than the river in other places, stretches beyond the town, and serves for its harbour, which is unfit to receive the vessels of the town, the musches from Cairo, chembecks from Cyprus, Syria, &c. scheomeone from Alexandria, and other small craft of this kind. The European vessels must anchor in the open road, without the mouth of the Nile, where they are no longer safe than whilst the weather favours them. In bad weather they have no other chance but slipping their cables and running to sea, or stretching for the harbour of Cyprus. On this account Damiata is a miserable place, and frequented by few European vessels; yet some Frenchmen, who from their youth have been used to the road, and are not frightened by these difficulties, but for the sake of the profit they get by the freight of the merchants goods, run all hazard.

The

The houses near the shore are tolerably well built after the Egyptian manner, but those in the town are the most miserable huts one can any where see. I counted about twelve Mosques. I afterwards sailed to the other side of the town, where I went on shore to look for plants, and there found in great plenty the handsomest in Egypt, and perhaps of all plants, viz. the Plaintain tree, which, with Vines, Mulberry and Peach trees, made part of a hedge round a field, in which Sugar and different sorts of Cucumbers were planted. A more valuable hedge will scarce be found in any other place. If it was even made of valuable metals, it would not equal this. The Plaintain tree was now in blossom, and had already at the lower end of the Pedunculus, fruit of two inches long, on a stem two spans thick and about three fathoms high. Clifford's Plaintain tree was too valuable for our Linnæus to anatomise. To me was left the business of anatomizing and describing it, which I could do with ease in a place where I might cut down the whole plant with blossoms and leaves for fourpence: I therefore dissected it, and found its construction as wonderful as the other parts which my master described. The Vines had lately put forth leaves. The Egyptians don't cultivate them for the sake of wine, their religion forbidding them to drink it. They keep a few for the sake of the grapes, which they eat fresh. The Peach tree was in blossom, but the Mulberry tree in the same situation as the Vine, nor is it applied to that valuable purpose for which it is so useful to other countries.

The Maltese cruizers frequently keep in the road before Damiata, when they are at sea, which is commonly about this time of the year, when the pilgrims go to the holy land. One of them was seen in in the morning of the 20th, at the very mouth of the Nile, where it seized three of this countries chebecks, laden with wood from Caramania for Egypt, and having on board a number of Turks and Greeks. The Turks taken on such an occasion are made slaves, and the Greeks are set at liberty, but their goods are deemed a lawful prize. These cruizers are all equipped at Malta, but they seldom carry a Maltese flag, except the ordinary religious vessel which is commanded by a Knight, and constantly kept at sea. The others carry the flag of Sardinia, Spain, or the Prince of Morocco, as these powers are never at peace with the Porte, or the Republics of Barbary; that above-mentioned carried a Sardinia flag, but was from Malta. Six others cruized at the same time on the coasts of Syria and Caramania.

On the morning of the 21st, I had the pleasure of seeing from my window one of the most remarkable sights in nature. A female Palm (Phœnix dactylifera Linnæi) had in the night put forth its blossoms from the spatha. I went thither at sunrise to see it, whilst the dew was yet falling. I saw a gardener, the proprietor of the Palm, climbing up the Palm, which equalled our largest firs in height. He had a bunch of male flowers, with which he powdered the female, and by these means fecundated them. After he had done this, he cut away the inferior boughs or leaves, between which the flowers of the preceding year had come out, together with the remarkable web which covers the basis of the leaves, and goes from one edge of a leaf to the other.

On one side of Damiata is a large river, or rather gulf, which empties itself into the sea, and likewise receives an arm of the Nile; by which the land

land whereon the town is built becomes an island. On the 22d, I went out to see this gulph. The mixture of sea and river water causes this water to be neither salt nor sweet, but between both. A number of fish keep here, which are caught near Damiata, and consist chiefly of the Burri (Mullet) of the Egyptians, and different species Sciænæ Artedi, which I have already described. In returning home I saw a single tree of Cassia fistula, which had ripened its pods, but had not yet put forth leaves. This valuable tree is rarely seen in these lower parts of Egypt, but more common round Cairo: it grows now spontaneously, but was first brought from India. On this excursion, I found the most remarkable Date tree I had seen in Egypt; it was composed of two trees, which had grown together at their basis, but parted two feet from the ground, one stem being larger than the other. It sometimes happens that several of these trees grow up so near to each other, as to join with their basis; but they are always distinct trees, nor does ever one root emit two stems. But at Tajum I saw a Date tree divided into two crowns near the top, which happens very rarely. Entering the town, I saw the house in which the French Consul dwelt during his stay at Damiata. It was entirely destroyed, and now uninhabitable. It has been in this situation ever since the Consul and his merchant were expelled the town for a riot which they had raised for an affair of gallantry; so dangerous and unpardonable an offence is this amongst the Turks. From that time there has not been a French Consul or merchant in Damiata. No other nation hath ever had any business here. The Greeks alone have a church in Damiata, by which I afterwards passed. It has a number of priests and a pretty large congregation,

gregation, particularly since a number of those Greeks, who were driven from Cyprus by the tyranny of the Turks, have taken refuge here. There are some rich Greek merchants in Damiata, and the inspector of the customs is a Greek, who pays 400 purses for his office; but in most of the Greeks here, their national misery shews itself. The Papists have neither chapel nor missionaries here, which is the only place of any consideration in Egypt destitute of this kind of apostles. The Syrian merchants, about 200 in number, and all considerable people, have two monks from the mountain of Libanon, of the order of St. Anthony, who read mass in their chambers, which even the French Captains frequent. The principal part of the inhabitants consists in Turkish Janissaries, who are all merchants, governed by Serdas; most of them are rich, but then they are chiefly knaves and run-aways, who, for great misdemeanors having quitted Constantinople, Caramannia, or the islands, took refuge in Egypt, and there live in safety. There are many Greeks here; a few families of Coptites; about 200 rich Syrian merchants already mentioned; of Jews a pretty large number. The brokers are all Jews, a few of them rich, but the greatest part poor. They have no synagogue here, but worship God in their own private houses. The Franks were obliged to quit the place entirely, after the French had been expelled.

On the 24th, we had the finest weather I had seen for twelve months, as it rained pretty hard in the afternoon. One should live a considerable time in the climate of Cairo, where there constantly reigns a scorching heat, and scarcely ten drops of rain fall in the year, to be sensible of the refreshment both the body and mind receive from a cooling rain.

THE 28th, I left Damiata with pleasure, as it is the most miserable place in Turkey for a Frank to live in. We had two hours voyage on the Nile from Damiata to the sea. The shore on the right hand consisted of sand-hills, with reeds near the water, and on the left rich land. At the mouth of the Nile, on the left hand, was a tower which, they say, was founded in St. Louis's age. On the right was a village, near which we brought to with our boat, and rested over night.

THIS was the last night I slept on the Nile, and the following day we went to sea with our ship, and sailed three leagues. We were at sea four days.

# TO THE HOLY LAND.

THE first of April, 1751, we anchored before Jaffa, called Joppa in the Holy Scripture, after four days voyage from Damiata. This town has no harbour, and the vessels must anchor in the open road, which obliges them to put to sea in the least bad weather, as is the case at Damiata. The water was so shallow on this coast, that our boat could not reach land, and we were obliged to be carried on shore. We were set down at the fine stone wharf lately built on the shore: it is the only one I have seen of this kind in the Levant. I went first with my Captain to a French factor, who is kept here by the merchants in Rama, and is the only Frank who dwells in Jaffa, being an old man, and having two sons.

I went from thence to the quarters of the Latin monks, who are here to receive Pilgrims, and take care to forward them. They were two Monks, one Priest and one Layman, who was Procurator. I had a bad lodging, because their building was very small, and the avarice of the Turks did not permit them to extend it, though they ought to have the largest lodgings in the Levant, on account of the number of travellers that land there; but I was well treated. The Procurator began directly to make preparations for my journey to Jerusalem. He commenced with a question which I should willingly

lingly have avoided. It was, Whether I came to visit the holy places out of devotion? I answered without ambiguity, No. What, continued the Monk, who was a Spaniard, travel to the Holy Land without devotion? I was for putting an end to this disagreeable conversation, and began another subject, by talking of money. I counted to him sixty-two piastres for myself, and the like sum for my servant. This money every Frank pays in Jaffa, for his whole journey to Jerusalem and back again. I left all my things in his charge till my return, only a suit of cloaths and some books, to dry plants in, which were sent to Jerusalem before me; and I then put on a Levant coat and a Greek cap, carrying nothing with me but my memorandum book. After these preparations had been made, the Procurator sent a messenger to Jerusalem to advise them of my arrival, and I was obliged to wait his return. I was well pleased with this delay, as it gave me time to rest myself, after a disagreeable voyage, before I set out on a journey yet more disagreeable by land. I was now come into the Holy Land, therefore had reason to expect continual informations of holy things. The Monks began with their hotel, by informing me that it was the holy place where St. Peter had his fishing hut, and where he threw the famous ring into the sea. Every thing, even to the table on which we supped, was holy. The wine we drank came from the holy desart where St. John dwelt; and the olives grew on the Mountain of Olives near Jerusalem. These, independent of their holiness, were of the best kind I had tasted in the Levant, being such as Palestine, always famous for Olive-trees, affords. Amongst those who visited me, during my stay in Jaffa, was a clerk of the customs, who on the third day came to receive

receive the twenty-two piastres, which every Frank is obliged to pay to the custom-house of Jaffa, for the privilege of coming on shore and travelling in the country. The inhabitants of the country, Armenians, Greeks, &c. pay only half the sum. But as 4000 persons arrive yearly, besides as many Jews, who come from all quarters of the world, this may be esteemed a considerable revenue for the Turks; and indeed they receive no other from this uncultivated and almost **uninha**bited country. The greatest part of this money is **by** legacies left to Mecca. A shrewd disposition, which appropriates the revenue arising from one kind of superstition to the maintenance of another.

**The** 4th of April, I went out to take a view of **Jaffa.** This place, which may be called **a** little **town,** is **situat**ed near the sea, on a rising ground, having a castle on a rock, garrisoned by an officer and some soldiers, which commands the road; but some of the ordnance were honeycombed with rust, and others sunk in the ramparts: in this negligent manner the Turks keep their forts. The place was some years ago in a much worse condition than at present; but an Armenian from Constantinople, for reasons to me unknown, obtained liberty to improve the buildings, which he did by rebuilding the wharf already mentioned, and erecting some **stone** houses and magazines on the shore, which **give the place** an appearance from the sea side, much preferable to the miserable prospect it formerly afforded. The other houses in the town are poor huts, **chiefly** inhabited by Turks and Arabs, together with some Greeks and Armenians, whose **Monks** have each an hotel here for the reception of Pilgrims. The country round the town is not very agreeable: the roads are broad and level, but inconvenient

venient from the quantity of loose sand which covers them: the handsome plain, which reaches as far as Rama, begins at a small distance from the town, near which are some pleasant gardens after the manner of the country, where in particular I found some Fig-trees, as beautiful as any I had seen in the Levant. Here were likewise several Sycamores, which are scarcer as you advance in the country. The hedges were overgrown with different kinds of prickly plants, in which the wild beasts had their passages and habitations, particularly the little Eastern Fox Jackal, who is to be found in large numbers in this neighbourhood.

## TO JERUSALEM.

THE 5th of April, about noon, I travelled from Jaffa, accompanied by my merchant from Leghorn, and two French Monks. We got from the Monks in Jaffa, whose business it is to accommodate with necessaries those who intend to visit Jerusalem, miserable asses, and yet worse saddles, together with ten Arabs and two Turkish horsemen to conduct us, who received us at the town's end. The whole country from Jaffa to Rama consists of little hills; between these are level and handsome vales, which extend in large plains. A part is turned into corn fields, but most of it lies waste. The ground here consists of a loose reddish sandy mould; and I have never seen in any place the ground so cast up by moles as in these plains. There was scarce a yard's length between each mole hill. This is an advantageous circumstance for all sorts of self-sown wild plants; therefore entire plains were covered with Buphthalmum foliis oblongis dentatis; or Oxeye, with oblong dentated leaves; which made them much yellower than our Swedish meadows are in the month of June, from the Caltha Palustris and Ranunculus, or Marsh-marygold and Crowfoot. In other places the fields were white with a sort of Matricaria, or Feverfew. In three places, we had fine vales abounding with Olive-trees. Cranes, the inhabitants of uncultivated countries, were here to be found
in

in great numbers. At four o'clock we came to Rama, and alighted at the fine convent, which, if we except Jerusalem, is the best in the Holy Land.

In the afternoon of the 7th, the President at the Holy Sepulchre in Jerusalem went with the greatest part of the Monks to the church, where the Holy Sepulchre is, to remain there till Easter day, after they had first made a holy visit in the morning of the 4th, to the place where the garden Gethsemane had been. About three o'clock in the afternoon, the Monk, who was appointed to wait on me, conducted me to the famous temple where the places were shewn, which Christ, by his sufferings, death and burial, has immortalized in memory. Before the door of the temple is a little place, to which one descends by a stair case of ten or twelve steps. This serves for a market, in which Paternosters were the chief commodity. The place on which the temple is built, is said to be that which formerly was called Golgotha, or the place of Skulls. The Europeans imagine this is a hill or rising ground; it is quite the contrary, a vale or deep ground. We now went into the temple, which at its entry had two doors, one beside the other, but one of them was walled up. Before the entry we found three Turks, a Scherif or Lawyer, a Janissary, and a Bostangi, who were ordered thither by the Regency of the country. The business of the first is to mark down the names of those who go in, for sake of the payment, which the Turkish Regency takes from the Christians who visit this place, as it belongs to the Turks. The latter should take care and prevent quarrels between Christians of various denominations, who pay their devotions here. The first thing I was shewn at my entrance, was the stone on which Christ's body, as they say, was laid and anointed

anointed by the women, before it was placed in the grave. It is directly opposite the door, and a few steps from it, surrounded with high iron rails. It is a fine slab of white marble, about six feet long and three broad. This belongs to the Latins; for each kind of Christians, except Protestants, possess certain holy things. From thence we went into the holy Sepulchre, which is in the midst of the choir, being the **center of the** church, and belongs to the Latins.

In the afternoon of the 8th, I went to see some of the remarkable places in the **town.** 1. The Bazar, or market place, which is miserable, and contains few valuable goods. 2. A house, in which the mother of the sons of Zebedee lived, as the Monks report. The Maltese had it for their dwelling, whilst they were masters of Jerusalem. The Greeks have now turned it into an inn for pilgrims, and have a little chapel there. 3. A church of the Syrians, which is said to have been St. Mark's house. They shew a stone vessel, in which the Apostles are said to have baptized the primitive Christians. 4. The place where Annas's palace formerly stood, and where Christ was tried, which belongs to the Armenians, who have a little chapel there. Before the house stands an old Olive-tree, which these people have in great veneration: the stem **of it** is covered over with earth, and it has only **some** branches above ground. They say that Christ was **tied to this tree** whilst the trial continued. 5. Another Armenian chapel, said to be built on the place where Christ was examined before Caiaphas: this was not far from the other, but without the town gate. In both was a little separate chamber well ornamented, exactly over the place where the affair happened, which was painted

in

in it. In the chapel of Caiaphas, the altar consisted of a stone eight feet long and five feet high, said to be the same which had been laid on Christ's grave at his burial, and the women would have taken away, but found it too large. It was now covered with mortar an inch thick, and was of the hard limestone, common in Palestine. In some places they have left it bare, for devout Pilgrims to kiss: here was likewise painted Peter's denial of Christ. From thence we went out through one of the town gates, and came immediately on the holy mount Sion, so famous in the days of David. It is now a desart flat and level, situated immediately without the ramparts. It is occupied by, and left to the Christians for a burial place, where all denominations of them bury their dead. Hence we could see a Turkish Mosque, with a handsome cupola, erected over David and Solomon's grave. In this same place, they say, Christ instituted the Lord's Supper, and the Holy Ghost came upon the Apostles. No Christian can approach nearer to this most principal of holy places, than Sion, which is at two guns shot distance. I botanized on the dry and poor Sion, and found some common plants there, viz. *Allium pallens, Veronense;* **Betonica** *officinalis; Biscutella didyma; Trifolium globosum, tomentosum, resupinatum; Ephedra distachia\**.

The 9th in the forenoon, I paid a visit to the Patriarch of the Armenians, with whom I had been acquainted in Smyrna. He resided in the convent of this nation, which is the largest in Jerusalem, larger than that of the Latins, and the next to it in riches. It has above 1000 chambers for Pilgrims, beside those of the Monks. The rich Armenian nation, which is more inclined to devotion, if not

\* Two sorts of Garlick, Betony of the shops, Buckler Mustard, three sorts of Trefoil, and the Shrubby Horsetail.

superstition,

superstition, than any other nation of the East, hath by pilgrimages put this their spiritual dwelling in Jerusalem into so respectable a condition. There is not a year passes but more than 1000 Pilgrims arrive from Armenia, Persia, and Turkey, who never leave it without giving considerable alms. The chapel which they have here in the convent is the handsomest of all the private chapels in Jerusalem; the whole is adorned with rich hangings, fine paintings, and an innumerable quantity of valuable silver lamps, some gilt, and almost all made by eminent masters. Going home, I passed by David's castle, which at this time is the name of a Turkish fort, and the only one with which they think themselves able to defend Jerusalem. This is almost totally destroyed, as are all the fortresses belonging to the Sultan. On a platform lay a dozen of cannon, which must be cast over again before they can be used. This fort lies on a low ground, and is not situated so as to command the town. It serves only to give signals by firing some cannon on the festivals of the Turks. Jerusalem has amongst its inhabitants about 20,000 Jews. The Jew women go here with their faces uncovered; this the Turks have ordered, that they may be known from their own women. The greatest part of the Jews here are poor, as they have no opportunity of trafficking; for without it they cannot thrive in any part of the world. They have no other income here than what they can get from the Pilgrims of their nation, who come far and wide from all places to pay their respects to the seat of their forefathers. Their Rabbi has large revenues from his brethren throughout the whole world, of which the Turks draw the greatest part; for Jews as well as Christians must constantly bring offerings to their altars, if they will kiss their holy places in peace.

TO

# TO JERICHO.

EASTER day fell this year on the 11th of April, new style. After divine service, and all the ceremonies were ended at the holy Sepulchre, we went to St. Salvador to dine. At dinner the Superior broke the silence, which had lasted during the Lent; and at the same time proclaimed, that all who intended to make the journey to Jordan, and the remarkable places adjacent, should be ready to go with the Caravan after dinner. We assembled at the time appointed, and found a company of 4000 people, Greeks, Armenians, Coptites, Syrians, and a few Roman Catholics. From the Latin convent were the Superior, the Procurator, and Vicar, with about thirty Monks, the interpreters and Janissaries of the convent. The Caravan was led by the Governor of Jerusalem with 300 soldiers, and was accompanied by the Arabian Princes and commanders from the confines of those places through which we were to pass. The Governor makes a good deal of money by this journey, considering the short time and little trouble that is employed in it; for he receives from each of the inhabitants four, and from a Frank ten piasters. Bethany, famous for the raising of Lazarus from the dead, was the first remarkable place we came to, about three quarters of a mile from the town.

We

We were shewn the place where Lazarus's Sepulchre had been; over which was erected a little stone hut, and the ruins of an old house, but no other signs of a town or building, which formerly must have been there. After travelling two leagues, we rested at another old demolished house, which was reported to be a remarkable place by the Monks. It would make one smile to be shewn a place where an affair happened, which perhaps never did happen; for they say this was the place where the man fell in amongst the robbers, and was passed by the Priest, but taken up by the Samaritan: a parable which Christ delivered after his usual manner, and therefore cannot be assigned to any particular spot. Not far from this place, is a hill on which the Christians in the time of the Croisades had a fort. On this road the original situation of Judea may be seen, which is the same as it hath been from time immemorial; though many divines contend, that Judea hath undergone a change, or, according to their manner of speaking, hath been transformed since the death of Christ. Judea is a country full of hills and vales, and as such it has been described both in the Old and New Testament; where it is always called a hilly land, and is every where famous for its mountains. The hills are all of a moderate height, uneven, and are not of any mathematical figure, like many others, which are either of a conic, hemispheric, or some other such form. At first, and nearest to Jerusalem, they consist of a very hard limestone, which approaches to the nature of a flint, of a whitish colour, or pretty near a pale yellow. They afterwards, and nearer the Dead Sea, consist of a more loose limestone, sometimes white and sometimes greyish; between which are layers of a reddish micaceous stone, or *Saxum purum micaceum*.

*micaceum.* Near Jerusalem grow different sorts of plants on these hills, especially *Ceratonia,* Carob-tree; *Myrtus,* Myrtle; and *Terebinthus,* Turpentine-tree; but farther towards Jericho, they are bare and barren. The vales, like the hills, are not fruitful, but deserted and uncultivated, being full of pebbles, and without vegetables; nevertheless, the earth consists of a good red mould, and would amply reward the husbandman's toil. In the beginning they are somewhat narrow, but become wider nearer Jordan. These interchanges of hills and vales, make the roads in Judea as dangerous as in any place whatever; and they could not be travelled with any but Arabian horses, which are used to go upon such stony roads as seem impassable, and perform it with great sagacity. I have had such proofs of this as I should scarce believe, if I had not seen it myself, especially on the journey from Jericho to the Dead Sea: but though these creatures are used to trot in the hills, they will blunder unless they be well governed. This I saw by those on which the Monks rid, who were but indifferent riders, and therefore their horses seemed to have forgot the expertness and safety with which they went when managed by an able horseman. The sun had already hid himself behind the hills of Stony Arabia, and the moon come from her retreat; when we, at eight o'clock in the evening, arrived at our encampment, which was laid out on the great plain of Jericho, that extends two leagues in length along the Dead Sea. Here we found tents erected for us, which by the care of the Procurator had been brought thither; under which we had a pleasant and delicious supper, and rested during the darkest part of the night. My Herbarium served me for a pillow. I was happy in having this, when the rest of the company, and the superior himself, had nothing

thing to lay on but the bare earth. If our bed was not convenient, our rest was not long. We arose before day-break to go to the mountain where Christ fasted and was tempted by the devil: we came thither at sun-rise, and began to ascend before the heat should incommode us. The mountain is high and pointed; and on our left, as we ascended, was a deep valley, towards which the rock was perpendicularly steep. It consists of a loose white limestone, mixed with another that is greyish and harder. The way up to its highest point is dangerous beyond imagination. It is narrow, steep, full of rocks and stones, which obliged us frequently to creep over them before we could accomplish our design. The difficulty is encreased by the valley on one side; which, beside its terrible aspect, is dangerous in case one should slip, as in such case it would be impossible to escape death. Near the top of the mountain are the ruins of an old Greek convent, which shew how the Monks and Anchorites of the ancient Christians lived, and what places they inhabited, viz. such as really inclined them to lead a lonely, detached, and devout life: therefore deserts and inaccessible rocks were chosen by the primitive Christians for their dwellings, where they might offer up their prayers in solitude. The former are yet occupied by the Coptite Monks in Egypt, for they have two convents in the deserts; and with respect to the latter, the Greeks preserve the ancient dwellings of their forefathers in Mount Sinai, Saba, St. Elias, and other places in the East. I went as far up on this terrible mountain of temptation as prudence would permit, but ventured not to go to the top, whither I sent my servant to bring what natural curiosities he could find, whilst I gathered what plants and insects I could find below; of the

latter

latter I found a very curious and new Cimex, or bug. I had time enough to view the mountain and adjacent country, when we broke up at nine o'clock, and continued our journey to Jericho, and travelled over a part of its large plain, which was entirely defart and uncultivated, bringing forth a number of the trees that afford the oil of Zacchæus, and some Rhamnus call'd **Chrift's Thorn**. We came, after a little time, to the fountain of Elisha, which is the name of a fine spring of fresh water, situated in a vale, and furrounded with divers fine trees, viz. Salix safsaf, Loniceræ affinis floribus coccineis; and, amongst the rest, some Fig-trees, which grew there wild. We continued our journey over a vale of this plain, in which the Arabians had sown barley for their horses; and this was the only cultivated spot of ground I had seen between Jerufalem and Jericho, a country of a good day's journey in extent. We came towards noon to Jericho, or two stones cast from the place where they shew some remains in memory of this famous town. At this time there is not the least building, except the walls of an old house, which the Monks, who are apt to sanctify every thing, have called the house of Zacchæus, who, as they say, climbed up in a Sycamore tree, growing on this road, to see Chrift. But the Chriftians of the East say that he climbed up in a different kind of tree, which now grows common here, and of whofe fruit the Arabs exprefs an oil, which the Pilgrims purchafe under the name of Zacchæus's oil. The Grecian text plainly calls it Sycomorus; which in the Swedish tranflation, and by Luther, is erroneoufly called a Mulberry tree. The Sycamore does not grow near this place at prefent, but is to be found in other parts of Judea nearer the fea; and might have been planted here when the country was inhabited

K

habited and cultivated. We returned in the afternoon to our tents; and after dinner I walked out to search for Natural curiosities around Jericho, especially near the rivulet that runs across the plain. The famous Asclepias gigantea of Judea, and the tree whose flowers resemble a Honeysuckle, and hath thick leaves, were the most remarkable plants I found.

We broke up from Jericho directly after midnight, to go to Jordan. We travelled over the remaining part of the plain of Jericho, and therefore had a good road. We came before day-break to the shore of Jordan, three leagues from the Dead Sea. Here mass was read by seven Priests. I observed the different breadths of Jordan. Here it was about eight paces over, the shores perpendicular, six feet high, the water deep, muddy, rather warm than cold, and much inferior in goodness to the Nile. On the shores grew Rhamnus, Vitex Agnus Castus, a Willow of which Pilgrims make staffs. We travelled hence to the Dead Sea, accompanied by an Arabian Prince. The plain reached to the sea, and was three leagues long, level, with some small rising grounds dispersed in different places; between which were narrow vales, uncultivated and barren. The soil is a greyish sandy clay, so loose that our horses often sunk up to the knees in it. The whole surface of the earth was covered with salt, in the same manner as in Egypt. The soil therefore was Egyptian, and might be as fruitful if it were tilled; and, without doubt, it was so in the time of the Israelites. The river had thrown up a quantity of Willow at its mouth. The shore consisted of the same clay as the large plain over which we had passed. In several places were perpendicular strata formed of a reddish brittle earth; which, without doubt, will in time become slate, inclosed in limestone, such as

is

is to be found in the different parts of Judea nearest the Dead Sea. The stones on the shore were all Quartz, of different colours and sizes. We followed the whole length of the sea shore. Here I found Quartz stones in the form of a slate, which is one of the rarest Natural curiosities I got in my travels. If it was burnt, it smelt like Bitumen; which proves that it had its origin from it, like all the slate of this country. We took another road to our encampment, and followed the foot of that mountain, which at this time divides Arabia Petræa from the Holy Land; and was formerly the boundaries of the Israelites who lived on this, and the other side of Jordan. A Lichen covered in several places the clay ground in this large plain, which was somewhat strange in an open desart. There grew in several places of this desart, the Tamarisk tree; Reaumuria; a kind of the Arabian Kali, and a labiated flower of Linnæus; clafs of Didynamia; this had a fœtid smell, and is called Basel by the Arabs, which signifies a Leek. I found but one shrub of the Mimosa Nilotica, or true Acasia; which has been brought hither by birds from Arabia, its proper and native country. In a place near the foot of this mountain, is a river that has its shores covered with Reed, which does not grow near the Dead Sea. We saw on the top of a mountain, the Greek Convent St. Saba, famous in former times; and where, in the first ages of Christianity, 4000 Monks were maintained, who lived there in caves. The Greeks continue to make pilgrimages hither, and have Monks sent hither as a punishment for some transgressions. As we continued our journey, I found the Partridge of Arabia, or the Holy Land, which hath never been before described; and I think it alone worth a journey to the Dead Sea. These birds are undoubtedly the Quails of the Israelites.

GOOD Friday fell on the 12th of April, new style. Every one may imagine that it was particularly celebrated in Jerusalem, as being the place where those things happened, which make this day sacred to all Christians. The ceremonies at the holy Sepulchre were these: 1. We went in the church at three o'clock in the afternoon, when the officium began as usual; and ended when the Superior fell on his knees before the door of the holy Sepulchre, and said his prayers. 2. At six o'clock we went into the little convent, which the Latins have beside the church, through which they go into the vestry room. Here we supped, which was the miserablest meal I ever eat: it consisted of a head of lettuce; the deficiency was to be made up with bread and wine; two material articles for the refreshment and sustenance of man, and which the Monks always had very good. To be more at liberty, which is hard to obtain in a cloister, I went with a Jesuit, who was a Pilgrim, into another chamber, where we were refreshed with Hebron wine, and excellent bread, baked with oil, that we might support a whole night and day's fatigue in beholding the ceremonies. A Capuchin, who came immediately after to us, made a better supper than either of us; in virtue of a Canon used by the Monks, which he rehearsed:

" Humidum

"Humidum non rumpit jejunium;" but he added "modice fumtum." 3. At eight o'clock, the procession began to the moſt remarkable places in the church. Whilſt this was doing, ſeven ſermons were preached in different languages, which was the beſt of any thing that was done. The firſt was preached in the veſtry room, before the proceſſion went out; during which the Monks underwent diſcipline, as they call it, or whipt themſelves in memory of the ſufferings of Chriſt. They had ſermon and diſcipline amongſt themſelves, without any ſpectators. Upon this the proceſſion came out into the church, and halted firſt, where the cloaths of Chriſt had been divided; and here the ſecond ſermon was preached in French, by a Monk from the Low Countries.

We afterwards went to the place of crucifixion, belonging to the Greeks, under which they have their magnificent choir. Here they preached a third ſermon, on the place where Chriſt was nailed to the croſs; and the fourth, not far from thence, where the croſs was ſet down, and where they ſhew the hole which is open, round, of half a ſpan diameter, and lined with ſilver, over which the Greeks have built a fine altar. Here the firſt was preached in French by the ſame Monk, and the other in Italian by a German. We deſcended hence, and came to the ſtone where Chriſt's body was anointed: here was preached a ſermon in Arabian, and at eleven o'clock we finiſhed the proceſſion at the grave, where a ſlow and zealous Spaniard tried our patience.

The 15th, I went to ſee thoſe places in the town which had hitherto eſcaped my notice, and which were thought remarkable. 1. Where the old city formerly ended, which is now in the middle of the new. 2. Where St. Veronica dried the face of Chriſt

with the famous napkin. 3. Where Christ's judgment was read, "Jesus Nazarenus Rex Judæorum," where now stands a broken column, erected by St. Helena, in memory of the place. 4. Where Christ fell down, tired by the weight of the cross. 5. The place where Pilate shewed Christ to the people, and said, "Ecce homo;" where are the ruins of a theatre and an arch pretty high. 6. Where Mary Magdalene obtained the Remission of Sins: here the Turks have a wretched Mosque. 7. The palace of Herod, now the stable of a Turk. 8. The Tower, which defended itself longest again Vespasian. 9. The place where one of the gates to Solomon's temple stood. 10. The grotto where the Virgin Mary is said to have been born: over this the Turks have a large well-built Mosque, which before was a fine church. Here was a fine court; and in it grew Iris florentina, Jasminum fruticosum, Amygdalus and Rhus coriaria. 11. An old square, and formerly-magnificent cistern or pool; in which the angel stirred the water at Bethesda, that came from Fons Signatus. 12. A gate of the town St. Mary, which was shut, like all the others, during the time of pilgrimage. 13. The hospital of St. Helena, formerly a magnificent building, now an house for the poor, possessed by the Turks: here were seven large copper kettles, which are said to have been here from the first foundation, and two were yet serviceable. 14. The palace of Pilate, now the seat of the Turkish Governor, but almost ruined. 15. Hence we saw the temple of Solomon, which is an octangular well-conditioned Mosque, with a fine court before it. In going out from the court of Pilate's house, the place is shewn where Sancta Scala stood, which is preserved in Rome as a valuable relique. 16. The prison of
Peter,

Peter, which is yet used by the Turks, to imprison those guilty of great crimes. 17. A Greek chapel, where Abraham intended to offer his son Isaac on the place of Skulls. The holy Sepulchre is in the middle of the church, which is built over the holy places, in the middle point of that choir which belongs to the Latins, and which is the middle part of the church. The chapel round the holy Sepulchre, is quadrangular, consisting of two apartments; the exterior can hold twelve people, and the interior six. In the interior apartment is a coffin of marble, on one side of the wall, over the burial place: over this hang a number of lamps, belonging to all the different sects. The chapel is ruinous, and cannot be repaired on account of the dissensions of the sects. Directly opposite the door of this chapel, the Greeks have their magnificent choir; and over it is the place where Christ was fixed to the cross, belonging to the Greeks, built in a half cylindric form. The large choir adjoins also to a gallery, of which the Armenians have a share, consisting of a space, containing seven columns for their chapel. The Syrians have under this their chapel. The Coptites have theirs behind the chapel of the holy Sepulchre. The vestry room of the Latins is under their gallery; from which they go into their little convent, where they have constantly ten or twelve monks.

On the 16th, I saw what I do not esteem the least curiosity in Jerusalem. This was the Pharmacopœa of the Latins; which, on account of the rich stores of Drugs and Medicines, may safely be reckoned one of the most valuable in the world. It was amazing to see what quantities of the dearest Drugs their magazine contained. All sorts of

balsams were to be found here, to the value of some thousand piasters. Here were several pounds of the valuable Mumia mineralis from Persia, which is sold at three ducats. The Indian and American drugs come all from Spain, and are chiefly given as presents. Here is prepared the Jerusalem Balsam, famous in these countries, which is a preparation made of all kinds of balsams, and a number of aromaticks dissolved in spirit of wine. Of this they make yearly, in the summer solstice, a quantity that costs 150 ducats at Jerusalem. It is very useful in all fresh external wounds; but too hot to give internally. However, they give it in blood-spitting and contusions, from ten to twelve drops. The whole Pharmacopœa is valued at 100,000 piasters. The Greeks, Armenians, Syrians and Coptites, who all follow the Julian Calendar, had **Easter eve on** the 17th. At two o'clock in the afternoon, we went to see the famous sacred fire; one of the most remarkable rites to be seen at any place of divine worship. All the Christians of these denominations believe, that on Easter eve a supernatural fire comes up out of the holy Sepulchre, and this they call holy or sacred. They believe, that their priests, by a miracle, call it down from heaven on this day. One priest of each sect goes down into the holy Sepulchre at two o'clock. The Greek priest goes into the innermost apartment, and the others into another chapel, behind that apartment belonging to the Coptites. They there say prayers by themselves; and to those the common people ascribe the coming of the fire. In the mean time the Greeks, who are the most disorderly Christians, use various inventions in the choir round the Sepulchre; such as the ancients describe to have been used at their Bacchanals. Boys dance and skip about, representing the death and
resurrection

resurrection, and practice a thousand other follies of which the heathens would have been ashamed. This they do, at least so they say, to warm the earth, that the fire may come up more easily. At four o'clock, all the three nations began a procession; and a little while after, a lamp was brought out of the grave, which they believed to have been lighted by the sacred fire. There was such a fighting with torches and flambeaux, because every one was desirous of lighting his at the sacred fire, that it occasioned a greater and more detestable noise, than is even heard in a market place or a bear garden. The most entertaining sight was the manner in which the Turks treated the Greeks on their festival. About twelve stout men posted themselves at the entrance of the Sepulchre: some had whips, other sticks, with which they laid on the crouding multitude, without paying any regard to great or small, spiritual or temporal: they even spared not the Bishop's gown; for as the Greek Bishop was carried out on the shoulders of his congregation, with the holy lamp in his hand, he received unexpectedly a hard stroke with a stick over one hand: yet they must bear this treatment; and, blind with superstition, they suffer it with pleasure. If the Turks did not use precaution, and banish as much as possible the disorder that would ensue, this scene would never end without some unhappy accident. The Franks or Latins look with disdain on this superstition, and those who think rationally do the same; but here the stupid vulgar must be kept in the superstitious imagination they have long had; besides, it is certain, that of 1000 Pilgrims who now yearly arrive, not ten would come, were it not for the sacred fire: to let it go over their faces, and the women over their breasts; to let some of their whiskers

and

and beards be burnt, in order to sanctify themselves. Another powerful motive for their pilgrimages is, to wash themselves in Jordan, the water of it being no less sanctifying than the former element. It is a matter of consequence to receive the sacred fire from the Bishop first; and consequently it costs much in a place where holy things are so valuable. Some rich merchant, for the most part an Armenian or Syrian, as the Greeks are generally poor, offers himself for this purpose. He goes into the outward apartment, and is the first who receives from the Bishop in his torch, the fire out of the lamp, which he hath lighted at the sacred fire in the inward room. Three years ago an Armenian from Persia paid for the first fire 30,000 sequins, a sum which perhaps never was given for an answer from the Delphian Oracle. These revenues are divided between the four Convents to maintain them; it is therefore no wonder that they should be sollicitous to keep them in force. The Convent St. Salvator in Jerusalem, belonging to the Latins or Roman Catholics, is the most powerful and richest. This is possessed by the Franciscan Monks of the Observation Order; consisting of all the different Catholic European nations. Their number is considerable, but varies according to the times. They may be always reckoned 100, more or less, seculars and regulars. They remain there for three years, except the Spaniards, who are permitted to remain six. They are governed by a Guardian, Vicar, and a Procurator: the first of these is always an Italian, and keeps his office six years; the second is a Frenchman, and the third a Spaniard. The business of the latter is the most important, as he has the entire management of every thing that relates both to the holy Sepulchre, and

the

the Convent; on which account there yearly passes through his hands, at least half a million of livres. These are the revenues of the Sepulchre and Convent, of which little remains at the year's end. The revenues arise from alms, the greatest part from Spain and Portugal; from those people who permit the Barbarians to ruin their trade, and plunder their country, without supplying one piaster for their chastisement; but send yearly a considerable sum to Jerusalem, to be devoured by Turks, their inveterate enemies, and by Monks, who are useless inhabitants in Europe, and unnecessary at Jerusalem, where they are of no sort of advantage to Christianity, unless we can believe that their devout kissing of stones has some hidden virtue. France gives a little. A thinking nation by degrees leaves off all absurd customs; but the French, since the time of Louis the Saint, have something else to do besides making pilgrimages to Jerusalem. The presents to the holy Sepulchre from Germany are sparing. A German Monk told me, that the Canon, " Primum quæ necessaria, deinde quæ opus sunt," prevented works of piety in that country. Alms from the Polanders, though such zealous Catholics, are quite out of the question, and few Pilgrims come from that country.

On the 18th, when I took leave of the Armenian Patriarch, he ordered me to be conducted into his church of St. James, which is in his Convent, to see its ornaments. They are well worth seeing, being, past all doubt, the richest and most valuable that any church in the East can boast of, and perhaps equal to the ornaments of the largest and richest Christian churches in Europe. They consist of Palls, Bishops Mitres, Surplices, Chalices, Staffs, Ostensoria, &c. Some of pure gold, the

others

others of silver gilt, and all enriched with precious stones. The Priest's garments are all made of the most magnificent stuffs from India, and a great part of them adorned with precious stones. The lamps in the church are all of silver, well wrought, and hung in fine order, being worth a considerable sum. All these ornaments were this day put on a large table in the choir, in order to their being exhibited to the public on St. James's day. The ornaments of the Latins are magnificent, and perhaps made in a better taste; but they themselves own that the Armenian are richer. The Greeks in this respect are not to be compared with either of them.

WITHOUT the town I saw, 1. The Sepulchres of the Kings, cut in a limestone mountain; but they are not to be compared to those of Alexandria. The doors were of a harder limestone, and turned upon two hinges in the nature of axles. 2. The cave of Jeremiah, where he wrote his book of Lamentations. 3. The prison of Jeremiah, which is a ditch full of water: here stood the coffin of an ancient King, out of which the Turks water their horses. 4. St. Stephen's gate, and beside it the place where this Martyr was stoned, which is a little remarkable rock. 5. St. Mary's Sepulchre, over which is erected an handsome church, but without ornaments. Before it is a fine court, in which grew a Bird Cherry tree, or Cherry Laurel (Padus) three fathoms round. You descend to the church, by a stair-case five fathoms broad, containing forty-six steps. I saw a sanctuary belonging to the Latins, in which is dug a coffin of marble; and the graves of St. Ann and St. Joachim on one side of the stair-case, and St. Joseph's on the other. 6. The cave where Christ sweated blood, cut out in the mountain, with some
thick

thick columns to support it. Gethsemane, a place where Christ exhorted his Apostles. 7. Gethsemane, at the foot of the mountain, a handsome little spot, with six old olive-trees, belonging to the Latins, who have them guarded by a Turk. 8. The spot where Christ was taken, a corner between two walls. 9. The place where the disciples slept, when Christ was taken, not far from thence. 10. The place where Thomas received the girdle of St. Mary, when she ascended into heaven. 11. A narrow road up to the mountain of Olives, full of flint stones; on the top of which is a chapel on the spot whence Christ ascended into heaven. This chapel is round, with a cupola, has no ornaments, but a fine yard surrounded with a wall. 12. Near this last is the place where the angel appeared to Mary, and foretold her death. 13. A cave where St. Placida lived thirty-seven years on bread and water. The Turks have here a house for prayers, which no Christian dare enter. 14. From a place on the other side of the mountain, we saw the Dead Sea and Jordan. 15. I saw the place where the disciples questioned Christ about the last judgment. 16. Where Christ taught the disciples the Lord's prayer: here was a ruined column. 17. A little cave, wherein it is said the apostles composed the confession of faith. 18. The Sepulchres of the prophets, nearer the foot of the mountain. 19. Jehosaphat's Vale with his Sepulchre. 20. Beside it the grave of Absalom; a small building, with a conic steeple. In this vale the Jews had one of their burial places. 21. Lower down in the vale, the place where Christ fell, when he was taken. 22. On the decline of a hill above the vale, a cave, wherein the disciples hid themselves when Christ was taken, near which were two columns. 23. The Sepulchre of Zachary the

the son of Barach, cut in the mountain. 24. The **Virgin** Mary's well, which yet hath water, but it is unpleasant. **25.** Hence was seen on the top of the mountain, on **the left hand, the** remains of Solomon's **town Silvia,** where he kept his 300 concubines. The houses are now inhabited by indigent peasants. 26. An old pool, wherein it is said the **blind man** washed himself. 27. The tree where Isaiah was **sawed asunder.** (Morus alba) a white Mulberry **tree, stood here in blossom.** It is a fable of the Monks, that **this** bears no fruit. 28. The Well of Nehemiah, where he kept the sacred fire. 29. I likewise saw the grotto on a rising ground, where the seven apostles lay hid. 30. Passed by Porta **Aurea, which** was walled up, and returned over **Mount Sion.**

# TO BETHLEHEM.

I WAS determined to see Bethlehem, and therefore received from the Governor an officer, and from the Procurator a Monk, to conduct me: with these I set out from Jerusalem the 19th in the morning. The country was at first pretty level, and the earth till'd and sown with corn; besides which, some plantations of tobacco presented themselves to our view. When we had reached half way, I was shewn the place where, it is said, Elias slept, when the angel revealed himself to him. It was an oblong pit in a rock, the length of a man, shaded by an olive-tree. I know not whether the prophet found this rock cut out in the manner it now is, or whether the people of these latter ages have cut out this kind of a bed, to give the story a better appearance of truth: but whatever it be, the place was very convenient to sleep in. The Greeks have on the left hand, near this place, an old Convent, bearing the name of the prophet Elias, which they frequently visit; but the Latins do not. Directly beside it they shew a grave, said to be Rachel's: this is an ancient structure, large and well built, with a dome over it. The other half of the way, the country was stony and uncultivated, and produced little else besides some olive-trees; and the best of these were destroyed some years ago, in a tumult the Bethlehemites had amongst themselves. After a journey of two hours, we came to Bethlehem at nine o'clock: this is a large village, situated on a high ground, the houses ruined, and the inhabitants lawless; partly **Christian Catholics**, partly Mahometans, and all Arabian peasants. I went to take my lodging in the Latin Convent, which is large, well built, surrounded with strong walls, situated below the village on the left hand. In this Convent are constantly ten or twelve Monks. I was here very well received, and entertained by the Superior, a Monk from Dunkirk, who had been chaplain in the French army when it took Bergen op Zoom; and by the organist, a Monk from Thuringia, eighty years old, sound and healthy, who had known and spoken to the present Archbishop of Sweden, Doctor Henry Benzelius, when he was at Bethlehem. I employed the forenoon in beholding that which made this obscure place famous throughout the whole Christian world; I mean the place which is here shewn, and said to be that where Christ was born and laid in the manger. We descended some steps under ground, to come into the cave where these two places are shewn, viz. on the left hand the place where the infant was born, and on the right where he was laid in the manger. Over both are erected small altars, on which lamps are kept constantly burning. Over the cave is erected a very fine church, of a particular architecture; after which, they say, St. Paul's church in Rome is built. The cave is under the choir. Without this church is another, through which one can likewise go into the Convent: this church is large, well built, with two rows of fine marble columns. Here they also shew the room, where St. Jerom is said to have kept his school and chapel. The Latins are the sole possessors of these holy places in Bethlehem; nor can the Greeks, though they have a little Convent here, or other sects, visit them, without their permission. In the afternoon, we went to see some remarkable places on the other side of Bethlehem, where some monuments were shewn, which, they said, were erected at the time in which the Jews were in their splendour. We then followed the foot of a mountain, which lay on the right hand. Another hill extended itself towards the left side: between these was a vale, in which it is supposed Solomon had one of his gardens (Hortus Solomonis); and according to the relation, this should have been his private garden, of which he speaks in chap. iv. 12. of his Canticles. The place will well admit that Solomon might have formed a garden here, though it is not by nature an agreeable situation, being in a bottom; but perhaps this great Prince might chuse to improve nature by art, as many other potentates have done. What seems most to have contributed to adorn this place, is the aquæduct from the well, of which I shall speedily make mention. It was carried by this place to Bethlehem, and therefore could well have served to have watered a garden on the way. In one place of the vale, some ruins of ancient buildings are to be seen. After two hours travelling, we came to the spring of water which is shewn under the name of Solomon's Sealed Well. This is a fountain, which flows up out of the earth in a cave, cut in a mountain. The cave consists of several apartments, all cut out and worked according to the rules of art. A little below this fountain, and nearer Bethlehem, are the three square reservoirs, one after the other; which, by means of a subterraneous aquæduct, receive the water from the fountain. Whence, in the days of

L             Solomon,

Solomon, an aquæduct is also supposed to have gone to Jerusalem, conveying the water to the city, and to the cisterns in the temple. The water is yet conveyed from hence to Bethlehem, and might with ease be conveyed to Jerusalem, if the Bethlehemites, sworn enemies of the Hierosolymites, would permit it. The water of this fountain is wholesome, and not of the coldest kind. Not far from the fountain is an old castle, without doubt founded in the time of the Croisades, and yet in a tolerable repair, but unoccupied. On our return to Bethlehem, I was shewn a mountain of a conic figure a great way on the right-hand of us, which the inhabitants to this day call the Frank's mountain, in memory of the Croisades; when the Christians left marks of their prowess in the very heart of the country. We travelled by Bethlehem; and a little on the other side, came to the place where the angel appeared to the shepherds: there is a cave into which those descend who are inclined to say their prayers. Whilst my companions were doing this, I had an opportunity of viewing a kind of a Plough; here used to turn up the earth, on which I saw something which I had never seen in any other place, viz. They fix a reed along the Plough-handle to the share; at the upper end of the reed is fixed a leather funnel. The workman, by this invention, waters the earth at the same time he is ploughing it. Under his left arm comes a pipe from a leather bag, filled with water, which hangs on his shoulders: out of this he lets the water run into the funnel, which through the reed waters the ground as he is ploughing: a compendious method of watering the earth in dry weather. I lay this night in Bethlehem, and next morning, after I had botanized in this neighbourhood, returned to Jerusalem. A disease had

had got amongst the Monks in Bethlehem, which would have been strange to me, if I had not made myself acquainted with it in the North. The Scurvy, which I had never seen in Egypt, or the Levant, had taken root in the Convent. The Monks, who were constantly shut up within their walls, for fear of the Arabs, were obliged to eat salt fish on their fast days, being at a distance from the sea, and thus brought this sickness upon themselves. They were not ignorant of the virtues of Cochlearia (Scurvy Grass) which is the greatest remedy, in this disease, of any Art hath yet discovered; but it was not to be found. I therefore advised them to try another plant of the same tribe, which has been found of service in that distemper; this was the Nasturtium aquaticum (Water Cresses) which I saw growing in great quantities, in the moist places, near the wells of Solomon. I desired the Monks afflicted with the Scurvy, to press out the juice of this plant, and drink it with milk, which they did, and found themselves relieved by it, as I was afterwards informed in Cyprus. Bethlehem is by legacy left to Mecca, and therefore is not under the Governor of Jerusalem's command; but is under him who governs Jaffa, which likewise belongs to Mecca. This certainly contributes much to the licentious life the Bethlehemites lead, and which hath risen to a height, scarce to be equalled by any nation. They are almost in constant quarrels with the Hierosolymites, or with the inhabitants of Hebron, or some other of the neighbouring villages; and their differences are seldom adjusted without the effusion of blood, which sometimes is considerable. Five or six years ago, the inhabitants of Bethlehem and Hebron carried on such a war, as destroyed the greatest part of the best inhabitants of both villages; and the neighbourhood of Bethlehem was entirely laid waste, its Olive-trees cut down, and the stumps of them yet shewn in woeful remembrance of those dissensions. The Bethlehemites scarce ever go to Jerusalem, at least they take care not to come within its gates, at a time they are at difference with the Regency or inhabitants of it; for these last would soon find means to revenge themselves of an enemy within their walls: and on the contrary, those of Jerusalem must take heed not to venture too far out into the fields, towards the side of Bethlehem, in unpeaceable times; especially as, on such occasions, to be an inhabitant of Jerusalem, is sufficient to make a person unhappy, who hath not at all deserved it. These people have likewise constant dissensions amongst themselves, not for the sake of religion, which in other places is the source of many evils. The Bethlehemites have not narrow consciences in this matter. Here live Christians and Mahometans, one with the other, without ever quarrelling for the sake of religion; but they have other reasons for quarrelling: for example, their right to provide Pilgrims with horses; to take caffar from the travellers, of which one party is in possession, and the other would willingly be so. Besides this, the Bethlehemites, like all other inhabitants of Palæstine, both Christians and Mahometans, are divided into two parties, which are called the white and red ensigns, and who only study to suppress one another. The Turks take advantage of this; and with a handful of men keep in subjection a country, whose inhabitants are at variance, which would cost them much trouble if they were united. But none suffer more from these wicked Bethlehemites, than the Monks, their neighbours. These would be happy, if they were safe by being shut up within the walls of their Convent;

but

but they every day apprehend being attacked in their own chambers, by these robbers. They surprise the Monks, either to obtain provisions, which like most other robbers they want continually, or attack and force them to buy a quantity of Paternosters, models of the grave of Christ, crosses and other wares of this kind, which is the only employ of all the inhabitants of this village. Of these they have so large a stock in Jerusalem, that the Procurator told me, he had to the value of 15,000 piasters of reliques in the magazine of the Convent; a sum which one would scarcely believe could be expended in such things. An incredible quantity of them goes yearly to all the Roman Catholic countries in Europe, but most to Spain and Portugal. Great part is bought by the Turks, who come yearly for these commodities. A number is yearly sent by the Monks in Jerusalem, to be given as presents to the patrons of their order; and these are best paid for by other presents they receive in return. No Pilgrim goes away, without carrying with him a store of these wares; and therefore the making of these holy things is a constant and certain employ for the inhabitants of Jerusalem and Bethlehem, with which they may drive on a monopoly as lasting as the Dutch do, with Nutmeg and Cinnamon. The dexterity and art with which they make these things, especially the Paternosters, and a Bull from the Pope, which grants indulgencies to those who have Paternosters brought from these holy places, are circumstances which add to their credit. On my return to Jerusalem, I was shewn the place where the angel took the Prophet Habakuk, and carried him to Babylon, and another place, with some ruins of a building, which my guide told me was the house in which the Patriarch

Jacob

Jacob dwelt. If the palace of this Patriarch was like those most used to this day in Palestine; namely, a tent made of a coarse rugg; these ruins do not deserve the honour of his name.

The 21st, in the afternoon, I set out from Jerusalem, in company with a number of Monks; and had terrible roads for four leagues from the city. The Convent of St. Jeremiah was quitted and destroyed, after the Monks had long ago been murdered there. Here we paid caffar. We had now another view of the Mediterranean Sea, from the mountains of Judea. This was a very hard day's journey, and which scarcely afforded us a drop of water to cool our throats. In the evening we came to Rama.

The 22d, we saw St. George's church in Rama; which is an ancient magnificent building under ground, with well-conditioned columns, covered with a dark green Mucor, and well situated in a handsome place. The church of forty martyrs had likewise been a fine building under ground in its time, but was now ruined. They further shewed us the remains of a Benedictine Convent, which was now turned into a Mosque. Its magnificent steeple was yet preserved, from which all Judea might be seen. The Turks say, that these forty martyrs were forty robbers, who were punished with death, and regard them as saints in their religion, as well as the Papists do in theirs; wherefore they, at this time, began the pilgrimage, which they make every year to this place, in memory of their robbers.

The 24th, I set out early from Rama; and after three hours returned to Jaffa, over the fine and fruitful plains which are between these two towns. Rama is a small, but pretty handsome town, extremely well situated on a fruitful plain, which affords wine, cotton, and corn. Tho' it be an inland

land town, they carry on a good trade. Here is a French consul to three merchants houses, who buy cotton, both raw and spun, ashes, and large quantities of soap. Rama is now chiefly noted for being the residence of the Turkish commander, who, under the title of Bey, governs Jerusalem, Gaza, and Rama, and to whom all Christians, as well as the subjects of the Turkish emperor, who go to and from Jerusalem, must pay a duty of some piasters, which makes a fine revenue. The Franks alone are exempted from this.

The 30th, in the forenoon, I came to the Town of Acra, after a voyage of twenty-six hours from Jaffa. We went with the little boat, which brought us over, into the harbour, which is a gulf between the mountain Carmel and the mountain of Galilea, at the foot of which Acra is situated, close by the entrance of the gulf. Here lay three French merchant ships, which is the only nation that continues to trade to this port, and fetch its goods, of which the greatest part consists in raw cotton, which some years amounts to ten thousand bales, each bale of a cantar of one hundred rottoli of the country. I took lodgings at the convent of the French monks, which is the only European house in this town, and depends, as all others in Syria and Egypt do, on the Spaniards in Jerusalem; I was here treated to my entire satisfaction. The board and lodging in the other convents of Syria and Palestine are preferable to those of Jerusalem. In the afternoon I paid a visit to the French vice-consul, who is here for the sake of five merchants, who carry on a trade to Marseilles. Towards evening I went about the town, to see the most remarkable things here: I mean the work which a common Arab, who hath lately usurped the government of Galilee, ordered to be made round the town.

town, consisting of a wall four fathoms high, furnished with two strong gates; he began a bastion at one corner without the wall, and a palace within. This work, compleated by a rebel in six months, the Turkish emperor would not be able to perform in any place of Syria, of which he is lord, within some hundred years. Since the knights of Malta became masters of Acra, nobody ever thought of fortifying the place, tho' it is the key of Galilee. This Arab made use of the remains of their ruin'd palace and castle, and dug up the subterraneous ruins of old Ptolemais for the continuation of his work; and, according to the common report, some of the buried treasures he found were of use to him in accomplishing his design. A broken granite column, of the thickness of the Egyptian, was shewn me, which had been dug up out of the ruins. Thus was this stone so highly valued by the ancients as to have been formerly carried as far as Syria to adorn their splendid buildings. Over one of the new city gates, which leads to Nazareth, the Arab had ordered two lions to be cut in stone, which are very bad, being done by a Mahometan, who, by his religion, is forbid to suffer images; but the Turks of this age are not so scrupulous in the less material points of their religion, as their ancestors. In returning to our lodgings, we went into the subterraneous vaults of the convent of St. Clara, possessed by the Franciscan monks before the Turks took it, and is said to have been founded by a lady, who, to avoid her obstinate lovers, had the courage to cut off her nose, and live in solitude with a mangled face, rather than please herself and others with such an one as nature had given her.

The 2d of May, I travelled from Acra to Nazareth. Without the town, on the right hand, we

met

met with the remains of a town formerly built here. Round these the fields were in tillage, from whence they were carrying home the barley, which in this country ripens about this time. To these ruins belong the large mounts that are seen here, over-grown with grafs, which are said to be artificially made, for the better building the town. We afterwards came to a field, about three miles wide, which bears every year a quantity of good cotton, and had now been lately sown, as this was the proper time. We travelled by a village called Rama, inhabited by Christians. On the other side of it the country consisted of small hills, or rather rising grounds, covered with plants, and fine vales between them. At the end of this field, the country round us consisted of the finest groves of the eastern Oak (Quercus coccifera) whose fly, called Tenthredo, had made its hard gaul, in which lay its caterpillar, with others dried up, which the insects had already quitted. The country here was like our East Gothia. From these groves we came into the fine plains of Zebulon, above three miles long and three-quarters broad, yet quite uninhabited, but not uncultivated, as the greatest part of it is planted with cotton. We travelled directly acrofs it, and on entering it we met with one of the wells of the Israelites, destroyed, and at the end a fine grove of Oak, in which were also some Beech trees (Fagus sylvatica); here we found small hills and vales, which we followed to Safuri, a village inhabited by Greeks. In this place the monks, who were with me, alighted, to honour the ruins of an old destroyed church, which is said to have been built in memory of the mother of St. Anne and St. Mary, who are reported to have dwelt here. The inhabitants breed a great number of bees, to their considerable advantage, and with

little

little trouble. They make their bee-hives of clay, four feet long, and half a foot diameter, as in Egypt: They lay ten or twelve of them on one another on the bare ground, without any thing under them. Over every ten they build a little roof, which makes their bee-hives exactly resemble the dog-kennels of our peasants. They wall up the opening of those in which the bees are at work, and leave only a little hole for them to go in and out. In the empty hives, the opening is not shut. The dwellings of the people were miserable huts, made of clay walls, in which they lay on the bare ground; they have a little entrance on the earth, and no windows, or other openings, except a hole for the smoak to go out. A little distance from this village, we came to a soil quite different, being hilly and full of hard lime stones, such as we met with in Judea, of which this is a continuation under the same meridian thro' several countries, which is somewhat remarkable. The same plants are seen here as in Judea, which before were not very common, and some scarce to be seen, as Kali fruticosum. We came to Nazareth at three o'clock in the afternoon, after having made an agreeable journey, in a country where there are good roads and one may travel in safety.

As soon as we were come to Nazareth in the evening of the 2d, we went to see its remarkable places. These are, a handsome church in the convent over the sanctuary of this place, where the angel announced the Virgin Mary's pregnancy; a stone in the village without the convent, which the monks said was the table of Christ, at which he eat several times with his disciples. This is large, sticks fast in the ground, and its upper surface declines: it is made of the hard lime-stone
common

common in Judea. This stone is said to have been formerly covered with iron plates, the marks of which are yet to be seen. We went from thence to a little church, which they say stands in the place where formerly a synagogue stood, in which Christ frequently preached when he was in Nazareth. It once belonged to the Greeks, but was taken from them by the Arabians, who intended to convert it into a mosque: they sold it however to the Latins for a certain sum of money, and it is now in their possession. This is a late transaction; so that they have not yet had time to embellish it, but intend soon doing it. We next were shewn the place where the house of Joseph, the foster-father of Christ, hath stood, on which now stand the remains of an Arabian hut. The place itself is possessed by Arabians, who have good houses there. Below the village, and near the road to Acra, is a good well belonging to the village, where the monks say Ave-Maria, for seven years indulgence, as the Holy Mother is said to have fetched her water here. We went from thence to a fine large cave, made by nature in a hard lime-stone mountain, which is a fine natural curiosity, but is not holy. Nazareth is at this time a large village, situated in a vale, with stone houses in the manner of the country, strong and well built, but far from elegant. This village can raise 100 fighting men, in case any troubles arise between the Galileans and Samaritans, which frequently happens. The inhabitants consist of Arabians and Christians, the greatest part papists, and some few Greeks, who have only one priest. The convent of the Franciscans is large, surrounded with strong walls, is rich, and hath constantly from fifteen to twenty-two monks, which have more privilege here than in any other place in the Holy Land,

Land, or perhaps in the East. They farm, from the Bashaw of Seyde, Nazareth, and two other villages in Galilee, for 4000 piastres per annum. For this they are at liberty to tax the inhabitants of the villages, and punish the wicked. In a word, to govern both Arabians and Christians as they think proper; for which purpose they have an Arabian officer of the village under them, who governs by their direction.

We travelled from Nazareth to Mount Tabor: it is a fine country, and consists of forests, through which we could see Samaria on our right upon a hill, a little on this side of Mount Tabor. Below this hill is the road that leads from Egypt to Damascus and Constantinople, which is large, broad, and fine. After travelling two hours we began to ascend Tabor, cooled by its agreeable dew, and refreshed by the milk of its fine herds of goats. It was a league up to the top, stony and difficult; but we did not however dismount. On the top of it was a fine plain, the sides of it rocky: between these rocks are the remains of a church and building, erected in former times by the Christians, where pilgrims pay their devotion. We could hence see the beauty of Galilee and Samaria. We descended the hill after remaining there six hours, when I had botanized there. The hill is round, hath no precipices, is about four leagues in circumference, beautiful and fruitful. On leaving the mount we came to a little plain, at the end of which was a Chan with a market-place, where the Arabs sold and bought horses, asses, camels, oxen, sheep, goats, &c. Here began the plain of Esdralon, and extended three miles to a village. At the entrance of it we could plainly see Tabor and Hermon. On this extensive plain, but little of which is cultivated, the

Arabs

Arabs sometimes fight their battles; and the present rebel Daker stood for several months the Bashaw of Seide. I met here an Arabian huntsman with a falcon and fine dogs. The Arabs are great proficients in what relates to hunting. On leaving Esdralon, we came to almost naked hills and dales, having only shrubs of Christ's thorn on them. With this plain began the singular stone, of which the Tiberian mountains consist. We had much trouble with our horses in this plain, being tormented by flies and heat. We refreshed ourselves in the shade of a Fig-tree, under which was a well, where a shepherd and his herd had their rendezvous, but without either house or hut. Here I beheld the oxen and cows of Galilee, which constitute a remarkable part of this country's riches. They are all of a very small size, which shews that the climate does not occasion any difference in the growth of those animals; mountainous countries and low lands sooner occasion a difference in size; in the former the black cattle are less than in Galilee, and in the latter larger, as in Scania and Egypt. The same prospect of hills and plains continued till we came to Tiberias, where we arrived towards evening before sun-set. We went immediately, without alighting from our horses, to the hot baths in this town, where I tarried long enough to describe the water, its sediment, and the places that were adjacent. We took our night's lodging in an old church built over the place, where Peter received the important keys, which his successor asserts are in his possession: we eat, drank, and slept in this holy place, which now has scarcely a roof, and serves the Arabians only for a stable. We afterwards went out to the shore of the sea Tiberias, and had some fish brought us by the fishermen. I thought it remarkable, that

the

the same kind of fish should here be met with as in the Nile, Charmuth, Silurus, Boenni, Mulsil, and Sparus Galilæus. The water in this river is sweet, but not very cold, though wholesome.

TIBERIAS is a little town, half of it inhabited by Arabs, who are the masters, and the other half by Jews, who pay taxes to the former. The Christians have no liberty here; and if there are some few, they are not known to be such. The town has lately been fortified by the frequently-mentioned Scheck Daker, who was born here, and reigns also supreme lord. He has ordered the town to be surrounded with a wall, and built a castle on a hill without the town. He had, however, no more than six small iron cannon in this work of defence; but he used another method, more antient than cannons for defending forts. He ordered loose stones to be laid on the top of the wall four feet high, which, in case of a siege, might be rolled down and crush the besiegers. Since he has fortified the town, it has been once besieged by the Bashaw of Seide, the marks of which are yet to be seen in the wall, but it was not taken.

THE 4th early we left Tiberias, and saw on the right Bethulis or Saphet, whither the Jews go out of devotion to spend their vacant time. We afterwards followed the broad ridge of a hill which had dales on each side. On the right hand side, about a league from Tiberias, the place was shewn where Christ gave food to 4000 men; on which lay a heap of stones in memory of it. Farther on we saw the mountain or hill where Christ preached his sermon: it is high, stony, and rugged. At the foot of the mountain the Arabians had an encampment; to these I went to see the manner of living of these uncivilized people. Their women are hideous; half

their

their faces are bare; they are dressed like the men, and have their under lip painted blew. They made butter in a leather bag, hung on three poles erected for the purpose, in the form of a cone, and drawn to and fro by two women. We were next shewn the place where the disciples plucked the ears of corn; here was also a heap of stones. We now met with limestone and Olive-trees, which are not to be seen farther in the country of Galilee.

Cana in Galilee is a little village, inhabited by Roman Catholic Greeks: the church over the place where Christ changed water into wine has nothing left but the walls, being without a roof. The vestry room is inhabited by peasants. In the church of the village they shew a stone vessel, three feet in diameter, and half a foot in height, which they say is one of the jars filled with water, that was changed into wine, and a skull, which they revere for that of St. Athanasius.

The 5th, in the morning, we went out to see the hill, from which the inhabitants of Nazareth were for throwing down Christ when he preached to them. This is a high stony mountain, situated some gun-shots from Nazareth; consisting of the limestone common here, and full of fine plants. On its top, towards the south, is a steep rock, which is said to be the spot for which the hill is famous: it is terrible to behold, and proper enough to take away the life of a person thrown from it. Jaffa is a village comprehended in the number of those the monks rent; thither we went in the afternoon. The monks make devout journies hither in reverence to the place, where they say Zebedee lived: they shew it in a garden full of pomegranates and Fig-trees, which the monks have planted here; and it was the only one I saw in Galilee, being agreeable

able enough on account of its pleasant situation and fine young trees. We were shewn some stones in a place in this garden, which they say distinguished the spot where the house of Zebedee stood. But what I found most remarkable at this village, was the great quantity of Mandrakes, which grew in a vale below it. I had not the pleasure to see this plant in blossom; the fruit now hanging ripe to the stem, which lay withered on the ground; but I got several roots, which I found it difficult to procure entire, as the inhabitants had no spades, but a kind of hoe or ground ax; with this they cut up the earth, and hurt the root, which in some plants descended six and eight feet under ground. From the season in which this Mandrake blossoms and ripens fruit, one might form a conjecture that it was Rachel's *Dudaim*. These were brought her in the wheat harvest, which in Galilee is in the month of May about this time; and the Mandrake was now in fruit. This plant grows in all parts of Galilee; but I never saw or heard any thing of it in Judea. The Arabs in this village call it by a name, which signifies in their language the Devil's Victuals. I likewise found in the Olive-trees here a Cameleon, which I carried alive with me to Acra, and learned, as I carried him in the easiest manner, to make him change from black to a speckled or yellow colour: the method consisted in covering or rolling him up in a cloth, and as soon as he then was taken out, he was quite changed.

I left Acra early in the morning of the 14th, having rested there for several days after my return from Galilee. I took the road to Scide, accompanied only by one horseman. There is no occasion for more company in Syria, where the roads are as safe

safe as in any Christian country, especially for a Frank. We followed the sea shore, and for the first two leagues had good roads, and a fine country, producing the common plants, and Salix (*Safsaf*) which I had not seen before, with an incredible quantity of Wormwood. We rested at a rivulet under a fig-tree, the leaves of which were covered with the little white Moth, called Phalæna gregaria. Here began the terrible mountains, over which we travelled for several hours, sometimes on foot, at other times on horseback. These shoot forth three great points into the sea, one of which is by the seamen called Cape Blanc from the white lime-stone, of which all these mountains consist. On this is an old castle, fallen to ruin since the Maltese left this country: there are several of them to be seen on this coast. On the other side of this mountain, the road was exceedingly bad, but pleasant on account of the many plants which grew here. Having passed the first hills, we got a fine road along the sea shore. I was now very near the sea, and could not refrain from going on the shore to look for natural curiosities; but the terrible heat which struck me, occasioned by the redoubled force of the sun-beams near the sea, made my stay very short. This was the most dangerous place I had been in for a long time. If I had not soon drawn near the mountain into the shade, I should have paid dear for my curiosity; for my head began to swim, and my legs failed me, when I rested myself comfortably under a Bay tree (Laurus) which I observed to grow here, and not in Galilee and Judea. In one place of this level road we came to a spring of water, where we paid caffar; and in another I saw some few ruins of Scanderette, one of Alexander's magnificent cities: it was entirely destroyed, and even the place

place uninhabited. A Rubus (bramble) grew in the ruins, which I had not seen before. The hills commenced again, through which Alexander the Great made a road for his army to pass. We followed this road above half an hour; it was of different breadths, from half a fathom to three fathoms in some places. This was a labour which required an Alexander to accomplish. It is certainly one of the most advantageous places in the world to obstruct the passage of an army; for on one side are inaccessible rocks, and on the other the great ocean, whose shores are fortified with perpendicular hills, by which there is no escaping. At four o'clock in the afternoon we came to the most remarkable place on this road, viz. the famous wells, which are by travellers called Solomon's, from which Tyre formerly received water through an aquæduct. They are three, all cut out in a mountain of sand-stone, at the distance of a gun-shot from the sea. Two of them are square, one situated below the other, each of about six feet square. The third is the most remarkable: this is round, and is at least 100 feet in diameter: it hath two outlets, each consisting of a narrow channel, to which the water runs through two round apertures, and falls into a small bason; from this place the water at present serves to turn some mills; but it formerly ran into the aquæduct, cut out in the sand-stone hill, which carried the water for the space of two leagues to Tyre; the remains of this being still to be seen. The inside of the ruins of this aquæduct is covered with a stalactite, such as is to be found in the eastern aquæducts, having been there deposited by the water: this is a noble piece of antiquity, the work of a great king, and the remains of a potent people. They knew not whence

whence the water came, which conſtantly fills theſe reſervoirs; but I naturally conclude, that it comes from ſubterranean ſprings, and riſes in their bottoms. The reſervoirs are ſurrounded with various plants, large trees of Salix Safſaf, a quantity of Ricinus and Vitex Agnus Caſtus. A number of the common little Piſmires were at work in the wall; and if Solomon hath ever travelled this way, he might have had an opportunity of making his obſervations on theſe animals. We followed the ſea ſhore, which here had formed a little plain, and after travelling two hours, came to Tyre, now called Zur, where we lay all night. None of theſe cities, which formerly were famous, are ſo totally ruined as this, except Troy. Zur now ſcarcely can be called a miſerable village, though it was formerly Tyre, the queen of the ſea. Here are about ten inhabitants, Turks and Chriſtians, who live by fiſhing. Time has in ſeveral places left pieces of broken walls, in teſtimony of the magnificent ſtructures with which this city was once adorned. Of theſe I ſaw ſome fine pieces of marble, porphyry and granite. Zur might yet be in a much better condition than it is. Its harbour, which is doubtleſs to be prefered both to thoſe of Acre and Saide, might contribute towards it. The French merchant ſhips frequently find ſhelter here in the winter ſeaſon, when they cannot have it elſewhere. The reigning Scheck Daker in Acra has determined to erect a magazine here for the reception of cotton, and houſes for merchants, which might contribute towards bettering the condition of this now wretched place: he would at leaſt do ſome ſervice to travellers, who are now indeed very badly accommodated here. All travellers complain of Fleas in Zur, which, they ſay, aſſemble here from all quarters

ters of the world. I shall not contradict their assertions. This, and other inconveniencies, made the lodging so disagreeable, that I rather chose to mount my horse, and travel all night on a fine and level road, crossed by several brooks and rivers, till I came to Seide in the morning. Nerium Oleander, which I had not hitherto seen, began now to appear on the road between Zur and Seide.

We came to Seide (Sidon) on the 14th. The gardens in this town are the most remarkable things in it, and in these consist its riches; wherefore my first business was to see them. They extend an entire French mile round the town, and contain Pomegranate-trees, Apricots, Figs, Almonds, Oranges, Lemons and Plums, in such quantities, that the town can yearly furnish other places with considerable cargoes of these fruits; but the most numerous, and in which their riches chiefly consist, are Mulberry-trees, on which they feed an infinite number of silk worms. Cordia Sebesten is a rare tree in Egypt, grows wild in Palæstine, is not seen in Natolia, but is so common in the gardens of Seide, that the bird-lime, which is made of its fruit, is one of the principal articles of trade in this town. Rhus Sumach, and a three-leaved Bramble (Rubus) grew spontaneously here. No vine grows near Seide; but it is produced in considerable quantities on the mountains of Antiliban and Caschevan. Some authors reckon the Tamarind amongst the trees of Seide, but I know not what tree they mistook for it, as it grows not near this place, and not wild even in Egypt.

The 16th, we saw the Sepulchres of the ancient Kings of Syria, which are at a small distance from the town. They are cut out in a limestone mountain, and have their apertures level with the earth, which in most is so large, that one may enter them with

with ease. They consist of vaults some fathoms square, worked in the mountain, with oblong niches in the walls. In several places may be seen obscure remains of carved work in basso relievo, over the niches, and of red painting, such as is seen in the Sepulchres at Alexandria. These vaults are of a workmanship much inferior to those of the Israelites at Jerusalem, and in nothing resemble those of Alexandria, though they seem made after their model. A great part of them are now open, and serve as huts for shepherds, or dens for wild beasts; but it would certainly be worth while for an Antiquarian to search along this hill, to discover some not yet opened, of which there is beyond doubt a great number. The town is not large, but has some fine houses towards the sea side, of which that of the French is the largest and handsomest. The harbour was ruined by the famous rebel Emir Fackardin; for which reason European vessels must anchor in the road, and resort to the harbour of Zur in the winter season. Near the harbour stands a ruinous castle, with a few cannon and a small garrison. The town is governed by a Bashaw of three tails, whose command extends over the country to Acra, over Galilee, and the adjoining mountains of Antiliban. The principal part of the inhabitants are Turks, together with a great number of Maronites, many Papists, and some Greeks. The Armenians have neither church nor house: here there is a Franciscan and Capuchin Convent in the French Kan, and an hospital for the Jesuits, who have their Convent on mount Libanon. The French is the only nation that trades hither; they have nine merchant houses with a Consul, who has under him the Vice-Consul of Acra. Their commerce is considerable, in regard to the place, and keeps Sidon

from

from falling into the same state as her sister Tyre. They load yearly twenty and more vessels for France. The goods exported from this place consist chiefly in spun cotton, with some silk, and amount annually to at least a million of livres. Next to them must be reckoned the silks, particularly the fine watered half-silks which come from Damascus, and are brought hither in considerable quantities for the French, who carry them to Italy; for they are prohibited in France, though the French make none equal to them in goodness. Ashes, Oil and Galls, make likewise a small part of this town's produce. They import Cloths, Spices, Spanish Iron, and Drugs for dying, the greatest part of which is sent to Damascus, which town supports Seide and Baruth, to be considered only as its harbours. They receive also a large quantity of Piasters yearly from Marseilles, which mostly go to Damascus; where, as well as on the whole Syrian coast, this coin has the greatest circulation, but most of all, the Quarter piasters, called Patines, which are valued at fifteen Med. On the road from Acra to Seide, we saw a herdsman, who rested with his herd of goats, which was one of the largest I saw in this country. He was eating his dinner, consisting of half ripe ears of wheat, which he roasted and eat with as good an appetite, as a Turk does his Pillaus; he treated his guests with the same dish, and afterwards gave us milk, warm from the goats, to drink. Roasted ears of wheat are a very ancient dish in the East, of which mention is made in the book of Ruth. In Egypt such food is much eaten by the poor, being the ears of Maize or Turkish wheat, and of their Dura, a kind of Milium. When this food was first invented in the earliest ages of the world, art was in a simple state; yet the custom is still continued in some nations, where the inhabitants have not, even at this time,

time, learned to pamper nature. After all, how great is the difference between good bread, and half ripe ears of wheat roasted!

Without the town, towards the sea side, is shewn a Sepulchre, in which three Bashaws are buried; and not far from thence a demolished Kan, where the Venetians lived at the time they traded to this town, and in a war were all cut to pieces by the Turks. Not far from the town is a well, which receives its water from a subterranean spring, like that of Solomon, and is called Sidon's well; as the old town of that name extended to it, though it is now a league from the sea. The village of Elias is one of the nearest to this town, where this prophet is said to have dwelt and performed miracles, especially that with the widow of Zareptah [a].

Superstition, common amongst unpolished people, has its principal seat in the East. I have particularly found it amongst those who breed silk worms, especially women, who have, almost through the whole world, a taint of the religion of the ancient Egyptians, as far as relates to omens and superstition. They believe in almost all parts of the East, that if a stranger sees their silk worms, all hope of success is lost. This was the reason I could never see any Silk-worms before to day, the 18th of May, neither during my stay in Smyrna, nor in all my travels in Natolia and the Archipelago, where silk is produced. There is a hut made of boughs of trees in every garden round Seide, in which they are at this time fed, grow, spin, and are transformed. My servant, who was a daring Armenian, procured me an opportunity of entering one of these huts, where I contemplated this noble worm, so common and yet so much esteemed in the East, but never to be enough admired.

[a] 1 Kings xvii.

The 21ft, I viewed the aquæducts of the town, an ancient work, and the nobleft that has been preferved. The water has been by them conveyed twelve miles from the hills into the town, and is by pipes carried to every part of it, which is not uncommon in thofe places of the Eaft, where there are no refervoirs. Near the town there is fomething curious in this aquæduct. It runs on walls through great part of the town gardens, and has on each fide a grove, of all the different forts of trees to be found here. In fome places the channel is open, but for the moft part covered; in a few places are openings on both fides, through which the water runs to the gardens, making pretty cafcades, which have an agreeable effect amongft the green trees.

# TO CYPRUS.

I LEFT Seide on the 23d of May, 1751, and at the same time the Syrian coast, of which I could not see any more for many reasons. I went on board a small French vessel, in which I sailed to Cyprus. On the 28th, we anchored in the road of Larnaco, a village, where the European Consuls dwell; part of which lies on the shore, but the greatest part a quarter of a league from it. In the former lives the Consul from Naples; in the latter the Consuls from France, England, Venice and Ragusa, have their houses. I lived at the house of the Venetian Consul, who was also Consul for Sweden, during the time I waited for an opportunity of continuing my return. As this was the reason of my coming to Cyprus, I had no notion of travelling through the island, for which this season of the year is not the best, as one can hardly cross the street in the day time, on account of the heat, and therefore must travel by night. The season to botanize was likewise over; and besides, the country affords little extraordinary in botany; wherefore I found it not worth my while to make long excursions in the country. For this reason I made only two short journies in Cyprus. St. Crux, the highest

mountain

mountain on the island, was the first thing I went to see.

I UNDERTOOK this journey on the evening of the 9th, having only my servant and a guide with me, not being incumbered with armed companions, who are not wanted in a country in which a robbery has never been heard of. We rid on mules, the common equipage of this country, where, they say, they have the best beasts of this kind to be found in the Levant: wherefore they are bought up for Syria, which in return sends small Horses, for the few who have a privilege of riding them. The road to the mountain is broad and level; hills of a moderate height, and large vales, fill the country round it. The mountain consists of a rusty limestone, saturated with vitriol. In the vales I found also some grey limestone, pure and unmixed, in large quantities, in the dried-up beds of rivulets. In many places the craggy mountain afforded lead and copper ore, and a quantity of small mountain crystals. Of these stones a fine sort is found towards Paphos, which is large and clear, of which I saw a fine cluster at the French Consul's. They were shewn some years ago by a person at the court of the Turkish Emperor, who said they were Diamonds. This discovery was much approved of by those who knew no better than himself; and the Grand Turk was persuaded he had within his dominions, a Diamond-mine. He therefore sent workmen to Cyprus, to fetch these treasures. They began to work, and the place was strictly guarded, but they left off in a short time. Myrtle, Pine, Oriental Cistus Ladanifera, and Arbutus Andrachne, grew altogether in the woods, with the Oleander, which was now in blossom. On this journey we saw several villages, better built than they commonly are in the Levant. We went into one of them, not far from the

the mountain, after midnight, where a shepherd gave me np his resting place, under an olive-tree, as it was too late to get a lodging in any of the houses. The night was extremely clear, which afforded me an opportunity of viewing an eclipse of the Moon, which proved almost total; and before sun-rise I continued my journey. In a level inclosure beneath the mountain, stood a little Greek church on the right hand. After we had passed it, we began to ascend the mountain, and in half an hour came to the top of it. The road was good, even and broad, therefore we could ride all the way. On the highest top of the mountain is a little Greek hermitage, with three or four rooms, and a small church. I there met with a Monk, who quitted his hut to accommodate me. I scarcely believed myself in Cyprus, every thing was so different on this mountain. Instead of a burning heat, almost enough to make one faint, I was refreshed with a most agreeable cool air. The thick, sickly, and I may almost say, poisonous air of Cyprus, but especially of Earnacas, is not felt here; and I could, by the easiness of my breathing, find that I was come into a thin and sound air. When I add to this, a prospect of the sea on one side, and on the other the whole island, as far as I could see, one may easy imagine, that this is the most pleasant place in Cyprus. After my return, I blamed the Franks, and was surprised, that they who inhabit the most disagreeable and unwholesome place in the island, should not furnish themselves with summer houses on this mountain, to which they might go for the change of air. They all said, that as they had never thought of summer houses, they could not look out for a place; but that this would be the properest. One obstacle to making this mountain an agreeable dwelling, is, the want of a

level

level place on the top of it, which confists of nothing but rocks and ftones, amongft which the Monks have fcarce found a little level fpot for their dwelling; but towards the foot of the mountain, numbers of fuitable places might be found. Some ftone moffes (Lichenes imbricati) were the only natural curiofities I found on the top of the hill, which I have not feen in greater varieties and quantities at any place in the Levant.

It is worth while for a perfon who is in Cyprus, to fee Famagufta, as it has formerly been the ftrongeft place in the country, and the moft famous in hiftory. I travelled thither on the 13th, in company with an Englifh merchant from Aleppo, and the Englifh Conful's interpreter. We kept along the fea fhore, and travelled almoft all night, coming to the town before day-break. The gates are not opened before fun-rife, we therefore refted at the houfe of a Greek Deacon without the town. The Turks have the fame cuftom here as in Jerufalem and Damafcus, not to fuffer any Chriftian, whether he be Frank or born in the country, to ride thro' the gate of the town. To obferve this foolifh order, we alighted at the Draw-bridge, as is cuftomary, and walked through the gate, mounting again within it. As foon as we were entered, we rid through all parts of the town, and round the ramparts. Mr. Frudrord, an Englifh merchant, had built a houfe in Larnaco, the fineft and largeft at this time in Cyprus, which has the handfomeft and moft fpacious hall I faw in the Levant. We faw many houfes on the road, between Larnaco and Famagufta, which he had built for his pleafure; but the greateft part of them were in ruins. In Famagufta, we went firft to pay a vifit to the Governor, and get his permiffion to fee the fortrefs. The Governor made the

fame

same appearance as the town and fortress do, a very mean-looking person, without any token of his being a commanding officer, which the Turks never fail shewing, at least by a number of servants which they keep about them, if they have any money; but this, the post of a Governor of Famagusta will not admit of. A Turkish officer must always pay himself, i. e. he must take, right or wrong, as much, and often more than he wants, from those under his command; but this Governor had only 2 or 300 good for nothing soldiers under him, and from them little was to be got. The fort has not been repaired since the Turks took it from the Venetians, and is therefore ruinous. Here were about 200 pieces of cannon, which were taken with the fort, but scarcely one of them is fit for use. The garrison consisted of about 300 men, of those called Levanti: these are soldiers who serve in the fleet, and are the worst men in the Porte's service. The harbour for the gallies, which is well situated, and defended by the fort, was entirely ruined. I have never seen such quantities of Aloe vera, as I saw on the ramparts of this fort. We went from the fort to see the church of St. Sophia, which is used by the Turks for a Mosque. It is of Gothic architecture, large, and was once handsome. It received, some years ago, considerable damages by an earthquake; and the Turks, who are the most ignorant architects in the world, have in a miserable manner repaired it. The tombs, monuments, and chapels, erected by the Christians, were entirely demolished: I could only see some epitaphs on the pavement in the church, some in Latin, with old Gothic letters, others in modern Greek; and even of these I could only see those nearest the threshold, which a Christian, according to the superstitious custom of the Turks,

must

muſt not paſs. Oppoſite the church were the ruins of the palace, formerly inhabited by the Venetian Governors. Here were ſeveral columns of Granite and Porphyry, and in ſeveral places of the wall the Venetian lion; in ſome places carved in relief, in others entire. The town of Famaguſta is now in a worſe condition than the fort. All the houſes, built by the Venetians, are either entirely demoliſhed or uninhabitable. There are now no more than 300 inhabitants in the town, moſt of them Turks, who poſſeſs the miſerable remains which are left of the once fine and famous Famaguſta.

I HAVE always, ſince my departure from Sweden, with much attention examined the ſea birds. I had ſeen many of them during my voyage to Smyrna, but from that time they had been inviſible to me. The firſt I ſaw afterwards, was on the 28th towards evening: this was a little bird, of the ſize of a Sparrow, of a greyiſh colour, with a brown breaſt, and white under his wings; he ſometimes ſettled on the ſea, and then flew up again, but not at any diſtance from the ſurface of the water: it followed the veſſel till dark. This bird had gone out to ſea when it was fine and calm, in ſearch of food, by catching ſome ſmall inſects which fly above the ſurface of the ſea. The diſtance would not permit me fully to deſcribe him, but the inſects were a kind of ſmall Water-flies.

THE 30th, we ſailed by Carams and Chateau Rouge in Caramannia. At both places are harbours, whence they load wood for Egypt, which is cut in abundance in the woods of Caramannia. I was told, that in the former place a town was to be ſeen under water, and the ruins of another on the land. In the latter are the remains of a caſtle, which is one of of the many founded by the Maltese Knights from Gaza, quite to this country.

The 2d of July, at sun-set, we came in sight of Rhodes, after a voyage of fifteen days: we were yet twelve miles from it, at which distance the mountain St. Catherine appears first.

After a constant calm which had occasioned a long and disagreeable voyage, we got on the 5th in the afternoon the wished-for gale, which in the night carried us past this island: during the gale, we saw a number of Flying-fishes, about two fathoms above water; and we had before seen a number of dolphins swimming on the surface of the sea: these always are a sign of a change of weather. We viewed the town of Rhodes in the evening at some distance, with its fortifications, kept in good repair since the Turks took them from the Knights of St. John of Jerusalem. Rhodes has a good harbour, and always contains some Turkish men of war. Here are also vessels built for the Porte, for which purpose this island is very proper, having plenty of timber. There are no Franks, only a French Consul, who is appointed by the French Ambassador at the Porte, in the same manner as other small Consulships. The island, which is fruitful, is governed by a Bashaw; but the greatest part of its inhabitants are Turks, and some Greeks, who carry on the trade of the island, which is not very important, and consists in some cotton, tar, and small ship rigging. Himia is a little, and almost unknown island, directly opposite Rhodes: we saw it in the morning on our right hand; it is worth notice, on account of the singular method the Greeks, inhabitants of the island, have to get their living. In the bottom of the sea the common Spunge (Spongia officinalis) is found in abundance, and more than in any other place

place in the Mediterranean. The inhabitants make it a trade to fish up this spunge, by which they get a living, far from contemptible, as their goods are always wanted by the Turks, who use an incredible number of spunges at their bathings and washings. A girl, in this island, is not permitted by her relations to marry, before she has brought up a certain quantity of spunges, and before she can give a proof of her agility, by taking them up from a certain depth.

We had been at sea twenty days, when on the 8th we came in sight of Stanchio. Our voyage began to grow tedious. They never take much provission on board for a voyage through the Archipelago; but imagine they can always run into some of the islands, and get what they want. We had these thoughts at our departure from Cyprus, with provisions for some days; and intended to provide ourselves in Rhodes, or Stanchio, for the remaining part of the voyage; but we were much dissatisfied to find ourselves without water, and with very little other provision, being at the same time informed, by a vessel which met us, that the plague raged violently in both the places we intended to run into, and therefore were inaccessible. Our circumstances gave me an opportunity of making a good observation. We had on board a Dervice (Turkish Monk) who came to us, and complained bitterly, not for want of Bread, though he had been without it for several days, but for something more necessary to him than Bread. He had been two days without Opium, and now found himself in a condition which made him fear he should find his grave in the sea. I with pity saw a young man become lean, emaciated, with a trembling body, seized with weakness and swimmings. This is the case of those, who by a destructive

tive custom, have made it necessary to eat Opium, which however is not so common amongst the Turks now, as it was formerly. The use of Opium is now mostly confined to those who officiate in religious ceremonies, or who would be strict followers of Mahomet, being prohibited the use of strong liquors. The Janissaries have found means to explain the law, and admit the use of Brandy, which, they say, was not forbid by their Prophet; as it is prepared by fire, and every thing that passes through fire is pure and clean. Wherefore almost all the Turkish soldiers have, in virtue of this excellent explanation of the law, given over eating Opium, which made them stupid and trembling, taking to Brandy, which makes them mad and dropsical. Our Captain was persuaded to put the Dervice on shore, on the coast of Natolia, or Lesser Asia, where he might find Opium, so necessary to his support, which was not to be had on board. He tried, in the mean time, as a palliative, to take an uncommon large dose of Venice Treacle, but without effect. A body, used to strong medicines, is not moved by those of less power. A person, accustomed to take Scammony, is not at all moved by Manna; we sometimes see what terrible effects Opium hath on those who have been accustomed to take it, when they refrain from it. My fellow traveller, Mr. Titzyon, who had been long an English factor at Aleppo, related the following story: a Prince of Persia was accustomed to take Opium at certain hours; his servants, on a journey the Prince made, had forgot to take with them Opium; his hour came, and he desired Opium, which was not to be had. The Prince, who knew what the consequence might be, if he did not take Opium at the accustomed hour, dispatched several servants by different roads, to fetch in haste what their neglect had left at home; but,

N to

to his and their misfortune, the Prince was dead when one of the servants returned, though within two hours. An English merchant, who had long lived in Ispahan without company, took Opium to pass away his melancholy hours. This pernicious refreshment became at last so necessary, that, to avoid any misfortune which might happen, if he were once to be without it, he ordered small bags of Opium to be sewed in his apparel and bed-clothes, that he might always have a sufficient quantity about him.

We anchored before Stanchio the 12th of July, having been informed that the plague was not there, but on the opposite coast, and in the country of Natolia. However, to be more careful, we did not venture on shore, but only sent our boat for water, which was the most necessary article that we wanted. Stanchio has no harbour, but the vessels must anchor in the gulph, at the distance of a cannon-shot from the shore between the island and the continent, to which the entrance on both sides is pretty narrow; but its road is wide and open, for which reason vessels seldom anchor before Stanchio in the winter, but rather go to the opposite shore, where they find small harbours in the continent, in which they lie more secure. There is a spring on Stanchio, six miles from the town, which the inhabitants call the fountain of Hippocrates: I could not learn whether this name is to be attributed to the ancient Grecians, in which case it would be the only monument now remaining, in the place of the nativity of this great father of physic. It is also possible, that some Venetian physician, when the Venetians possessed this island, gave the fountain this name, to revive the name of the greatest man the island ever produced. The Greek Bishop of this island hath 5000 piasters revenue a year,

year, which the Turks left him, when they took possession of the island. This is one of the most considerable fixed revenues that any Greek prelate, at this time, has. The Bishop in Smyrna may sometimes receive 15,000 piasters a year, but at other times not half that sum; as it depends on alms, and especially those that he receives on the day when he visits every house, and presents them with the holy water. He receives on this day from six to 10,000 piasters, according to the generosity and wealth of his flock.

# DESCRIPTIONS

OF THE PRINCIPAL

NATURAL CURIOSITIES,

FOUND BY

FREDERICK HASSELQUIST,

ON HIS

TRAVELS TO THE EAST.

# CLASSIS I.

# MAHHALIA.

## QUADRUPEDES.

1. Simia Cynamolgos. The dog-headed Monkey.
2. Simia Æthiops. The Æthiopian Monkey.
3. Canes varii. Several sorts of Dogs.
4. Viverra Ichneumon. The Ichneumon of the Nile.
5. Vespertilio Egyptiacus. The Egyptian Bat.
6. Mus Jaculus. The Jumping Mouse.
7. Hippopotamus Amphibius. The River Horse.
8. Camelus Dromedarius. The Dromedary.
9. Equus Caballus. The Horse.
10. Cervus Camelopardalis. The Camel Deer.
11. Capra Cervicapra. The Rock Goat.
12. Capra Angorensis. The Mohair Goat.
13. Ovis Aries. The Sheep.

1. Simia Cynamolgos [a]. The dog-headed Monkey.

IT is of the size of a young Bear, above two feet in length, and almost one foot and a half high, and two feet broad; it makes an horrid appear-

---

[a] Linn. System. Nat. Pag. 28. No. 16.

ance, and is very ugly towards the back parts: in outward appearance, it resembles a Bear. It is a cruel, perfidious, and almost untameable animal. It is found in Æthiopia. I have seen it brought to Cairo by vagrants, and led about to be shewn to the people at the inundation of the Nile.

2. Simia Æthiops[b]. The Æthiopian Monkey.

It is about as big as a common Cat, and is found in Æthiopia, whence the Negroes bring in numbers to Egypt. The female menstruates. It is very docile.

3. Canis Vulpes[c]. The Fox.

This animal is common in Palæstine; they are very numerous in the stony country about Bethlehem, and sometimes make great havock amongst the Goats. There is also plenty of them near the Convent of St. John, in the desart, about vintage time; for they destroy all the vines, unless they are strictly watched.

Canis aureus[d]. The Jackcall. Chical of the Turks.

There are greater numbers of this species of Fox to be met with than the former, particularly near Jaffa, about Gaza, and in Galilee. I leave others to determine, which of these is the Fox of Sampson. It was certainly one of these two animals.

Canis familiaris[e]. The Dog.

The magistrates at Leghorn in Italy have authority to issue out orders for killing Dogs, if they

---

[b] Lin. Syst. Nat. P. 28. N. 14. [c] P. 40. N, 4. [d] P. 40. N. 7.
[e] P. 28. N. 1.

abound

abound too much in the streets, and molest the inhabitants. The men entrusted with the execution of these orders go through the city in the night, and drop small bits of poisoned bread in the streets; these are eaten by the Dogs, and instantaneously kill them: before sun-rise, the same men go thro' the streets with a cart, gather hundreds of the dead Dogs, and carry them to the Jews burying-ground without the town.

4. *Viverra Ichneumon* [f]. The Ichneumon of the Nile.

It is met with both in Upper and Lower Egypt, living, during the inundation of the Nile, in gardens and near the villages; but in the dry season it lives in the fields, and near the banks of the Nile. It creeps slowly along, as if ready to seize its prey. It feeds on plants, eggs and fowls; killing the latter in the night, when it frequents the villages. In Upper Egypt it searches for the eggs of the Crocodile, which lie hid in the sand on the shore, and eats them, preventing by that means the increase of that dangerous animal. The Ichneumon may easily be tamed, and frequently goes about the houses like a Cat. Mr. Barton, who has been the English Consul nineteen years in Egypt, has kept a tame one for several years. It makes a growling noise, and barks when it is very angry. The Arabians call it Nems. The French in Egypt, who give every thing they don't know names of their own making, have called this Rat de Pharaon, which the Latin writers of Egypt, viz. Alpinus and Bellonius, have followed, and called it Mus Pharaonis

[f] Lin. Syst. Nat. P. 43. N. 1.

(the

(the Moufe of Pharaoh.) The refemblance it has to a Moufe (Mus terreftris) in regard to the colour and hair, might have induced ignorant people, who know nothing of natural **hiftory, to** call it a Moufe; but I cannot conceive why they fhould call it **Pharaoh's** Moufe. The Egyptians were too intelligent, **in the time** of Pharaoh, to call it a Moufe, having **knowledge** enough to give true defcriptions and fignificant names to all natural bodies; nor is it at **this** day **called Phar by the** Arabs, which **is the** name for Moufe, but **they call it** Nems, as I have **before** obferved. What is related concerning its entering the jaws of the Crocodile, is **fabulous.**

5. Vefpertilio Ægyptiacus. The Egyptian Bat.

It is **of the fize of a fmall Moufe, and** lives in the gardens of **Rofetta, near the** banks **of the Nile.**

6. Mus Jaculus[t]. **Jumping** Moufe.

This animal **is of the** fize **of** a large Moufe: it **fupports** itfelf **only on its** hind legs, and therefore hops or jumps **in its** progreffive motion. When it refts, it clofes its feet to its belly, and **fits on** its knees, bent; it holds its victuals with its fore-feet, **or paws,** as do the reft **of** this tribe; **it is** fond of **fleep,** fleeping in the day and **waking at** nights; it eats wheat, wheat bread, and the feeds of oily grain (Sefamum.) Though it is not much afraid of a man, yet it is not eafily tamed: for this reafon, it is always kept in a cage; and I have known one of thefe animals kept for fome months, and even a year, in this manner at Cairo. It is met with in Egypt, or be-

[t] Lin. Syft. Nat. P. 63. N. 15.

tween

tween Egypt and Arabia. The Arabians call it Garbuka; the French, who live in Egypt, Rat de Montagne.

N. B. If one should follow the method of the ancients in describing this animal, we might say it had a head like a Hare, whiskers like a Squirrel, the snout of a Hog, a body, ears, and fore legs, like a Mouse, hind legs like a bird, with the tail of a Lion. What a monstrous animal would this seem to be! And had it been delineated 2000 years ago, it would at this day have been accounted a monster. To this manner of describing, do most monstrous animals owe their origin; as Griffins, Unicorns, &c. &c. For instance, when the parts of a new-discovered animal are compared to those of other animals already well known; painters, from this method of describing, receive an idea of a form of nature, which they always draw out of character. This matter certainly merits a farther enquiry.

7. Hippopotamus Amphibius [h]. The River Horse.

Some observations related to me by a credible person, who lived twelve years in Egypt.

1. The hide of a full grown Hippopotamus is a load for a camel.
2. The River Horse is an inveterate enemy to the Crocodile, and kills it whenever he meets it. This, with some other reasons, contribute much to the extirpation of the Crocodile; which, otherwise, considering the many eggs they lay, would utterly destroy Egypt.
3. The River Horse never appears below the Cataracts in Egypt, wherefore the inhabitants of Upper Egypt only can give any account of it;

[h] Lin. Syst. Nat. P. 74. N. 1.

and as very few Europeans, none at least who understood natural history, have travelled into those parts of Egypt, we know little of the history of this animal; such as have travelled in India, have had better opportunities of informing themselves in this matter. The Egyptians very seldom bring the hide of it to Cairo; and it is impossible to bring thither the living animal. A hide has been sent to France, which, I am informed, is preserved in the Royal Menagerie.

4. The River Horse does much damage to the Egyptians, in those places he frequents. He goes on shore, and in a short space of time destroys an entire field of corn or clover, not leaving the least verdure as he passes; for he is voracious, and requires much to fill his great belly. They have a curious manner of freeing themselves, in some measure, from this destructive animal: they remark the places he frequents most, and there lay a large quantity of peas; when the beast comes on shore, hungry and voracious, he falls to eating what is nearest him, and filling his belly with the peas, they occasion an insupportable thirst; he then returns immediately into the river, and drinks upon these dry peas large draughts of water, which suddenly causes his death; for the peas soon begin to swell with the water, and not long after the Egyptians find him dead on the shore, blown up, as if killed with the strongest poison.

5. The oftener the River Horse goes on shore, the better hopes have the Egyptians of a sufficient swelling or encrease of the Nile.

6. The Egyptians say, they can almost distinguish the food of this animal in his excrements.

8. Camelus

8. Camelus Dromedarius[i]. The Dromedary.

The Dromedary commonly weighs 1000 lb. in Egypt. They feed him, for want of better food, with bruised kernels, or stones of dates: they copulate in Egypt in the month of December.

9. Equus Caballus[k]. **The Horse.**

Horses are found wild in the defarts of **Crim Tartary**, and differ from **those** that are **tame, in** having much larger tails, **according to Justi, who** travelled in those parts.

10. Cervus Camelopardalis[l]. The Camel Deer. Bellon. 179. Camelopardalis Giraffa. Alpin. Ægypt. Zurnap. Arab.

The colour of the whole body, **head and legs of** this animal, is variegated with **dark brown spots;** the spots are as large as **the palm of** a man's hand, of an irregular figure, and in the living animal are of various shades. This Deer is of the bigness of a small Camel; the whole length, from the **upper lip** to the tail, is twenty-four spans. It is met with in the shady and **thick woods of** Sennar and Æthiopia.

N. B. This is a most elegant and docile animal, it has been **seen** by very few natural historians, and indeed scarcely by any, except Bellonius; but **none** have given a perfect description, or good figure of it. I have only seen the skin of the animal, and have not yet had an opportunity of beholding it alive.

[i] Lin. Syst. Nat. P. 65. N. 1. [k] P. 73. N. 1. [l] P. 66. N. 1.

11. Capra

11. Capra Cervicapra [m]. The Rock Goat.

This is larger, swifter, and wilder, than the common Rock Goat, and can scarcely be taken without a Falcon. It is met with near Aleppo. I have seen a variety of this, which is common in the East, and the horns appear different; perhaps it is a distinct species. This animal loves the smoke of tobacco, and when caught alive, will approach the pipe of the huntsman, though otherwise more timid than any animal. This is perhaps the only creature, beside man, that delights in the smell of a poisonous and stinking plant. The Arabians hunt it with a Falcon (Falco gentilis, Linn.) I had an excellent opportunity of seeing this sport near Nazareth, in Galilee. An Arab, mounting a swift courser, held the Falcon on his hand, as huntsmen commonly do: when he espied the Rock Goat, on the top of a mountain, he let loose the Falcon, which flew in a direct line, like an arrow, and attacked the animal, fixing the talons of one of his feet into the cheek of the creature, and the talons of the other into its throat, extending his wings obliquely over the animal; spreading one towards one of its ears, and the other to the opposite hip. The animal, thus attacked, made a leap twice the height of a man, and freed himself from the Falcon; but, being wounded, and losing its strength and speed, it was again attacked by the Falcon, which fixed the talons of both its feet into the throat of the animal, and held it fast, till the huntsman coming up, took it alive, and cut its throat; the Falcon drinking the blood, as a reward for his labour, and a young Falcon, which was

[m] Lin. Syst. Nat. P. 69. N. 7.

learning,

learning, was likewise put to the throat of the Goat; by this means are young Falcons taught to fix their talons in the throat of the animal, as being the properest part; for should the Falcon fix them in the creature's hip, or some other part of the body, the huntsman would not only lose his game, but his Falcon also: for the animal, roused by the wound, which could not prove mortal, would run to the deserts, and the tops of the mountains, whither its enemy keeping its hold, would be obliged to follow; and, being separated from its master, must of course perish.

12. Capra Angorensis[n]. The Mohair Goat.

THE Mohair Goats are a singular variety of the common Goats, being famous for their soft and silver-white hairs, the like of which are not to be found in any place but Angora. The English and Dutch have long, to their great advantage, made the Mohair Goats one of the principal articles of their Levant trade. The fine English camlets are made of the hair, which is commonly carried ready spun to Europe; and, being there woven, is afterwards exported to all parts of the world, even to those whence the yarn was originally brought. The French at present have some share of the profit resulting from this trade; but nobody could ever hit on a surer and more judicious method of making this valuable commodity serviceable to his country, than Mr. Alstroemer, one of the Swedish Lords of Trade, who got the animal to Sweden, with an intention to propagate it there. We received this day four of them, sent by Mr. Bioerling,

[n] Lin. Syst. Nat. P. 68. N. 13.

from Angora to Smyrna: he was sent thither by Mr. Alstroemer, for this purpose. This is the handsomest creature of the kind I ever met with, and differs from the common Goat, in having longer hair, a shorter body, shorter legs, broader and flatter sides, and less and straiter horns. I should almost conclude it to be a distinct species; and the rather, as it continues its breed without degenerating.

### 13. Ovis Aries[o]. The Sheep.

I have observed a crust growing on the teeth of the Sheep in Egypt, which hath entirely the appearance of a Pyrites. It appears chiefly at the time when they feed on grass, which is scarcely any thing but Lucern. I have heard that this is also common to the Sheep of Antiliban.

[o] Lin. Syst. Nat. P. 70. N. 1.

## CLASSIS II.

### AVES. BIRDS.

14. Vultur Percnopterus. The Egyptian Vultur.
15. Strix Otus. The Horn Owl.
16. Strix orientalis. The Oriental Owl.
17. Psittacus Alexandri. The Parrot of Alexander.
18. Psittacus obscurus. A Parrot from Africa.
19. Upupa Pyrrhocoax. The Black Hoop.
20. Corvus ægyptius. The Egyptian Crow.
21. Pirus minor. The Lesser Woodpecker.
22. Alcedo rudis. The Persian Kings-fisher.
23. Alcedo ægyptia. The Egyptian Kings-fisher.
24. Merops Apiaster. The Bee-catcher.
25. Ardea Ibis. The Ibis of the Egyptians.
26. Tringa ægyptiaca. The Egyptian Plover.
27. Tringa autumnalis. The Autumnal Plover.
28. Tringa subtridactyla. The Three-toed Plover.
29. Charadrius Himantopus. The Autumnal Dotterell.
30. Charadrius alexandrinus. The Alexandrian Dotterell.
31. Charadrius ægyptius. The Egyptian Dotterell.
32. Charadrius Kervan. The Oriental Dotterell.
33. Charadrius spinosus. The Armed Dotterell.
34. Fulica atra. The Coote.

35. Anas

35. Anas damiatica. The Damiatick Duck.
36. Anas nilotica. The Duck of the Nile.
37. Mergus Albellus. The White Nun.
38. Larus smyrnensis. The Smyrna Gull.
39. Larus canescens. The Grey Gull.
40. Sterna nigricans. The Black Sea Swallow.
41. Sterna nilotica. The Egyptian Sea Swallow.
42. Nuonida Meleagris. The Guinea Hen.
43. Tetrao orientalis. The Oriental Partridge.
44. Tetrao Coturnix. The Quail.
45. Columbæ variæ. Several sorts of Pigeons.
46. Alauda hispanica. The Spanish Lark.
47. Sturnus vulgaris. The Starling.
48. Emberiza melitensis. The Eastern Bunting.
49. Emberiza africana. The African Bunting.
50. Motacilla yvica. The Wagtail from Yvica.
51. Motacilla. The Red-breasted Wagtail.
52. Motacilla hispanica. The Spanish Wagtail.

14. Vultus Percnopterus[a]. The Egyptian Vultur.

THEY light in great flocks on the lay-stalls near the city of Cairo, and there promiscuously feed, together with the Dogs and other beasts, on dead carcases and other offal. They assemble with the Kites every morning and evening, in the square called Rohneli, below the castle (which is the place for executing capital offenders) there to receive the alms of fresh meat, left them by the legacies of wealthy great men.

THE appearance of the bird is as horrid as can well be imagined, viz. The face is naked and wrinkled, the eyes are large and black, the beak black and hooked, the talons large, and extended

[a] Lin. Syst. Nat. P. 87. N. 6.

ready

ready for prey, and the whole body polluted with filth: these are qualities enough to make the beholder shudder with horror. Notwithstanding this, the inhabitants of Egypt cannot be enough thankful to Providence for this bird. All the places round Cairo are filled with the dead bodies of asses and camels; and thousands of these birds fly about, and devour the carcases, before they putrify and fill the air with noxious exhalations. The inhabitants of Egypt, and after them Maillet, in his Description of Egypt, say, that they yearly follow the caravan to Mecca, and devour the filth of the slaughtered beasts, and the carcases of the camels, which die on the journey; but I have not been an eye-witness of this. They don't fly high, nor are they afraid of men. If one is killed, all the rest surround him, in the same manner as do the Royston crows; they do not quit the places they frequent, though frightened by the explosion of a gun, but immediately return thither. I am not of opinion that this bird eats insects or worms, as it is scarcely ever seen in the fields and lakes; nor do the other species of this genus admire that diet. Maillet imagines this bird to be the Ibis of the ancients; but, I think, his opinion has not the least appearance of truth. We can scarcely be induced to imagine, that a wise nation should pay such honours to an unclean, impure, and rapacious bird, which was not perhaps so common, before the Egyptians filled the streets with carcases. If the Ibis is to be found, it must certainly be looked for in the Ordo of Grallæ of Linnæus; and I imagine it to be the White Heron, which is so common in Egypt. The Arabians call it Rochæme; the French, living in Egypt, give it the name of Chapon de Pharaon, or de Mahomet: Maillet says, it is so called, because it re-

O 2 sembles

sembles a Capon; but, except its being larger than a Capon, what resemblance is there between them? This is not the only ridiculous denomination given to things.

15. Strix Otus [b]. **Horn Owl.**

I have seen this alive in Cairo, nor is it rare in Egypt.

16. **Strix** orientalis **facie pilosa sutura** crispato-plumosa in dorso rostri. The oriental **Owl.**

It is of the size of the common Owl, living in the ruins and old deserted houses of Egypt and Syria, and sometimes in inhabited houses. The Arabs in Egypt call it Massasa; the Syrians Bana. It is very ravenous in Syria; and in the evenings, if the windows are left open, it flies into houses, and kills infants, unless they are carefully watched, wherefore the women are much afraid of it.

17. Psittacus Alexandri [d]. The Parrot of Alexander.

It is of the size of a Dove, lives in Æthiopia, and is by the Æthiopians brought to Cairo for sale. This is a very pretty bird; it has a shrill and piercing voice, and can easily be taught to make it in some measure articulate. Its chief food consists in the seeds of Safflower (Carthamus tinctorius).

18. Psittacus obscurus [c]. A Parrot from Africa.

This is of the size of a Cuckow.

[b] Lin. Syst. Nat. P. 92. N. 4.   [d] P. 97. N. 9.
[c] P. 97. 3.

19. Upupa

# BIRDS.

19. Upupa Pyrrhocorax [f]. The black Hoop.

THIS is of the fize of the Jackdaw, lives in the fields and houfes of lower Egypt, during the months of September and October, on the decreafe of the Nile. It eats an infect peculiar to Egypt, and near a kin to the Cock-Roach (Blatta).

20. Corvus ægyptius viridi maculatus, dorfo medio cæruleo. The Egyptian Crow.

IT is of the fize of a lark; it lives in the trees of Egypt, feeds on infects. I have found the remains of Scorpions and Scolopendras in its ftomach.

21. Picus minor [g]. The Leffer Woodpecker.

THIS is of the fize of a Lark; the female is a little bigger than the male. The peafants of Natolia bring it to Smyrna. I can fcarcely believe that this bird migrates.

22. Alcedo rudis [h]. The Perfian Kings-fifher.

IT is found in Egypt, near the banks of the Nile, and catches fifh by diving with its long beak under the water, in the fame manner as do the Sea Gulls (Larus).

23. Alcedo ægyptia. The Egyptian Kings-fifher.

IT is found in Lower Egypt, and builds its nefts in the Date-trees and Sycamores about Cairo; feeding on the frogs, infects, and little fifh, which it

[f] Lin. Syft. Nat. P. 118. N. 4.   [g] P. 114. N. 12.   [h] P. 116. N. 6.

gets

gets in the overflown fields. Its voice resembles that of the Raven.

24. Merops Apiaster [i]. The Bee-catcher.

THIS bird is called Varuar by the Arabs, and is found in the plains of Galilee.

25. Ardea Ibis [k]. The Ibis of the Egyptians.

IT is of the size of a Raven Hen. This bird is found in lower Egypt, and is seen in great numbers during the overflowing of the Nile, in those places, which the water does not reach, and afterwards in the places the water has deserted. It feeds on insects and small frogs, which abound in Egypt, during the inundation of the Nile and for some time after, being, by this means, of great service to the country. They often assemble, especially mornings and evenings, in the gardens, in such numbers, as to cover whole Palm-trees. When this bird rests, it sits upright, so as to cover its feet with its tail, and raises the breast and neck.

N. B. I am inclined to believe this bird to be the Ibis of the ancient Egyptians, rather than any other; because it is: 1. Very common in Egypt, and almost peculiar to that country. 2. It eats and destroys Serpents. 3. The urns found in the Sepulchres contain a bird of this size.

[i] Lin. Syst. Nat. P. 117. N. 1.    [k] P. 144. N. 18.

26. *Tringa ægyptiaca longiroftris, fufco albidoque variegata.* The Egyptian Plover.

This bird is of the fize of a Hen, and is found in the moift places of Egypt, during the month of September.

27. *Tringa autumnalis longiroftris, dorfo abdomineque purpurafcente.* The Autumnal Plover.

It is of the fize of a Hen, and is found in Egypt, during the autumn.

28. *Tringa fubtridactyla.* The Three-toed Plover.

It is of the fize of a Pigeon.

29. *Charadrius Himantopus* [l]. The Autumnal Dotterell.

This bird comes to Egypt, in the month of October, and is found in the lakes.

30. *Charadrius alexandrinus* [m]. The Alexandrian Dotterell.

It is of the fize of a Lark: I found it the 24th of May, 1750, in the channel, which leads the water of the Nile to Alexandria. It feeds on infects.

31. *Charadrius ægyptius* [n]. The Egyptian Dotterell.

It is found in the plains of Egypt, feeding on infects.

[l] Lin. Syft. Nat. P. 151. N. 10.  [m] P. 150. N. 3.  [n] P. 150. N. 5.

32. *Charadrius Kervan* º. The Oriental Dotterell.

THIS bird is of the size of a Crow, and is met with in lower Egypt, in the Acacia groves, near the villages Abusir and Sackhara, near the Sepulchres of the antient Egyptians, and in the desarts. The Arabians call it Kervan. It has a shrill voice, somewhat resembling that of the Black Woodpecker (Pirus martius), which it raises and lowers successively, uttering agreeable notes. The Turks and Egyptians value it much, if they can get it alive, and keep it in a cage for the sake of its singing. Its flesh is hard, and of a very good taste, inclined to aromatic. It is a very voracious bird, catching and devouring Rats and Mice (Glires), which abound in Egypt. It seldom drinks, and, when taken young, and kept in a cage in Egypt, they give it no water for several months, but feed it with fresh meat, macerated in water, which it devours very voraciously. It is found in desarts, and is therefore accustomed to be without water. I kept one of these birds alive in Egypt two months, and then sent it to Smyrna.

33. *Charadrius spinosus* P. The armed Dotterell.

IT is of the size of a Dove: the French call it Dominicanus, from the resemblance it bears the dress of a Dominican Monk; as it has a black neck, but the sides of it are white.

34. *Fulica atra* q. The Coot.

º Lin. Syst. Nat. P. 151. N. 9. P P. 151. N. 11. q P. 152. N. 1.

35. Anas

35. Anas damiatica grisea, rostro apice plano lato rotundato. The Damiatick Duck.

It is of the size of the common Duck. It is found near the sea coasts of Egypt, and is very common in the Mediterranean; but particularly in the Bay near Damiata, and between Alexandria and Rosetta; near the harbour Bichie, where they are caught with nets alive.

36. Anas nilotica. The Duck of the Nile.

The neck and upper part of the head are white, with grey spots, and a grey line runs lengthways behind the eyes; the breast is greyish, with black stripes running across it; the belly and thighs are of the same colour, but at the sides of the belly are some grey oblong stripes. It is met with wild in Upper Egypt, and no where else, if not perhaps in the Red Sea. The Arabians call it Bah. It is easily tamed, and is kept in Egypt with the common Geese.

37. Mergus Albellus[r]. The White Nun.

I had this brought from the island Tinus: it lives in the North during the summer months.

38. Larus smyrnensis. The Smyrna Gull.

The upper parts of the beak, head, neck, back, wings and tail, are black, but the lower parts are white; the membrane of the toes, and the inward

[r] Lin. Syst. Nat P. 129. N. 4.

toes,

toes, are white, but the outward toe is black; the inside of the legs is white, and the outside black. This was caught in the harbour of Smyrna.

39. Larus canefcens [s]. **The Grey Gull.**

I saw this bird on the 26th of February, near the Nile, and suppose it came from the Mediterranean.

40. Sterna nigricans. The Black Sea Swallow.

41. Sterna nilotica. The Egyptian Sea **Swallow.**

The beak of this bird is black; the head and neck are greyish above, with small black spots; the part round the eyes is black, spotted with white; the back, wings, and tail, are grey; the belly, and under part of the neck, are white; the feet red, and toes black. It is of the size of a Dove, and is found in the Nile. The Arabs call it Abunures. It bears a great resemblance to a Gull; the lower part of the beak is somewhat thick, but being strait also, proves it to belong to this genus. This bird comes in great flocks to Trajan's canal (which runs near Cairo) in the beginning of January, and seeks its food in the mud left by the Nile. It hunts, especially for insects without wings (Aptera), small fish and filth; it is therefore of great service to Egypt.

42. Numida Meleagris [t]. The Guinea Hen.

I had this bird from Nubia, whence the Nubian merchants bring it for sale to Cairo, with Monkeys

[s] Lin. Syft. Nat. P. 136. N. 2. [t] Linn. Muf. Regis, tom. 2. p. 27.

and

and Parrots. When it raises its voice, it makes a singular creaking sound, easier to be imagined than described, somewhat resembling the cackling of a hen, but more sonorous: there is a peculiarity in it which almost penetrates the brain, and affects the head in a manner not to be described; this, at least, has happened to me. I never heard it make this loud noise but in the morning; but its constant noise is like a Turkey Hen. It chuses high places to sleep in, as Hens do: it is brought up tame in Nubia, and other places of Africa, as well as America, where it is very familiar, and feeds with other poultry. It is as pretty a bird as one would wish to see, and is certainly the third bird in beauty, after the Peacock and Humming bird: it does not, it is true, dazzle the eye with gaudy colours; but its elegant shape, and the regular disposition of the spots, make it appear perfectly handsome.

43. Tetrao orientalis [u]. The Oriental Partridge.

It is of the size of the common Partridge, and is found in the groves and woods of Natolia. It is taken in the winter.

44. Tetrao Coturnix [w]. The Quail. Tetrao Israelitarum, Hasselquist.

It is of the size of a Turtle Dove: I have met with it in the wilderness of Palæstine, near the shores of the Dead Sea and Jordan, between Jordan and Jericho, and in the deserts of Arabia Petræa. If the food of the Israelites in the deserts was a bird,

[u] Lin. Syst. Nat. P. 161. N. 12.  [w] P. 161. N. 13.

this is certainly it, being so common in the places through which they passed.

I have seen a species of Partridge, very common about the pyramids of Egypt, and in the deserts. It is of a greyish colour, and less than our common Partridge. This ought certainly to obtain a place amongst the birds mentioned in the Scriptures. The Arabians call it Katta. An Selaw?

### 45. Columba domestica[x]. The Pigeon.

I had three very singular and fine varieties of this species at Cairo, 1751.

#### 1. Columba area oculorum lata nuda rugosa pallide sanguinea.

A pigeon, which hath the circle round the eyes broad, naked, wrinkled, and of a flesh colour. This comes from Arabia.

#### 2. Columba crispa.

This bird is of the size of the common Pigeon; the pinions, or upper part of the wings, are covered with small erect curl'd feathers, somewhat like the petals of a flower. It is quite white; I have been informed, that it is likewise found of a black colour; but I never saw one of them. It is brought from India.

#### 3. Columba arabica tremula. The Fan-tail Pigeon.

It is of the size of a common Pigeon; it carries its neck very far back, and its head is in constant tremulation;

---

[x] Lin. Syst. Nat. P. 162. N. 1.

tremulation; the breast is very convex, and projects far out, especially in the female. I had it brought from Arabia Felix to Cairo. The head, belly, wings, throat, and upper part of the neck, were quite white, and a white fascia in the middle of the back; the shoulders, back, and under part of the neck, were of a shining changeable purple; this is the colour most common to this variety, yet I have seen others of a different colour, but of the same form and size. It is the most elegant and beautiful variety of all hitherto known; its position, when it walks, is very particular, for it elevates one half of the body, viz. the breast, and part of the belly; but the female does this in a greater degree than the male. The common Pigeon is by the Arabians called Haram; the Turtle Dove they call Jamara; the Ring Dove Josie. The latter of these migrates at Cairo; it lives in the holes of the adjacent houses, from the filling of the canal of Trajan until it is dry; but is not seen during the remaining part of the year. The common Pigeon builds her nests in the following manner: the male gathers straw, &c. and carries it to the sitting female; but he gives it to her in a very peculiar manner, leaning his neck over hers, so that she receives the materials from the opposite side, and lays them under her belly, building a round nest. It was in this manner, the first variety of the Pigeons, here described, proceeded in building its nest. I had it for some time in Cairo.

46. *Alauda hispanica.* The Spanish **Lark**.

I saw this in the Mediterranean, coming from the Spanish shore, the 18th of November, 1749, and

and gave an account of it in that part of my journal.

### 47. Sturnus vulgaris [y]. The Starling.

It comes to Egypt in the winter, from the Southern parts of Europe, France and Italy.

### 48. Emberiza melitensis. The Eastern Bunting.

I saw it in the Mediterranean, coming on board from Malta, and then described it.

### 49. Emberiza africana [z]. The African Bunting.

It came on board the first of November, 1749, from Africa; I then described it in my journal.

### 50. Motacilla (yvica) corpore fusco viridiscente, pectore ferrugineo. The Wagtail from Yvica.

It was caught on board the ship the 18th of October, 1749, and came from the island Yvica.

### 51. Motacilla corpore ex fusco viridiscente, pectore ferrugineo. The Red-breasted Wagtail.

I saw it in the Mediterranean, near the Spanish shore, whence it had come on board the 15th of October, 1749, and have already described it in my journal.

[y] Lin. Syst. Nat. P. 167. N. 1.   [z] P. 174. N. 20.

52. **Motacilla Hispanica.** The Spanish Wagtail.

It came on board the 15th of October, 1749, from the Spanish shore. It feeds on flies.

---

## The Arrival of Migrating Birds in Egypt, observed in the year 1750.

IN the months of September and October, at the end of the former, and beginning of the latter, I have observed the wading birds called Grallæ.

**Ardea Grus** [a] (Crane) from Greece and Turkey.

I know not whence this bird came. The Egyptians tell me, that it is an inhabitant of Egypt, and that it is met with in the Southern parts of the kingdom in summer, but comes to Lower Egypt in autumn. If this is true, it differs from the nature of other birds, which go from the North to the South at that time; but this, on account of food, comes to the North. The bird of this kind, which I described at Smyrna, was brought from Greece, according to the accounts of the Turks: but how can this agree with the relation of the Egyptians?

**Tringa autumnalis.** The autumnal Plover.

**Tringa ægyptia.** The Egyptian Plover.

**Tringa Vanellus** [b]. The Bastard Plover.

It comes in great numbers in the beginning of October, and remains all the winter. I saw it about

[a] Lin. Syst. Nat. P. 141. N. 2.   [b] P. 148. N. 2.

Cairo the 15th of December, 1750, where it is esteemed good eating.

SEVERAL other species of Plovers, which I have already described.

Pelecanus Onocrotalus [c]. The Pelecan.

THIS bird comes to Egypt in the middle of September. In flying, they form an acute angle, like the common wild Geese, when they migrate. In the summer they inhabit the Black Sea, and coasts of Greece; and, in their migration, remain for a few days near Smyrna, and the other parts of the coasts of Natolia, but never stray far from the continent: they fly very high. Some of them remain at Damiata, and in the islands of the Delta, in the Mediterranean, but the greatest part goes to Egypt.

The Motacilla Ficedula arrives in September.

THE Alaudæ (Larks) Fringilla Carduelis (Goldfinch) and domestica, with several others of the Sparrow tribe (Passeres Linnæi), remain all the year.

## NOVEMBER.

IN this month all sorts of water fowl abound in the places lately overflowed by the Nile; for here they find plenty of small frogs for food: they remain till near the end of the spring, and come, perhaps, from Europe; nor are they, at this time, less numerous in Natolia and the islands.

Anas Boschas [d]. The Duck.

THIS appeared on the tables about the beginning of this month: they are shot, but in no great plenty.

[c] Lin. Syst. Nat. P. 132. N. 1.   [d] Lin. Syst. Nat. P. 127. N. 34.

Anas

### Anas Penelope [e]. The Wigeon.

This kind was brought alive in great numbers, about the middle and latter end of this month: they are caught in nets at night, just before the water is entirely returned or dried up.

## MARCH.

### Tetrao Coturnix [f]. The Quail.

An amazing number of these birds come to Egypt at this time; for in this month the wheat ripens. They conceal themselves amongst the corn, but the Egyptians know extremely well that there are thieves in their grounds; and when they imagine the field to be full of them, they spread a net over the corn, and surround the field, at the same time making a noise, by which the birds are frightened, and endeavouring to rise, are caught in the net in great numbers, and make a most delicate and agreeable dish.

In December and January, 1749, I saw Tringæ, Charadrii, and other migrating birds, of the genus of Scolopax, such as Woodcocks, &c. at Smyrna; I afterwards saw in the following year, 1750, at the same time of the year, some of the same kind of birds in Egypt. Hence we see, that migrating birds are not at all obliged to go to the same climate or country; but it is sufficient for them to find a place where the air is temperate, and food in plenty, in which they may winter; neither do those which winter in Egypt, come from the same places as those that winter in Natolia; for I have found by experience, that birds go in a direct line from North to South, and never take their course

[e] Lin. Syst. Nat. P. 126. 24. [f] Lin. Syst. Nat. P. 161. N. 13.

from East to West, or West to East. Hence it seems probable, that those which winter in Natolia, come from the borders of Muscovy, Tartary, &c. and those which winter in Egypt, from the opposite parts of Greece and Southern Europe.

---

## The Birds of Damiata in Egypt, 1751.

### Fulica atra.   The Coot.

Anas grisea mediocris, rostro apice plano lato rotundato.   The grey Duck.

### Pelecanus Onocrotalus.

THE Pelecan, I saw at Damiata, was quite white; and that I saw at Smyrna was of a greyish, or dark colour. The inhabitants of Damiata make a vessel out of the upper part of the beak, with which they lade the water out of their boats.

### Anas Cygnus [g].   The Swan.

I saw this on the coast of Damiata, near Egypt.

### Poulle de Ris of the French.

THIS is of the Hen tribe (Ordo Gallinaceus Linnæi.) Corolla coccinea, reflexa in vertice. It is plentiful in the fields, during the growth of the Rice. The season was not yet come, in which it might be procured; for about this time these birds

[g] Lin. Syst. Nat. P. 122. N. 1.

# BIRDS.

are scattered over the desarts, and hatch their young. They come in May, and the following months, taking up their quarters in the Rice fields, eating the valuable food which nature designed for them.

---

## The ANIMALS which I saw in the Holy Land.

### QUADRUPEDES.

1. Hystrix cristata. The Porcupine.

IN the mount of Temptation near Jordan.

2. Canis aureus. The Jackcall. Chical of the Turks.

IN the hedges near Jaffa.

3. Canis Vulpes. The Fox.

IN the vineyards near Bethlehem and Philistæa, in great plenty.

4. Capra Cervicapra. The Rock Goat.

IN mount Thabor.

5. Cervus Dama. Fallow Deer.

IN mount Thabor.

## BIRDS.

6. Vultur Percnopterus. The Egyptian Vulture.
NEAR Jerusalem.

7. Falco Gentilis. The Falcon.
WITH the Arabs.

8. Falco Tinnunculus. Kestrell.
IN the mountains near Nazareth.

9. Vultur. A Vultur.
NEAR Cana in Galilee.

10. Corvus Monedula. The Jackdaw.
IN numbers in the oak woods near Galilee.

11. Picus viridis. The Green Wood Spite.
AT the same place.

12. Merops Apiaster. The Bee-catcher.
IN the groves and plains between Acra and Nazareth.

13. Motacilla Luscinia. Nightingale.
AMONGST the willows at Jordan, and Olive-trees of Judea.

14. Alauda arvensis. The Field Lark.
EVERY where.

15. Fringilla

15. Fringilla Carduelis. Goldfinch.
In the gardens near Nazareth.

16. Tetrao rufus. The Red Partridge.

17. Tetrao Ifraelitarum. The Quail of the Ifraelites.
In the defarts near the Dead Sea.

18. Tetrao Coturnix. The Quail.
In Galilee.

19. Columba Turtur. The Turtle Dove.

20. Columba Palumbus. Ring Dove.
In Galilee.

# CLASSIS III.

## AMPHIBIA.

53. Lacerta crocodilus. The Crocodile.
54. Lacerta chamæleon. The Chamæleon.
55. Lacerta stellio. The Lizard Stellio.
56. Lacerta ægyptia. The Egyptian Lizard.
57. Lacerta gecko. The Lizard Gecko.
58. Lacerta scincus. The Scinc.
59. Lacerta nilotica. The Lizard of the Nile.
60. Coluber vipera. The Viper of the Shops.
61. Coluber cerastes. The horned Viper.
62. Coluber haje. The Viper Haje.
63. Colubri duæ species. Two Species of Vipers.
64. Anguis jaculus. The Snake Jaculus.
65. Anguis colubrina. The Viper Snake.
66. Anguis cerastes. The horned Snake.

### Lacerta Crocodilus[a]. The Crocodile.

THE Crocodile swallows stones to assist digestion, after the manner of seed-eating birds, which commit to the stomach the work of mastication, as well

---
[a] Linn. System. Nat. Pag. 200. No. 1.

well as concoction, being destitute of the instruments adapted to that purpose.

The Egyptians say that his excrements do not pass through the anus: this seems to be confirmed by the structure of the gut, which is near the **Pylorus**; for it cannot easily be conceived, that excrements should pass thro' so narrow a passage, seemingly destined for the conveyance of the Chyle only; but the structure of the parts, and the Gut being so near the **Pylorus**, seem to indicate that the excrements pass through it into the Ventricle, and are vomited up. The inhabitants above Cairo say, they see this daily, and observe that the Crocodile is obliged to come on shore as often as he has occasion to ease himself. There is a **Folliculus**, of the bigness of a Hazel nut, under the shoulders of the old Crocodiles: this contains a thick matter, which smells like musk. The Egyptians are very anxious to get this when they kill a Crocodile, being a perfume much esteemed by the grandees. I did not find one in any I dissected. When the male copulates with the female, he turns her with his snout on her back.

The eggs of the Crocodile are larger than a Hen's egg, but not so large as that of a Goose, being covered with a hard crust, of a rugged surface, and a cloudy white colour: these were taken out of a female 30 feet long.

The Egyptians use the fat against the Rheumatism, and stiffness of the tendons, esteeming it a powerful remedy outwardly applied.

They say the gall is good for the eyes: they make use of it as a certain remedy for barrenness in women, taking about six grains internally, and outwardly they apply a Pessus, made of cotton, and the gall of a Crocodile.

The eyes of the Crocodile are the best Aphrodisiac of any known by the Arabs, who prefer it to all confections of Dia-satyrii, Hyacinthi, &c. and even to Amber-grease.

The Crocodile does inexpressible mischief to the common people of Upper Egypt, often killing and devouring women who come to the river to fetch water, and children playing on the shore, or swiming in the river. In the stomach of one dissected before the English Consul, Mr. Barton, they found the bones of the legs and arms of a woman, with the rings which they wear in Egypt for ornaments.

He breaks the nets of the fishermen, if they come in his way, and they are often exposed to great danger. I found a fishing hook in the palate of the Crocodile which I dissected.

Job, in c. iv. v. 20, asketh, "Can a man draw up the Leviathan (Crocodile?)" And answers it in the negative; for it was known even in his time, that this animal possessed the art of destroying the hooks and other utensils of fishermen.

I took this description at Cairo from one alive, the 30th of January, 1751.

Linnæus hath given a description of the external parts of this creature, in the first volume of his Amœnitates Academ. p. 122.

54. Lacerta Chamæleon [b]. The Chamæleon.

I found the remains of various insects in its stomach, viz. Tipulæ, Coccionellæ and Butterflies. I saw part of an entire ear of Barley in the excrements, which is very singular. I could not find the Vesica Urinaria (Bladder).

This animal is very subject to the Jaundice, especially if it is made angry; it seldom changes unless

less it is made angry, from black to a yellow, or greenish colour, that of its gall; which last, being transmitted into the blood, appears very plain, as the muscles of the Chamæleon are very thin, and the skin transparent or pellucid.

This Lizard, of which the ancients have related so many true and fabulous stories, and which is known to all writers in Natural history, under the compound name of Chameleo, I procured alive about this time, when the spring had induced it to leave the retreat wherein it had passed the winter. This elegant creature is frequently found in the neighbourhood of Smyrna, particularly near the village Sedizeud: here it climbs the trees, and runs amongst the stones. The people of the country told me that it lived in hollow trees; I have not been an eye witness of this, but have often seen it climb on the branches of the Olive-tree, Plane, &c. Every one knows the qualities attributed to this animal; that it changes colour, and lives on air, without requiring other food.

I did not fail making all the enquiry I could concerning its nature, in a place where it is so frequently found. The inhabitants told me that it would assume the colour of a piece of cloth, or other painted or coloured substance, which might be put before it. Some have assured me that it lives only on air, but others have told me that they have seen it catching a sort of very small flies.

I will now relate what I observed myself, in one I kept alive a considerable time; and first concerning the colour. I could never observe that it assumed the colour of any painted object presented to its view, though I have made many experiments, with all kinds of colours, on different things, Flowers, Cloth, Paintings, &c. Its natural colour is iron-grey,

grey, or black mixed with a little grey. This it sometimes changes, and becomes entirely of a brimstone yellow: this is the colour I have seen it most frequently assume, except that first mentioned. I have seen it assume a darker yellow, approaching somewhat to a green, sometimes a lighter; at which time it was in colour more inclined to a white than a yellow. I have not observed him to assume any more colours; such as red, blue, purple, &c. I am, for this reason, inclined to believe, that all which has been said concerning the changing and shifting of colours in the Chamæleon, consists only in this, that on certain occasions it changes the dark colour, which seems to be natural to it, into yellow, of various shades. This change it makes frequently. I observed, that it more particularly did it on two occasions; one was when I exposed it to the hot beams of the sun, and the other when I made it angry, which I did by pointing at it with my finger. When it was changing from black to yellow, the soles of its feet (Plantæ & Palmæ Pedum) its head, and the bag under its throat (Gula saccata) began first to change, which was afterwards continued over the whole body. I saw it several times speckled, or marked with large spots of both colours over the whole body, which gave it an elegant appearance. When it was of an iron grey colour, it extended its sides, or ribs, and hypochondria, which made the skin sit close to the body, and it appeared plump and handsome; but as soon as it turned yellow, it contracted those parts, appearing thin, empty, lean, and ugly; and the nearer it approached in colour to white, the emptier and uglier it seemed, but it appeared worst in regard to shape, when it was speckled. I kept this creature alive for twenty-four

four days, from the 8th of March to the 1st of April, without affording it an opportunity of taking any food, yet was it nimble and lively during the whole time, climbing up and down in its cage, fond of being near the light, and constantly rolling its eyes, which are indeed admirable: I could however, at last, plainly perceive that it waxed lean, and suffered for hunger. It could no longer hold fast by the grating of the cage, but fell thro' weakness, when a Turtle, which was kept in the same room, bit it, and hastened its death. I have seen the Chamæleon of Egypt, but it is less than the Asiatic, and is not often met with.

55. Lacerta Stellio[c]. The Lizard Stellio.

This creature frequents the ruinous walls of Natolia, Syria, and Palæstine. The Arabs call it Hardun. The Turks kill it; for they imagine, that by declining the head, it mimicks them when they say their prayers.

56. Lacerta (Ægyptia) cauda verticillata squamis denticulatis, pedibus penta-dactylis. The Egyptian Lizard. Lacerta Cordylus[d]?

This is found in the mountains and plains of Egypt.

57. Lacerta Gecko[e]. The Lizard Gecko.

This is very frequent at Cairo, both in the houses and without them. The poison of this ani-

[c] Lin. Syst. Nat. P. 202. N. 10. [d] P. 202. 9. [e] P. 205. N. 21.

mal is very fingular, as it exhales from the Lobuli of the toes. The animal feeks all places and things impregnated with fea falt, and paffing over them feveral times, leaves this very noxious poifon behind it. In July, 1750, I faw two women and a girl, in Cairo, at the point of death, from eating cheefe new falted, bought in the market, and on which this animal had dropt its poifon. Once at Cairo, I had an opportunity of obferving how acrid the exhalations of the toes of this animal are, as it ran over the hand of a man who endeavoured to catch it; there immediately rofe little puftules over all thofe parts the animal had touched; thefe were red, inflamed, and fmarted a little, greatly refembling thofe occafioned by the ftinging of nettles. It emits an odd found, efpecially in the night, from its throat, not unlike that of a frog.

58. Lacerta Scincus[f]. The Scinc.

This is found in Petræa Arabia near the Red Sea, and in Upper Egypt, near the Nile. It is much ufed by the inhabitants of the Eaft as an aphrodifiacum, but not at this time by the Europeans. The flefh of the animal is given in powder, with fome ftimulating vehicle; broth made of the recent flefh, is likewife ufed by the Arabs. It is brought from Upper Egypt and Arabia, to Alexandria, whence it is carried to Venice and Marfeilles, and from thence to all the apothecaries fhops of Europe. It has been an error, common to almoft all authors, to imagine the Scincus to be a fifh.

[f] Lin. Syft. Nat. P. 205. N. 22.

# AMPHIBIA.

59. Lacerta (nilotica) cauda tereti longa, corpore toto glabro, squamis angulo obtuso notatis. The Lizard of the Nile.

This is met with in the moist places of Egypt, near the Nile. The Egyptians say, that this Lizard proceeds from the eggs of the Crocodile hatched in the sand, but that the Crocodile proceeds from those which are laid in the water. I need not add, that this is in every respect false.

60. Coluber Vipera g. The Viper of the Shops.

It is found in Egypt, and affords all those preparations which are to be had in the shops: Sal Viperæ, Viperarum caro exsiccata, Trochisci viperini, are prepared from this Viper, sufficient for the inhabitants, and for Europe. A considerable quantity is yearly carried to Venice, to make treacle; and this is the true Viper of the Shops.

61. Coluber Cerastes h. The horned Viper.

It is a native of Egypt.

62. Coluber Haje i. The Viper Haje.

The Arabs call it Haje. It is found in Egypt. When angry, it blows up its throat and neck to four times the size of its body.

g Lin. Syst. Nat. P. 216.   h P. 217.   i P. 225.

63. I saw

63. I saw two species of Vipers at Cyprus.

1. One is called Aspic; of this they relate:

(a) THAT it contains the most subtile poison, killing within a few hours, with a universal Gangræne.

(b) That it changes its colour to that of the ground on which it lies, using this faculty as a stratagem, the better to enable it to seize its prey.

2. Of the other they say:

(a) THAT it is at enmity with the first, and kills it.

(b) THAT one devours others of its own species.

(c) THAT it seizes on Larks, Sparrows, and other birds, with an incredible agility, whilst they are at rest, devouring them entire; and this I have myself seen.

64. Anguis jaculus [k]. The Snake Jaculus.

65. Anguis scolubrina [l]. The Viper Snake.

66. Anguis cerastes [m]. The horned Snake.

THESE three are all met with in Egypt.

[k] Lin. Syst. Nat. P. 228.  [l] P. 228.  [m] P. 228.

CLASSIS

# CLASSIS IV.

## PISCES. FISH.

67. Muræna anguilla [a]. The Eel.

68. Echencis neucrates [b]. Sucking fish. Alexandria. The Arabs call it Chamel or Ferrhun: it is very rare in these waters.

69. Gobius paganellus [c]. Gudgeon. Harbour of Smyrna.

70. Scorpæna porcus [d]. Harbour of Smyrna.

71. Chætodon nigrescens [e]. The Red Sea.

72. Spatus mormyrus [f]. Harbour of Smyrna.

[a] Lin. Syst. Nat. P. 225. N. 4. [b] P. 261. N. 2. [c] P. 263. N. 2. [d] P. 266. N. 1. [e] P. 274. N. 9. [f] P. 281. N. 20.

73. Sparus

73. Sparus aurata [g]. Gilt Head.

Smyrna.

74. Sparus orientalis.

Smyrna.

75. Sparus niloticus.

Nile. The inhabitants call it Giralle.

76. Sparus galilæus [h].

Lake Genazereth in Galilee.

77. Labrus Pavo [i].

THE Mediterranean, on the coasts of Syria.

78. Labrus niloticus [k].

THIS is the best fish of the Nile. The Arabs call it Bulti.

79. Labrus orientalis.

Smyrna.

80. Sciæna umbra [l].

THE Mediterranean sea, near Damiata. The Arabs call it Schifsch.

81. Perca ægyptia. Ægyptian Perch.

THE Mediterranean and Egypt. The Arabs call it Charms.

[g] Lin. Syst. Nat. P. 277. N. 1. [h] P. 282. N. 22. [i] P. 283. N. 8.
[k] P. 286. N. 24. [l] P. 289. N. 4.

82. Perca nilotica [m]. The Perch of the Nile.

The Nile, near and above Cairo. The Arabs call it Kefchr: the French, who dwell in Egypt, Variole. The flesh has a sweet and exquisite flavour, and is not hard, but very white. It is one of the best fishes of the Nile; and as it is of the largest size in Egypt, it adorns a table, if brought on it entire, and well fryed.

83. Perca Luth. The Damiatic Perch.

Damiata. The Arabs call it Luth.

84. Scomber Trachurus [n].

The Mediterranean sea; Smyrna.

85. Gasterosteus Ductor [o].

The Mediterranean.

86. Silurus Clarias [p].

It lives in the Nile, and is called Scheilan by the Arabians. If it pricks any one with the bone of the breast fin, it is dangerous, being poisonous. I have seen the cook of a Swedish merchant-ship die of the prick of this fish.

87. Silurus anguillaris [q].

It is found in the Nile, about Rosetta and Cairo. The Arabs call it Charmuth.

[m] Lin. Syst. Nat. P. 290. N. 5. [n] P. 298. N. 6. [o] P. 295. 2. [p] P. 305. N. 10. [q] P. 305. N. 5.

## 88. Silurus Myſtus [r].

The Nile, near Cairo.

## 89. Salmo niloticus [s]. The Salmon of the Nile.

The Nile, near Cairo. This fiſh frequently weighs 100lb. The Arabs call it Nefaſch. The fleſh is ſweet, and one of the beſt in the Nile.

## 90. Atherina Hepſetus [t].

The harbour of Smyrna. The Turks call it Jumiſch baluk, i. e. Silver fiſh.

## 91. Mugil Cephalus [u]. The Mullet.

The Mediterranean Sea; Smyrna; Nile. The Arabs call it Buri.

## 92. Clupea Aloſa [w]. A kind of Herring.

The Mediterranean Sea at Smyrna, and in the Nile near Roſetta. This fiſh goes up almoſt as high as Cairo, in December and January: they fill it with wild Marjoram, and fry it, when it almoſt intoxicates the eaters. The French call it Sardaine; the Arabs at Cairo, Sagboga. This fiſh eats very well, eſpecially if fried in olive oil, or butter.

## 93. Cyprinus orientalis.

## 94. Cyprinus niloticus [x].

The Nile.

[r] Lin. Syſt. Nat. P. 305. N. 4. [s] P. 312. N. 22. [t] P. 315. [u] P. 316. N. 1. [w] P. 318. N. 13. [x] P. 322. N. 9.

95. Cyprinus

95. Cyprinus Dentex [y].

THE Nile. The Arabs call it Kalb El Bar, i. e. Sea Dog.

96. Mormyrus anguilloides [z].

THE Nile. The Arabs call it Cafchive.

97. Tetraodon (Fahaka) corpore teretuifculo, abdomine inflato utrinque aculeato, infra anum glabro.

THE Nile, about Cairo, where it hath been found but of late, and never known in former times, according to the inhabitants. It came, perhaps, from the Mediterranean. The Arabs call it Fahaka, and fay that it grows to a prodigious fize. When it is juft caught, it pricks the fkin, if it is taken in the bare hands, and produces fmall puftules, in the fame manner as nettles. This I have been told by fifhermen; who likewife informed me, that the flefh is a fudden poifon. I have never had an opportunity of trying it.

98. Syngnathus marinus.

[y] Lin. Syft. Nat. P. 325. N. 25. [z] P. 327. N. 2.

# CLASSIS V.

## INSECTA. INSECTS.

99. Scarabæus Ceratoniæ. The Beetle of the Carob-tree.
100. Curculio Cypri. The Weevel from Cyprus.
101. Meloe Cichorii. The Blistering Fly of the Ancients.
102. Cerambyx smyrnensis. The Capricorn Beetle from Smyrna.
103. Gryllus arabicus. The Locust from Arabia.
104. Sphinx Atropos.
105. Phalæna ficus. The Moth of the Fig-tree.
106. Phalæna.
107. Phalæna amygdali fructus. The Moth of the Almond.
108. Phalæna Mori. The Silk Worm.
109. Panorpa Coa.
110. Cynips Psenes. The Gall Fly of the Fig.
111. Cynips Sycomori. The Gall Fly of the Sycamore.
112. Cynips ægypti. The Egyptian Gall Fly.
113. Tenthredo sodomitica.
114. Tenthredo dactyli.
115. Ichneumon natoliæ.
116. Ichneumon vitis.
117. Apis mellifera. The Bee.

118. Culex

118. Culex cypri. The Gnat of Cyprus.
119. Culex ægypti. The Gnat of Egypt.
120. Musca buphthalmi. The Fly of the Ox Eye.
121. Acarus citri.
122. Acarus testudinis.
123. Aranea galilæa. The Spider of Galilee.
124. Aranea vitis. The Spider of the Vine.
125. Aranea Coa. The Spider of Coa.
126. Cancer cursor. The Running Crab.

99. Scarabæus ceratoniæ [a]. **The Beetle of the Carob-tree.**

I FOUND this at Cairo, feeding on the leaves of the Carob-tree.

100. Curculio (Cypri) mediocris, fuscus, linea longitudinali atra in dorso. The Weevel of Cyprus.

This I catched at Cyprus.

101. Meloe cichorii [b]. The Blistering Fly of the Ancients.

This lives and feeds on the flowers of Succory.

102. Cerambyx smyrnensis. **The Capricorn Beetle of Smyrna.**

I FOUND this at Smyrna, in the burying place of the Jews.

103. Gryllus arabicus. The Arabian Locusts.

[a] Lin. Syst. Nat. P. 353. N. 57.   [b] P. 419. N. 5.

## The use of Locusts for Food in Arabia.

DURING my stay in Egypt, I used every means to learn whether Locusts are to this day eaten, either in this or the neighbouring countries. I was the more solicitous to be informed of this, as I thought the answer would determine what St. John lived on in the desart. Whether the ἀκρίδες of this holy man are Locusts, according to the literal sense of the word in all Grecian authors, or whether these ἀκρίδες are the fruit of some tree, or a kind of birds. The first has been the opinion of all interpreters of the scriptures, who attended only to the contents of them; others, who have translated the New-Testament, were for shewing their refined genius; asserting, that St. John never eat Locusts, as they are an unnatural food, never used by any body, and not adapted for sustenance. This is the strongest argument, by which they endeavoured to destroy the true meaning; and this feigned unnaturalness, has, as I imagine, occasioned an alteration, where there needs none, and induced some to crack their brains in finding for St. John other food, than what he really eat, during the rigorous course of life which he led in the desart. If it can be demonstrated, that Locusts are to this day eaten in the neighbourhood of the place where St. John dwelt, the impossibility and unnaturalness of this diet can no longer be afferted, and the weakest person will form the following conclusion:

If

# INSECTS. 231

If Locusts are to this day eaten in those places, where St. John dwelt, I cannot see why he may not have lived on the same insect, according to the evangelic history, which therefore needs no alteration. Ἀκρίδες will remain what they have been, and are neither changed to birds nor fruit.

A TRAVELLER is the only person who can learn whether Locusts are to this day eaten in the East; to accomplish his design, he must either be an eye witness, or receive informations from those, who have been on the spot, where they could know the truth of it; of whose veracity he must be as well assured, as if he had seen and eat them himself. Arabia is the place where these informations are to be obtained, a country inaccessible to Europeans: it is therefore evident, that no European ever could, or perhaps scarcely ever will, be an eye witness to the truth of this. Informations and relations therefore, procured from persons who have visited, and seen the customs of, the country, on which one may depend, are the only means we have left to come at the truth; and these I have earnestly endeavoured to obtain, during my travels in Asia and Egypt. I have asked Franks, who have long lived in the East, whether they ever heard that Locusts were eaten there? They all answered in the affirmative, and those of greatest veracity I got in Egypt (Chaffin, first French interpreter in Alexandria, who had lived thirty years in Egypt) and Aleppo (Bonard, French Chancellor in Smyrna, who had long lived at Aleppo) being the places where such informations may be easiest obtained. I have asked Christians, inhabitants of the country, Armenians, Grecians, Coptites, and Syrians, who were born here, and travelled in Syria, near the Red Sea and Egypt, if they knew whether the Arabians eat Locusts?

Q 4

All answered, that they have partly seen them eat them, and partly heard it said that they were a common food amongst the Arabians. But the informations I had from Greeks, who had travelled to mount Sinai, are those I can most depend on; for the Grecian church has a noted convent there. The Arabians live in the places adjacent and near it, wherefore they have a good opportunity of informing themselves of their customs: I at length met with a person who gave me better informations, and stronger assurances than all the rest. This was a Scheck, with whom I was acquainted at Cairo; one of the most learned and most ingenious of any there, who had been six years at Mecca. Him I asked, in the presence of Mr. Le Grand, the principal French interpreter at Cairo; and Mr. Fourmont (nephew to the learned Fourmont in Paris, who was sent hither at the expence of the royal French academy, to learn the Eastern languages) whether he knew that the Arabs fed on Locusts? And he gave me the following answer: "At Mecca, which is furnished with corn from Egypt, there frequently rages a famine, when there is a scarcity in Egypt. The people here are then obliged, as in all other places of the world, to support life with unusual food. Locusts obtain a place then amongst their victuals: they grind them to flower in their hand mills, or powder them in stone mortars: they mix this flower with water to a dough, and make thin cakes of it, which they bake like other bread, on a heated griddle; and this serves instead of bread, to support life, for want of something better." I further enquired whether the Arabs do not use Locusts, without being driven by necessity? He answered, that it is not uncommon to see them eat Locusts, when there is no famine: but then

then they boil them a good while in water, afterwards stew them with butter, and make a sort of fricassee; which, he says, has no bad taste, he having tasted them. I further enquired, whether the Locusts of the Arabians were different from those in Egypt? He answered, No; and said he had seen none in Arabia, but those he had seen in Egypt, of larger and smaller kinds; that they take little and big, without distinction, for this use; and that at certain seasons of the year, these insects are as common in Arabia, as they are scarce in Egypt, at this time; where they, at least, never occasion a plague to the country, as they do in other places.

### 104. Sphinx Atropos [c].

This is sometimes found in the houses of Cairo.

### 105. Phalæna (Ficus) minima gregaria candida. The Moth of the Fig-tree.

I found this between Acra and Tyre, sitting on the Fig-trees; near the road which Alexander made for the passage of his army.

### 106. Phalæna parva atra subtus ferruginea.

This I found on the mountain of Precipitation, near Nazareth.

### 107. Phalæna amygdali fructus.

It is odd, that Almonds cherish a Moth, when most other fruits nourish a Dermestes, Tenthredo, or some other insect.

### 108. Phalæna mori [d]. The Silk Worm.

[c] Lin. Syst. Nat P. 490. N. 8. [d] P. 499. N. 18.

## The manner of breeding Silk Worms in Syria.

THE eggs are laid in a warm room: the women often carry them in their bosoms, or lay them between the bolsters in a bed, where they are hatched; and to the Worms they immediately give Mulberry leaves, to which they stick fast. They eat and grow for forty days, all that time laying on stages made of reed, in an arbour formed of boughs of trees. The worms are covered once a day with Mulberry leaves; and creeping upon these leaves, they seem almost to cover them, by the time a new layer of leaves is to be put over them. When they begin to change colour, the people set up branches of various trees; these they climb up, and begin to spin. When they have left off spinning, they are taken from their habitations; such as are to be used for silk, which is by much the greatest part, are laid in hot water, and wound on a reel; the remainder are kept alive to be transformed into moths, for preserving the breed. When the Moths are come forth, the attendants spread a black carpet in the room; on this they lay their eggs, which are preserved in small bags. Thunder frequently destroys the worms, and Ants are their enemies, wherefore they cannot be bred in Egypt. Seyde (Sidon) exports yearly silk to a great value, as does also Tripoli. The former of these places sends the greatest part to Damascus, where they manufacture the beautiful watered half silks, viz. Cotton and Silk mixt, which are not to be equalled in any other part

part of the world. Tripoli sends most of its silk to Europe, which the French and English carry away. The silk which comes from Baruth, and is manufactured on Antiliban, is said to excel all the silks of Syria.

### 109. Panorpa Coa [e].

This I found on the island Meteline and Stanchio (formerly Cous) in the Archipelago.

### 110. Cynips Psenes [f]. The Gall Fly of the Fig.

I saw this at Smyrna. It lives in the female Figs, the germina of which I have observed to be eaten by this insect, finding one of them in almost every germen.

Is this insect the Cupid of the Fig, carrying the pollen to the female? The Fig is to be considered as its gall; it eats the germen of the figs, and does more harm than good. When it is hatched, does it do the office of a mediator? (Vid. Amœn. acad. tom. p. 41.)

### 111. Cynips Sycomori [g]. The Gall Fly of the Sycamore.

It dwells in the fruit of the Sycamore.

### 112. Cynips Ægypti. The Gall Fly of Egypt.

I have found this in the leaves of various trees in Egypt, but particularly the Sycamore.

[e] Lin. Syst. Nat. P. 552. N. 3. [f] P. 554. N. 13. [g] P. 554. N. 14.

113. Tenthredo

### 113. Tenthredo sodomitica.

I have found this in the Mad Apples, near mount Thabor and the Dead Sea.

### 114. Tenthredo Dactyli.

This I found in the stem of a Date tree at Damiata.

### 115. Ichneumon Natoliæ.

Natolia.

### 116. Ichneumon Vitis.

I saw this on the vine at Smyrna.

### 117. Apis mellifera [h]. The Common Bee.

The Egyptian Bee-hives are very singular in their kind. They are made of coal dust and clay, which being well blended together, they form of the mixture a hollow cylinder, of a span diameter, and as long as they please, from six to twelve feet: this is dried in the sun, and becomes so hard, that it may be handled at will. I saw some thousand of these hives, at a village between Damiata and Mansora; they composed a wall round a house, after having become unserviceable in the use they were first made for.

[h] Lin. Syst. Nat. P. 576. N. 17.

118. Culex cypri minimus subfuscus, antennis breviſſimis faſciculis plumoſis, alis ovatis. The Gnat of Cyprus.

This is an inſect peculiar to Cyprus, and occaſions great uneaſineſs, by its painful bites in the night; which leave puſtules more inflamed, and longer of duration, than thoſe made by the common Gnat.

119. Culex ægypti articulationibus candidis. The Gnat of Egypt.

120. Muſca Buphthalmi. The Fly of the Ox Eye.

This is found in the common Ox Eye, near Damiata in Egypt, in great numbers.

121. Acarus citri.

I have ſeen this inſect in a rotten lemon.

122. Acarus teſtudinis.

This lives on the Land Turtle at Smyrna.

123. Aranea galilæa. The Spider of Galilee.

This I found near the Fountain of Solomon in Galilee.

124. Aranea vitis. The Spider of the Vine.

This I found on the vines in Natolia.

125. Aranea

125. Aranea coa. The Spider of Coa.

Island of Stanchio, in the Archipelago.

126. Cancer curfor[i]. The Running Crab.

This lives in the sea, and on the coasts about Egypt and Syria: I took it on the coast of **Alexandria**, in the month of May.

This animal is very singular, coming up from the sea about sun-set, and running very fast on the sandy shore, in great numbers. The situation of the eyes in the feelers (Antennæ) is very remarkable; the same may be said of the structure of the Antennæ, and the appendices to the tail.

# CLASSIS VI.

## VERMES.

127. Sepia octopodia [k]. The Cuttle-fish.

128. Pinna muricata [l].

THE Cuttle-fish (Sepia octopodia) is the most inveterate enemy of this animal, rushing in, and devouring it as soon as it opens the shell, unless prevented; but there being always one or more Craw fish (Cancer pinnotheris) in the shell, which always keep in the mouth of it, when the animal opens it; and as soon as the enemy advances, the Craw fish gives notice of the danger, and the Pinna shuts her shell. The Craw fish is permitted to live within the shell, as a recompense for its trouble. This is a wonderful institution of the most wise Creator. The Greeks eat this during Lent, and almost all other shell fish and vermes; as they are not only forbid meat, but all kinds of fish.

The tentacula, or the fibres which compose the beard of this shell fish, are as fine as silk, and seem well adapted to be woven or manufactured, if they were collected.

[i] Lin. Syst. Nat. P. 625. N. 1. [k] P. 658. N. 1. [l] P. 707. N. 225.

PLANTÆ.

## PLANTÆ.   PLANTS.

1. Iris tuberosa.   Flower-de-Luce.
2. Cornucopiæ cucullatum.   The Horn of Plenty Grafs.
3. Hypecoum procumbens.
4. Anagallis monelli.   Pimpernel.
5. Mirabilis jalappa.   Marvel of Peru.
6. Solanum sanctum.   The Night Shade of Egypt.
7. Cordia myxa.   Sebesten.
8. Lycium atrum.   Boxthorn.
9. Chenopodium ægyptiacum.   Ægyptian Goose Foot.
10. Cicuta virosa.   Water Hemlock.
11. Linum usitatissimum.   Flax.
12. Ornithogalum umbellatum.   Umbellated Star of Bethlehem.
13. Aloe perfoliata.   Mitre-shaped Aloe.
14. Lawsonia spinosa.   Alhenna.
15. Anagyris fœtida.   Stinking Bean trefoil.
16. Cassia Sophera.   Wild Senna.
17. ——— Fistula.
18. ——— Ketschta.   The wild Senna of Egypt.
19. Punica granatum.   Pomegranate.
20. Rosæ variæ.   Roses.

21. Nymphæa

21. Nymphæa lotus. The Egyptian Water Lilly.
22. Mimosa lebbeck. Acacia of Upper Egypt.
23. Mimosa nilotica. Gum Arabic Acacia.
24. Anemone coronaria. Wind-flower of Natolia.
25. Clematis orientalis. Oriental Virgins Bower.
26. Origanum ægyptiacum. Wild Marjoram of Egypt.
27. Nepeta syriaca. Syrian Nep.
28. Orobanche lævis. Broom rape.
29. Draba verna. Common Madwort.
30. Lathyrus ægyptiacus. Ægyptian Chickling Vetch.
31. Dolichos lablab.
32. Carthamus tinctorius. Safflower.
33. Artemisia dracunculus. Tarragon.
34. Viola odorata. Sweet-scented Violet.
35. Arum colocasia. Colocasia.
36. Urtica dioica. Great Egyptian Nettle.
37. Platanus orientalis. Oriental Plane.
38. Momordica luffa. Balsam Apple of Egypt.
39. ———— Balsamina. Balsam Apple.
40. Cucurbita lagenaria. The Bottle Gourd.
41. ———— Citrullus. Water Melon.
42. Cucumis sativus. Cucumber.
43. ———— Melo. Melon.
44. ———— chate. The Queen of Cucumbers, or Egyptian Melon.
45. Ruscus aculeatus. Prickly Knee-holly.
46. Ceratonia siliqua. Carob-tree.
47. Musa paradisiaca. Plaintain-tree.
48. Ficus sycomorus. The Scripture Sycamore.
49. Phœnix dactylifera. The Date-tree.
50. Bryum ægypti. Ægyptian Bryam Moss.

R 1. Iris

# PLANTS.

1. Iris tuberosa [a]. **Tuberous** Flower-de-Luce.

I FOUND this at Smyrna.

2. Cornucopiæ cucullatum [b]. The Horn of Plenty Grafs.

I FOUND this plant the 22d of March, in the neighbourhood of Smyrna, towards Barnaba: this is one of those which I was very desirous of seeing. It is a grafs, in appearance quite different from all of its tribe. I was the more rejoiced to find it, as it has been seen and described by very few botanists in its natural state. It is to be found in the vales round Smyrna, and has not been met with growing wild in any other place; nor has it ever entered any botanical garden. I have described it well, gathered the roots of it, and used all my endeavours to have it sent to the botanical garden at Upsal, as Professor Linnæus had thought proper to charge me with this in particular.

3. Hypecoum procumbens [c].

THIS grows near the garden walls at Smyrna, and is by the Turks called Blebleli Tchidgeck. The Bees collect much honey from the nectarium of the blossom.

4. Anagallis monelli [d]. Blue Pimpernel.

THIS grows about Smyrna.

[a] Lin. Syst. Nat. P. 58. N. 19. [b] P. 79. N. 1. [c] P. 181. N. 1. [d] P. 211. N. 2.

5. Mirabilis

5. Mirabilis jalapa [e]. Marvel of Peru.

This is cultivated in the gardens and walks at Cairo.

6. Solanum sanctum [f]. The Night Shade of Egypt.

The Egyptians call it Meringam. The fruit is much eaten in Egypt.

7. Cordia myxa [g]. Sebesten.

This grows in the gardens of Egypt; the fruit ripens in November, and is the Sebesten of the shops.

8. Lycium afrum [h]. Box Thorn.

This grows on the banks of the Nile near Cairo.

9. Chænopodium ægyptiacum. Ægyptian Goosefoot.

This grows in the ruins of Alexandria, near the coasts of the Mediterranean Sea, and flowers in May. The Egyptians use it in sallads, on account of its saltish-aromatic taste, which is agreeable. Kali is possibly made from this in other countries; but here they use a Fig-Marigold (Mesembryanthemum) which likewise grows in the ruins of Alexandria.

---

[e] Lin. Syst. Nat. P. 252. N. 1. [f] P. 269. N. 26. [g] P. 273. N. 1. [h] P. 277. N. 2.

10. Cicuta virosa [i].  Water Hemlock.

This grows in plenty on the banks of the Nile, and on the coasts of the islands. I saw it in November, 1750, growing on an island, opposite that on which the Nilometer (the house where the height of the Nile is taken) stands, and though all the other plants on the island were greedily devoured by the oxen and cows, yet they never offered to touch this. I must in this place refer to the Dissertation de Viribus Plantar. in the first volume of Linn. Amœn. Acad. where I treated on the Marsh Hemlock and Water Hemlock. The above circumstance confirms what I there asserted, and proves, that nature acts always consistently with her own designs.

11. Linum usitatissimum [k].  Flax.

This is much cultivated in Egypt, especially the island of Delta, and near Damiata. A considerable quantity is yearly exported to Venice and Leghorn. It is soft and good, but not better than the European. They make to this day, cloth of it in Egypt, which is coarse, and of little value, when compared to what is made in Europe; however, the Turks purchase it, as do the Europeans, on account of its cheapness. By what we can see from the linnen wrapt round the Mummies, the famous linnen of the ancient Egyptians, was not better than what is made at present in this country. But it was then the best, as Egypt alone possessed the art of cultivating and manufacturing Flax. The Egyptian linnen is not so thick as the European,

[i] Lin. Syst. Nat. P. 336. 1.   [k] P. 397. N. 1.

being

being softer, and of a looser texture; for which reason it lasts longer, and does not wear out so soon as ours, which frequently wears out the faster, on account of its stiffness. The common people in Egypt are cloathed in linnen only, dyed blue with indigo; but those of better fortune have a black cloak over their shirt, or linnen. Flax grows very high in Egypt. I have seen a stem four foot high, and as thick as the stem of the common Rush. It flowers in winter.

12. Ornithogalum umbellatum [1]. Umbellated Star of Bethlehem.

I FOUND it in Smyrna.

13. Aloe perfoliata vera [m]. Mitre-shaped Aloe.

THIS is a kind of symbolick plant to the Mahometans, especially in Egypt, and in some measure dedicated to religion; for whoever returns from a Pilgrimage to Mecca, hangs this plant over his street door, as a token of his having performed this holy journey. The superstitious Egyptians believe, that this plant hinders evil spirits and apparitions from entering the house; and on this account, a person who walks the streets in Cairo, will find it over the doors of Christians and Jews, who have in all ages been fond of trifles. I scarcely remember to have seen this custom any where but in Cairo. It is a plant very common in the gardens of Egypt.

THE Egyptians distil a water from this plant, which is sold in the apothecaries shops at Cairo, and

[1] Lin. Syst. Nat. P. 441. N. 9. [m] P. 458.

is recommended in coughs. It is likewise given with good success in hysterics and asthmas. I have myself seen its good effects in the beginning of a jaundice, unaccompanied by a fever. An experienced French chirurgeon gave a Coptite, forty years old, afflicted with the jaundice, four tea-cups full of the distilled water of Aloe, and cured him in four days. This is a remedy unknown to our apothecaries, but it certainly merits their attention; nor is it difficult to obtain it, as the plant might easily be raised in the Southern parts of Europe. The Arabians call it Sabbara.

14. Lawsonia spinosa [n]. The true Alhenna.

This plant grows in India, and in Upper and Lower Egypt, flowering from May to August. The leaves are pulverized, and made into a paste with water: they bind this paste on the nails of their hands and feet, keeping it on all night. This gives them a deep yellow, which is greatly admired by the Eastern nations. The colour lasts for three or four weeks, before there is occasion to renew it. The custom is so ancient in Egypt, that I have seen the nails of the Mummies died in this manner. The powder is exported in large quantities yearly, and may really be reckoned a valuable commodity. The Arabians call it Chenna. The dried flowers afford a fragrant smell, which women who have conceived cannot bear.

15. Anagyris foetida [o]. Stinking Bean-trefoil.

This grows near Smyrna, and flowers in January.

[n] Lin. Syst. Nat. P. 498.    [o] P. 534. N. 1.

16. Cassia

16. Caffia fophera P.   Caffia or Wild Senna.

This tree is cultivated in the gardens at Cairo, and by the Arabs called Sopher.

17. Caffia fiftula q.   The Caffia Fiftula.

I have seen and defcribed this plant in a fertile plain, near the canal, which leads from the Nile to Alexandria. There were feveral of them growing amongft the Date-trees, being about twelve feet high, and from two to three fpans thick. It flowers in May. The Arabs call it Hearfciambar.

18. Caffia Ketfchta.

This plant is a native of India and Arabia, but is very feldom to be met with in the gardens of Egypt, where I faw only one tender fhrub of it. I have been informed that the fruit of it is full of a thickifh white juice. The Arabians call it Ketfchta.

19. Punica granatum r.   Pomegranate-tree.

I met with a variety of this. The ftem was fmaller than in the common fort; the leaves greener, and the flower barren. The inhabitants of Cyprus called it Balauftia, and fhewed it me as a fingular tree, becaufe it bore no fruit, for which they could not account, being ignorant of the myfteries of nature.

[p] Lin. Syft. Nat. P. 542. N. 22.  [q] P. 540. N. 14.  [r] P. 676. N. 1.

### 20. Rosa [s]. The Rose.

The Arabians call this at present Uard, which does not at all agree with the Hebrew name Barkanim *Celsii hierobotanicum* 2. p. 192. Perhaps the people of the East have given different names to the different varieties, so that the Hebrew name may have been formerly given to Rosa damascena hort. Ups. (Rosa centifolia Linn.) but the Arabian to the Rosa rubra (Red Roses) which is common in Arabia. At this time Uard is the name given to all the varieties in Egypt, where they are almost all to be had.

### Rosa gallica [t]. Red Roses.

These are common in the gardens at Rosetta and Damiata, where they plant them for the purpose of making rose-water. This rose bears small flowers, and those of no strong scent; for which reason it is of no great value at Cairo.

### Rosa Cinnamomea [u]. The Cinnamon Rose.

This is somewhat scarce. It is cultivated at Damiata and Upper Egypt for its beauty.

### Rosa alba [w]. White Rose.

This is cultivated in considerable quantities in the province Fajhum, of Upper Egypt, not far from the Pyramids. It is of a pale colour, not quite

---

[s] Linn. Hort. Upf. 132. 1. Spec. Plant. 704. [t] Spec. Pl. 8. Rosa Rubra Multiplex Hort. Upf. 13. [u] Spec. Pl. 4. Rosa odore Cinnamonic, simplex Hort. Upf. [w] Sp. Pl. 13. Rosa alba flore Pleno Hort. Upf.

white,

white, but rather inclining to red; the flower is double, being frequently of the size of a man's fist, and emit the most fragrant odour of any I have seen. The shrubs live to a great age. From this sort the Turks and Egyptians distil the water. An incredible quantity is distilled yearly at Fajhum, and sold in Egypt, being exported to other countries. An apothecary, who kept a shop in the street of the Franks, bought yearly 1500lb. (about 180 gallons) which he caused to be brought to the city in copper vessels, lined with wax, selling it to great profit at Cairo.

The Eastern people use the water in a luxurious manner, sprinkling it on the hands, face, head, and cloaths, of the guest they mean to honour, afterwards perfuming them with frankincense, the wood of aloes, &c.

21. Nymphæa Lotus [x]. Egyptian Water Lilly.

This grows in vast quantities in the plains of Lower Egypt, near Cairo, during the time they are under water. It flowers about the middle of September, and ripens towards the latter end of October. The Arabians call it Nuphar.

22. Mimosa Lebbeck [y]. Acacia of Upper Egypt.

This flowers in June, growing to be a large tree. It is cultivated in the gardens at Cairo; but I know not whether it is a native of the country. The Arabs call it Lebbeck.

[x] Linn. Sp. Pl. P. 729. N. 3. [y] P. 1503. N. 22.

### 23. Mimosa Nilotica [z]. Gum Arabic Acacia.

THE Arabs call it **Charad**. This plant, and not the Mimosa **Senegal Linn. Spec. Pl. 1506. 32.** as naturalists have hitherto imagined, produces the Gummi Arabicum (Gum Arabic) Gummi Thuris (Frankincense) and the Succus Acaciæ.

N. B. **This** species, **and the** Mimosa Senegal, grow together promiscuously: **hence** it happened, that the Mimosa Senegal having **been by** chance brought to Europe, instead of the Mimosa **Nilotica,** and Alpinus not having distinguished **one from the other, the Mimosa** Senegal was by all writers in **Botany, and Materia** medica, believed to be the **plant that produced the above-mentioned** gums; but **the true plant was only known to those who** cultivated it **in Egypt.** The Egyptians know one from the other **extremely well,** and have given them different names, **calling the true one** Charad, **and the other, which is neither of use nor value, Fetne.** They both grow in **Lower Egypt, where they are** planted **in gardens: I have, however,** seen them grow wild in the **sandy** desart, near the ancient Sepulchres of the Egyptians, and have been informed that the Mimosa nilotica (Acacia **vera) grows** plentifully in several parts **of** Upper Egypt. The **gum is gathered in vast quantities from the trees** growing **in Arabia Petræa, near the North Bay of** the **Red Sea, at the foot of mount Sinai,** whence they bring **the Gum** Thus (Frankincense) so called by the dealers **in drugs in** Egypt, **from** Thur **and** Thor, which is the **name of a harbour in** the North **Bay of** the Red Sea, **near mount Sinai,** thereby distinguishing

---

[z] Linn. Sp. Pl. Pag. 1506. N. 34.

tinguishing it from the Gum Arabic, which is brought from Suez, another port of the Red Sea, not far from Cairo. Besides the different places from which these gums are brought, they differ also in some other particulars. The Gum Thus is more pellucid, white, or of no colour at all; but the Gum Arabic is less pellucid, and of a brown or dirty yellow colour.

24. Anemone coronaria [b]. Wind-flower of Natolia.

I HAVE seen this growing in the plains and bottoms of mountains, near Smyrna in Natolia.

25. Clematis orientalis [b]. Oriental Virgins Bower.

THIS grows in the hedges round Smyrna.

26. Origanum ægyptiacum [c]. Wild Marjoram of Egypt.

I HAVE seen this in the gardens at Cairo, being introduced there on account of its smell; which is stronger than that of the Dittany of Crete (Origanum veticum) aromatic, and comforts the head. The Arabians call it Zatarhendi, i. e. Origanum indicum.

27. Nepeta syriaca, Syrian Nep.

THIS grows in great plenty in the gardens, and near the walls at Smyrna.

[a] Linn. Sp. Pl. Pag. 760. N. 8. [b] P. 765. N. 4. [c] P. 822. N. 1.

28. Oronanche

28. Orobanche lævis [d]. Broom-rape.

This grows in moist places round Smyrna.

29. Draba verna [e]. Common Madwort.

About Smyrna.

30. Lathyrus ægyptiacus pedunculis unifloris, cirrhis triphyllis, foliolis ensiformibus.

This grows in the fields of Damiata.

31. Dolichos lablab [f].

Alpinus says, that this grows wild in Egypt; but it is cultivated in gardens, and I am certain does not grow wild in Lower Egypt. The Egyptians call it Ful Frangi, i. e. the European bean: hence one might conjecture that the Europeans first brought it to Egypt. The Egyptians make pleasant arbours of this in their houses and gardens, by supporting the stem, and leading it where they think proper. They not only support it with sticks and wood, but tie it with cords, by which means the leaves form an excellent covering and an agreeable shade.

32. Carthamus tinctorius [g]. Safflower.

This is cultivated in large quantities in Egypt. The flowers are gathered thrice a year. The flowers are much used for dying, and are a valuable commodity to Egypt. The manner of preparing them is as follows: they are gathered fresh, and

[d] Linn. Sp. Pl. P. 881. N. 1. [e] P. 896. N. 2. [f] P. 1019. N. 2. [g] P. 1162. N. 1.

pressed

pressed between two stones, to extract the crude juice which is thrown away: the flowers, after being pressed, are washed several times in spring water, which is brackish in Egypt; by this the remaining acrid juice is washed away: they are then taken out, as much at a time as a person can hold in his hand, and the water is so well pressed out, as to leave the impression of the fingers. They are then put on the flat roofs of houses, and laid on matts, being now of a yellow colour. In the day time they are covered with rushes or straw, lest they should dry too fast, and too much by the heat of the sun; but at night they are uncovered and exposed to the air and dew. The dew changes them into a deep yellow; they are dried by the moderate heat of the night; and for this reason there are people constantly employed in turning them. They are afterwards sold to France, Venice, Florence, and England, under the name of Saffranon. The young leaves are used for sallad in Egypt: at Smyrna they powder them, and put them into milk to coagulate it; and in this manner all cheese is made in Egypt. The seeds are eaten by the Parrot of Alexander, which is very fond of them: to other birds or beasts they would be a mortal poison.

33. Artemisia dracunculus [h]. Tarragon.

The Egyptians say, that if Flax seed is put into an onion, and afterwards planted in rich ground, it will produce this plant. A fine fable.

[h] Linn. Sp. Pl. Pag. 1189. N. 19.

34. Viola

34. Viola odorata [i]. The sweet-scented Violet.

THIS is one of the plants most esteemed by the Egyptians and Turks, for its excellent smell and agreeable colour; but especially for its great use in Sorbet, which they make of Violet Sugar, dissolved in water, and drink frequently; but especially when they intend to entertain their guests in an elegant manner. This is one of the many sorts of drink, which are originally Arabic, and by them called Sorbet; the other sorts are made with raisins, boiled in water; capillaire, mixed with water; the decoction of liquorize, and perhaps other things; the grandees sometimes add ambergrease, which is the highest pitch of luxury and indulgence of their appetite. The Arabians call these flowers Neps.

35. **Arum** colocasia [k]. Ægyptian Wake Robin, called Colocasia.

THIS is met with in the fields and gardens of Egypt.

36. Urtica dioica [l]. The greatest Ægyptian Nettle.

THE Arabians call it Curcis. It is found in Egypt.

37. Platanus orientalis [m]. The Eastern Plane.

[i] Linn. Sp. Pl. Pag. 1189. N. 19. [k] P. 1368. N. 5. [l] P. 1396. N. 6. [m] P. 1417. N. 1.

38. Momordica

38. Momordica luffa [n]. Ægyptian Balsam Apple.

The Arabians call it Liff and Luff. It is cultivated in gardens, and climbs up on Palm-trees, covering and elegantly adorning the stem of them.

39. Momordica balsamina [o]. Balsam Apple.

This plant is famous in Syria for curing wounds. They cut open the unripe fruit, and infuse it in sweet oil, exposed to the sun for some days, until the oil is become red, which they preserve for use. It is applied to a fresh wound dropped on cotton. The Syrians reckon this the best thing to cure wounds, next to balsam of Mecca; and have found by experience, that it often cures large wounds within three days. The leaves and stems are besides used for arbours or bowers. It is cultivated in gardens.

40. Cucurbita lagenaria [p]. Bottle Gourd.

The Arabians call it Charrah. The poor people eat it. They boil it, and season it with vinegar: they likewise fill the shell with rice and meat, and thus make a kind of pudding. It grows in all parts of Egypt, and the deserts of Arabia, wherever the mountains are covered with rich soil.

41. Cucurbita Citrullus [q]. Water Melon.

The Arabians call it Batech. It is cultivated on the banks of the Nile, in the rich claiey earth, which

[n] Linn. Sp. Pl. Pag. 1433. N. 4. [o] P. 1433. N. 1. [p] P. 1434. N. 1. [q] P. 1435. N. 5.

subsides during the inundation, from the beginning of May until the overflowing of the Nile, i. e. to the end of July, or beginning of August; and in the island Delta, especially at Burlos, whence the largest and best are brought. This serves the Egyptians for meat, drink, and physic. It is eat in abundance during the season, even by the richer sort of people; but the common people, on whom Providence hath bestowed nothing but poverty and patience, scarcely eat any thing but these, and account this the best time of the year, as they are obliged to put up with worse fare at other seasons: they eat them with bread, and scarcely ever taste them ripe. This fruit likewise serves them for drink, the juice refreshing these poor creatures; and they have less occasion for water, than if they were to live on more substantial food in this burning climate. They make a hole in the melon, in which all the juice is collected. This fruit also affords physic; but it is not every kind of melon that answers this end. There is a variety softer and more juicy than the common sort, and not so plentiful. This comes from Burlos. When this is very ripe, and almost putrid, they hollow part of it, gather the juice there collected, and, mixing it with rose water and a little sugar, they give it in burning fevers, being the only medicine the common people use in those distempers. It is, however, not so frequent as Alpinus and Veslingius relate; for it can be had at only one season of the year, and that is when the fruit is ripe, which does not continue above three weeks. This is very comfortable to the patient, for it cools and refreshes him. This variety is by the Arabs called Et-Naovi, which signifies water. Alpinus, therefore, mistook the origin of the word.

A

## A CAUTION.

This fruit should be eaten with great circumspection; for if this cooling fruit be taken in the heat of the day, when the body is very warm, bad consequences often ensue, and it occasions colicks, looseneses, fluxes, a foul stomach, &c. I have been told by a person from Europe, a man of veracity, that he last year saw a merchant from Damascus, die suddenly at Damiata, upon eating a whole water melon when he was very hot. When I came to Egypt I was much delighted with the appearance and taste of this fruit, having never seen it before; and tho' I was very cautious, eating only a little at a time, yet it chilled my stomach, as if I had swallowed a bit of ice, which obliged me to desist from tasting it afterwards, and I likewise advised others from it; for tho' it is very agreeable to the palate, yet it can't be eat without danger. It is well known that people are much troubled with worms, at the time this fruit is ripe.

42. Cucumis sativus. The common **Cucumber**.

This grows with the Water Melons. The vulgar boil and eat it with vinegar; the richer people fill it with flesh and aromatics, and make a kind of puddings, which eat very well. This ripens a little later than the Water Melon, but then it is in season longer, and until the latter end of the autumn.

### 43. Cucumis melo [b]. Melon.

This is cultivated in the same places, and ripens at the same time with the Water Melon: it is very near as large as the Water Melon, the flesh is softer than with us, but more insipid, and has not the agreeable sweetness of ours, especially when we procure the seeds from Siberia. The richer people eat them in the manner we do, to gratify the palate; the poorer sort eat them but seldom.

### 44. Cucumis Chate [c]. The Egyptian Melon, or Queen of Cucumbers. Abdellavi of Alpinus.

This grows in the fertile earth round Cairo, after the inundation of the Nile, and not in any other place in Egypt, nor does it grow in any other soil. It ripens with the Water Melons. This fruit is a little watery, the flesh is almost of the same substance as the Melons, it tastes somewhat sweet and cool, but is far from being as cool as the Water Melons.

This the grandees and Europeans in Egypt eat as the most pleasant fruit they find, and that from which they have least to apprehend. It is the most excellent fruit of this tribe, of any yet known. The Princes and grandees in Europe may wish they could get it into their gardens, for it is certainly worth a place on their tables.

### 45. Ruscus aculeatus [d]. Prickly Kneeholly.

[b] Lin. Sp. Pl. P. 1436. N. 5.   [c] Lin. Sp. Pl. P. 1437. N. 7.
[d] Lin. Sp. Pl. P. 1474. N. 1.

46. Ceratonia

46. Ceratonia Siliqua [e]. Carob tree.

47. Musa paradisiaca [f]. The Plaintain-tree.

This flowers in Egypt in the months of October and November, i. e. after the inundation of the Nile. It flowers, therefore, at a time when the air is temperate, and the earth moist, and the fruit ripens when the air is excessively hot. The fruit is sweet, rather hardish, or between a pear and a date, a little viscid and mealy, melting in the mouth without being chewed. It soon becomes sour, and can't be kept above six days in Egypt, after it is taken from the plant. It is to be had fresh from the latter end of May to the latter end of October, growing plentifully near Rosetta; but it is very scarce at Cairo, tho' it grows there, but the trees are almost all barren, producing but little fruit, which is kept for ladies of the first quality.

48. Ficus sycomorus [g]. The Scripture Sycamore.

This is a huge tree, the stem being often fifty feet thick. The fruit is pierced or bored by an insect (Cynips sycomori) about the time it ripens, in a very remarkable manner. There is an opening made in the Calyx, near the time the fruit ripens, which is occasioned in two different manners:
1. When the Squamæ, which cover the Calyx, wither and are bent back, as in the Ficus Carica (common Fig-tree) tho' this is not very common in the

---

[e] Lin. Sp. Pl. P. 1513. N. 1.   [f] P. 1477. N. 1.   [g] P. 1513. N. 2.

Sycamore. 2. What follows is worth attention, and may serve to excite our admiration. A little below the scales on the side of the flower cup, there appears a spot before the fruit is ripe; the fruit is affected with a gangræne in this place, which extends itself further, and frequently occupies the space of a fingers breadth; it withers, the place affected becomes black, the fleshy substance in the middle of the calyx, for the breadth of a quill, is corroded, and the male blossoms, which are nearest to the bare side, appear naked, opening a way for the infect, which makes several furrows in the inside of the fruit, but never touches the stigmata, tho' it frequently eats the germina. The wounded or gangrænous place is at first covered or shut up with the blossoms, but the hole is by degrees opened and enlarged, of various sizes, in the different fruits, the margin and sides being always gangrænous, black, hard, and turned inwardly. The same gangrænous appearance is also found near the squamæ, after the insect has made a hole in that place.

Of this tree the ancient Egyptians made coffins, wherein to lay their embalmed dead. The wood is very proper for this use, as it does not rot for several ages, and not until it is very old. The Mummies which I saw in Egypt, were all preserved in coffins made of this wood, which, as well as the corpse, had kept found for 2000 years. This large and branchy tree, by spreading out its boughs, affords excellent shade, being of great use to people living in a scorching climate, and travelling through deserts, as they may frequently rest their wearied limbs and drooping bodies, under the shade of a Sycamore. The fruit tastes pretty well; when quite ripe it is soft, watery, somewhat sweet, with a very little portion of an aromatic taste. After I once

once had tasted it, I could scarcely refrain from eating; and if I had thought the fresh fruit wholesome, I should certainly have eaten a great deal of it: tho' the receptaculum is fleshy enough, yet but little of it is good, the insect having eat much of it, and often made its furrows to the outward skin. This tree grows in the plains and fields of Lower Egypt, where I have seen it very common. It buds in the latter end of March, and the fruit ripens in the beginning of June; it is wounded or cut by the inhabitants at the time it buds, for without this precaution, as they say, it will **not bear fruit.**

49. Phœnix dactylifera [h]. The Date-tree.

This palm is of great use to the inhabitants of the East, &c. The fruit or Dates are commonly eaten. In Upper Egypt many families subsist almost entirely on Dates; in Lower Egypt they don't eat so many, rather chusing to sell them. **The inhabitants** here yearly sell a considerable quantity, **which** are chiefly carried to the towns in Turkey; for which reason we see Dates exposed to sale in every town. The Egyptians make a conserve of the fresh Dates, mixing them **with** sugar; this has an agreeable **taste.** The **stones** or kernels of the Dates are hard as horn, **and nobody would imagine that any** animal could eat them. But the Egyptians **break** them, grin'd them on their hand mills, and, for want of better food, give them to their camels, which eat them. In Barbary they turn handsome beads for paternosters, of these stones. Of the leaves they make baskets, or rather a kind of short bags, which

[h] Lin. Sp. Pl. P. 1658. N. 1.

are

are used in Turkey on journies, and in their houses. In Egypt they make fly-flaps of them, convenient enough to drive away the numerous insects which incommode a man in this country: I have likewise seen brushes made of them, with which they clean their sofas and cloaths. The hard boughs they use for fences round their gardens, and cages, to keep their fowls in, with which they carry on a great traffic: they also use the boughs for several other things in husbandry, instead of other wood, which they are destitute of. The trunk or stem is split, and used for the same purposes as the branches: they even use it for beams to build houses, as they are strong enough for small buildings: it is likewise used for firing, when there is want of better. The wood is soft and spungy, but burns well. They lay a whole tree across their cisterns, on which they wind the rope when they draw the water. The integumentum (covering) which covers the tree between the boughs, entirely resembles a web, and has threads, which run perpendicularly and horizontally over one another: it is of considerable use in Egypt, for of it they make all the ropes which they use at their cisterns, &c. They have also rigging of the same kind for their smaller vessels; it is pretty strong and lasting. They reckon in Egypt, that palm-trees afford to their owners a sequin annually of profit for each tree. It is common to see two, three, to four hundred fruit-bearing Date-trees all belonging to one family, and one may sometimes see three to four thousand in the possession of one man, which, at the above rate, bring in a considerable revenue to their owner, for the little spot of ground they occupy. A full grown Date-tree does not, at most, take up above

above **four feet** in diameter, so that they **may be** planted within eight feet one of another.

50. **Bryum** ægypti.  Ægyptian Moss.

This flowers in November on the walls, ruins, and cisterns in Egypt.

# PLANTÆ ÆGYPTI.

### MARCH 12, 1751.

THESE flowered near the Nile, on the banks of the branch that leads to Damiata.

Scorpiurus fulcata.   Caterpillar.
Medicago polymorpha.   Snail Trefoil.
Oxalis corniculata.   Wood Sorrel.
Pimpinella Anisum.   Common Anise.
Cichorium Intybus.   Wild Succory.
Citrus Aurantium.   Orange-tree.
Cnicus benedictus.   Blessed Thistle.
Cardui species foliis radicalibus ovatis, caulinis pinnatifidis.   A species of Thistle.
Convolvulus Scammonia.   Scammony.

### MARCH 14. DAMIATA.

Adianthum capillus veneris.   Maidenhair.
Ranunculus foliis trilobis. The trilobed Crowfoot.

IN the gardens.

Hypnum

Hypnum foliis crenatis.

In moist places and walls of the Aqueducts.

## MARCH 16. DAMIATA.

Petroselinum anisum.　A dubious Plant.
Sonchus oleraceus.　Sow Thistle.
Senecio jacobæus.　Ragwort.
Alsine foliis ovato-lanceolatis.　Chickweed.
Euphorbia peplus.　Spurge.
Phalaris panicula tomentosa.　Canary Grass.
Lathyrus ægyptiacus.　Ægyptian chickling Vetch.
Melissa hortensis.　Baum.
Citrus Aurantium.　Orange-tree.
Festucæ species.　Ægyptian Fescue Grass.

Common in Egypt.

## MARCH 19. DAMIATA.

Musa paradisiaca.　Plaintain-tree.

The fruit of this is often eat by Field Mice (Mus agrestis), who run on the tree and devour it.

Saccharum officinarum.　Sugar Cane.

Vitis vinifera.　Vine.

This is cultivated here for the sake of eating the grapes, and not for wine, which is brought from Candia, Cyprus, Scopuli, &c. and Europe, for the use of the Christians.

Æschynomene sesban.　Bastard sensitive Plant.

A Willow by the Arabians, called Safsaf.

Phœnix dactylifera.　Date-tree.

## MARCH 22. DAMIATA.

Solidago virgaurea.   Golden Rod.
Crassula portulacaria.   Lesser orpin.
Plantago major.   Plantain.
Vicia foliis obovatis acuminatis pubescentibus, stipulis deflexis laciniatis, laciniis acuminatis plurimis.   A species of Vetch.
Matricaria chamomilla.   Chamomile.
Festuca, Phalaris, Avena.   Fescue Grass, Canary Grass and Oats.
Rumex acetosella.   Sorrel.
Cassia fistula.
Phœnix dactylifera.   Date-tree.

Of this eleven trees were grown together at the basis.

Atriplex vulgaris.   Orach.
   Arenariæ species.   A species of Sand Grass.

   The Lichenes of mount St. Cruz in Cyprus.

Lichen crustaceus flavus.
Lichen crustaceus virescens.
Lichen lamellosus flavus.
Lichen lamellosus griseus.
Lichen crustaceus griseus.
Lichen crustaceus ater.
Lichen crustaceus ex flavo & atro per circulos variegatus.
Lichen foliaceus laciniis sinuatis.

   Pancratium maritimum.   The Sea Daffodil.
   This the modern Greeks call χρίνος. Did not the ancients know it by the same name?

*Crinum*

# PLANTS.

Crinum æthiopicum. The Asphodel Lilly from Æthiopia.

It flowers in August.

Polianthes tuberosa. Tube-rose.

This flowers in August. The Egyptians put the flowers in sweet oil, and by this means give the oil a most excellent smell, scarce inferior to Oil of Jessamine.

LAPIDES

# LAPIDES.
# STONES.

Opalus Gemma. The Opal.
Cos Damiatæ. The Whetstone of Damiata.
Natrum Ægyptiarum. The Nitre of the Ancients.

THE *Opal* is one of the rarest Gems to be met with. During my stay at Alexandria, I was shewn a stone by Mr. Roboly, the French Interpreter, which was of the size of a hazel-nut, in the form of a half globe, and set in a ring; if it was held horizontally, it had a very fine olive colour; but if it was held perpendicularly, between the eye and the light, it had the colour of the finest ruby. The present possessor had procured it by accident from a Peasant, who found it amongst some old ruins, and sold it for five or six pence. The Interpreter, who knew not what it was, set no great value on it, and asked me, whether I knew the stone, and how much I thought it worth? I answered, that it was an Opal; but could not tell him the worth of it, as I was not used to prize such things, the value being often proportioned to the taste and inclination of the purchaser; I however told him, that it was worth having and keeping, and might be of considerable value to a person who was fond of Gems; this being

one

one of the scarcest to be got. Some time after, Mr. Roboly came to Cairo, where Mr. Lironcourt, the French Consul, a learned and very curious man saw, admired, and easily obtained the Stone. Lironcourt accepted of the present with pleasure, without knowing its value; I was therefore asked the second time about it, and answered as before; upon which Mr. Lironcourt compared it with the descriptions which Pliny, and several other Authors, which he had in his fine library, had given of the Opal, and was by them confirmed that I was right. But he knew not yet the value, and soon after set out for Constantinople. He there shewed the Stone to a Connoisseur, who told him it was an Opal, and that he valued it at several thousand ducats. The Ancients knew the Opal perfectly well, and without doubt it was more common with them, than it is at present. This, which I have described, had probably lain concealed in the ruins of Alexandria, ever since the time when all kinds of Gems and Jewels were part of the riches of its powerful inhabitants. There is scarcely any kind of Stone, accounted precious by the Ancients, which is not to be found in the ruins of Alexandria and old Cairo; some of them polished, others rough. I have seen the Chalcedon, Aga-onyx, Sard-onyx, Cornelian, all found in those places. I forbear mentioning Emeralds, and Sapphires, which are frequently found there, and are not so scarce at present as the former. The attentive Tavernier, who was a great Connoisseur of Stones, says, that the Opal is not to be found in any place in the world, except in a mine in Hungary; but the Ancients, without doubt, had this and many other Stones, of which we know not the country or place

whence

whence they are brought, thofe places at prefent being buried in oblivion. But we, on the other hand, know the way to the diamond mines of India, with which the Ancients were unacquainted; therefore the Stone which in our times is moft efteemed, with its companion, the Ruby, was not fo common with the nations of the ancient world, as at prefent.

**Cos Damiatæ.** Whetftone. Lapis foraminibus ex cavatus, magnus, inæqualis, ex cæruleo nigrefcens. This large rugged and almoft black Stone, with many fmall holes, is found in Paleftine and Galilee.

It is brought to Damiata for mill-ftones, and ought to be better examined in the place from whence it comes.

**Natrum,** a falt dug out of a pit or mine, near Manfura in Egypt; it is by the inhabitants called Natrum, being mixt with a Lapis Calcareus (Limeftone) that ferments with vinegar, of a whitifh brown colour. The Egyptians ufe it, (1.) to put into bread inftead of yeaft. (2.) To wafh linen with it inftead of foap. I have been informed, that it is ufed with fuccefs in the tooth-ach, in the manner following: The falt is powdered and put into vinegar, it ferments immediately, and fubfides to the bottom. The mouth is wafhed with this vinegar during the Paroxfym, by which the pain is mitigated, but not taken off entirely.

# HISTORIA NATURALIS PALÆSTINÆ,

## THE NATURAL HISTORY OF PALESTINE.

### I. JAFFA.

Hyoscyamus aureus. Golden Henbane.

Parietaria officinalis. Pellitory of the shops.

Lycium *spinosum*. Boxthorn. The Latin Monks say, that the crown of Christ was made of this.

Euphorbia *foliis oblongis lanceolatis verticillatis*, **herbacea**, inermis, pedalis. This grows in hedges.

Buphthalmum *foliis duplicato-pinnatis*. Ox-eye.

Buphthalmum *foliis oblongis laciniatis, laciniis denticulatis oppositis*. Ox-eye.

Turritis *caule simpliciusculo, foliis radicalibus longis lanceolatis laciniatis; terminali maxima dentata*. Tower mustard.

Cnicus *tomentosus*, *foliis cordalis amplexicaulibus dentatis integris*. Thistle.

Papaver Rhœas. Poppy.

Malva **vulgaris**. Mallow.

*In hortis.* In the gardens.

Ficus Carica. The fig-tree.

Rosa damascena. The damask rose.

Terebinthus. The turpentine tree.

Sycomorus,

Sycomorus. The sycamore.
Citrus aurantia. The orange tree.
Amygdalus persica. Peach tree.
Cannabis vulgaris. **Hemp.** A few of these plants were growing in a garden being only used by the Mahometans: they powder the leaves, and make of them a Narcotick, which has the same effects on them as opium. The Confection is called Chaschis, and is much used by the Egyptians.

Animalia *loci*. The animals of the country.

Canis aureus. The Jackcal (Chical of the Turks.) This is common in Egypt and the East, but very numerous in Palestine. I saw many of its caves and holes in the hedges round the gardens. This is fatal to the herds and flocks of the Arabians, and is therefore hunted continually, and they often throw great numbers of them into the sea. This is past all doubt the Fox of Sampson.
A species of Mustela, which is very common in Palestine, especially during the vintage, and often destroys whole vineyards, and fields of Cucumbers.

Scarabæus *clypeo pedibus anticis dentatis*, on which were found numbers of little Acari.

Chrysomela *coccinea, elytris thorace medio capiteque nigrescentibus*.

## II. ACRA.

Silene *foliis obovatis lanuginosis crossis suculentis*. Viscous Campion.

Plantago *caule ramoso foliis integerrimis lineari lanceolatis, ramis brachiatis, spica foliosa*. Plantain.

Lagurus *spica ovata, compressa, arista tertia longissima intorta. Folia breviuscula lineari acuminata, a caule distantia, vaginantia*. The Hares-tail Grass.

Physalis

Physalis Alkegengi? Winter cherry. *Foliis ovata integerrima lanuginosa. Caulis lanuginosus. Filamenta non brevissima, sed longitudine laciniarum.*

### III. JERUSALEM. 1751. April 7th.

Festuca? Fescue grass. *Pedalis, foliis linearibus mollissimis.*

THIS grows on the dry grounds round the town, and is very grateful to sheep and goats.

Sisymbrium *foliis cordato-lanceolatis, siliquis semiuncialibus longis pendulis, pedunculis capillaribus basi tenuioribus.* Water cresses.

Geranium *calycibus pentaphyllis, foliis cordato-ovatis inciso crenatis.* Crane's bill.

Geranium *foliis compositis: foliolis alternis pinnatifidis. Calyx pentaphyllus.* Crane's bill.

Cynoglossum *foliis tuberculatis, scabris, hispidis.* Hounds tongue.

Asperugo *foliis ovatis.* Great goose grass.

Lamium *foliis albis.* Archangel.

Urtica pilulifera. Nettles.

### IV. Mount SION. April 8, 1751.

Ranunculus *lanuginosus, caule procumbente, foliis quaternis, foliolis pinnatifidis, receptaculo ovato-acuminato.* Crowfoot.

Betonica officinalis. Betony.

Marrubium *flore purpureo.* Hore hound.

Biscutella *siliquis orbiculatis didymis, foliis radicalibus lanceolatis dentatis lanuginosis.* Buckler mustard.

Trifolium *minimum montanum, flore purpureo.* Trefoil.

As this plant is here very small, one may safely conclude, that the soil is barren.

Thlaspi *foliis lobato-laciniatis: laciniis ciliatis.* Treacle mustard.

Draba *caule nudo, foliis lanceolatis integerrimis margine ciliatis.* Whitlow grass.

Anthemis *parva, foliis pinnatis capillaribus.* Camomile.

Festuca? Fescue grass. Spithamalis, foliis capillaribus. This grass grows in sand.

Hieracium *montanum parvum.* Hawkweed.

Buphthalmum *parvum, foliis oblongis dentatis.* Ox-eye.

Draba? *foliis caulinis ovatis basi angustatis minima.* Whitlow grass.

## V. JERICHO. In the Vale near the Town.
### April 12th.

Solanum *fruticosum quadripedale caule & foliis spinosis.* Night shade.

Frutex *foliis triangularibus splendentibus.* This plant is very common in all the desarts of Palestine.

Asclepias *scandens fruticosa, foliis cordato acuminatis.* Swallow-wort. This grows in the clayey desart between Jericho and the dead sea.

Lichen *lamellis convexis.* Liverwort. This grows on the surface of the earth.

Didynamica *graveolens, petalis reflexis, foliis viscosis, radice fibrosa magna.*

Allium Cepa. Onion. The Arabians call it Basal. It grows in the plains near the sea.

Tamarix. Tamarisk.

Kali fruticosum (Salsola fruticosa?) Glasswort.

Erica *simplex fruticosa.* Heath.

Mimosa.

Mimosa. Egyptian Acacia. *Schitta* of the Hebrews. I saw only one shrub of this in the plain, near the mountains of Arabia.

## VI. The Road of St. JEREMIAH, between Jerusalem and Rama.

Terebinthus. Turpentine tree.
Vitex. Chaste tree.
Tamarix. Tamarisk.
Ceratonia. Carob.
Sycomorus, only one tree at Rama. The scripture sycamore.
Cynara. Artichoke.
Cicuta. Hemlock.
Cardui & Cnici, six species. Thistles.

## VII. At the SEALED Fountain of Solomon near Bethlehem.

Columba Palestinæ. A dove.
Rana corpore ovato, dorso convexo, tota lucido-viridis. A frog.
Tenthredo fasciata, fasciis candidis atrisque.
Scarabæus *Buphthalmi parvus, ater lineis candidis.*

### PLANTS.

Adianthum. Maiden-hair. ⎫
Hypnum minimum. ⎬ in the well.
Nasturtium aquaticum. (Sisymbrium.) Water cresses.
Achilleæ *affinis lutea.*
Gramen *panicula arundinacea, radice bulbosa.* On the hills.

Anagyris

Anagyris fœtida. Stinking bean-trefoil. Upon the hills.
Ocymum. Basil.
Origanum. Wild Marjoram.

## VIII. Mount THABOR.

Cynoglossum hispidum. Hound's tongue.
Ononis fœtida. Stinking Rest-harrow.
Papaver rhœas. Poppy.
Papaver *flore flavescente parvo*. Poppy.
Buphthalmum dentatum. Ox-eye.
Cynara. Artichoke.
Ruta. Rue.
Umbellata *cum disco filamentoso*.
Carduina *caulo spinoso quadrangulari*.
Laserpitium latifolium. Laserwort.
Pimpinella officinalis. Burnet saxifrage.
Trifolium, *foliis ovato-lanceolatis, spica oblonga laxa*. Trefoil.
Syngenesista cum pericarpiis confertis.
Quercus foliis dentato-aculeatis. Oak.
Ceratonia. Carob tree, or St. John's Bread.
Salviæ variæ species. Sage.
Gramen *secalinum radice bulbosa*.
Absinthium romanum. (Artemisia.) Wormwood.
Ilex. Holly. In the vallies.
Terebinthus. The turpentine-tree. On the rocks.
Myrtus. Myrtle.
Scorzonera. Viper grafs.
Cichoreum Intybus. Succory.
Hedera helix. Ivy.
Cepa montana. Onion.
Avena montana. Oats.

## IX. In Mount TEMPTATION.

Cepa montana. Onion.
Cordia sebesten. Sebesten.
Ricinus Palma Christi.
Rhamnus spina Christi. Buckthorn, called Christ's thorn.
Vitex agnus castus. Chaste tree.
Elæagnus. Wild olive; of this is made the oil of Jericho.
*Arbor magna, floribus loniceræ labiatis laciniatis, totis sanguineis.* Foliis obverse ovatis succulentis lucido viridibus.
Ficus carica. The fig tree.
Euphorbia *foliis teretibus succulentis.* Spurge.
Ranunculus *aquaticus luteus.* Crowfoot.
Malva ruderum. Mallow.
Buphthalmum commune. Ox-eye.
Chenopodium ruderum. Goose foot.
Hystrix cristata. Porcupine.
Cimex *aculeata, lateribus abdominis valde protuberantibus, maculis ferrugineis.*

## X. At the Fountain of SOLOMON near Tyre.

Salix safsaf. Willow.
Vitex agnus castus. Chaste tree.
Ricinus communis. Palma Christi.
Convolvulus foliis trinis. Bindweed.
Solanum foliis hirsutis. Anel el dib of the Arabs. Night shade.
Mercurialis. Mercury.
Parietaria. Pellitory.
*Didynamica,* flore minimo rubro bipedalis.

XI. The

## XI. The HOT-BATHS of TIBERIAS.

1. *The fountain*, or source of them, is at the foot of a mountain, at the distance of a pistol-shot from lake Genazereth, and a quarter of a league from the coasts of Tiberias.

2. The *mountain* consists of a black and brittle sulphureous stone, which is only to be found in large masses in the neighbourhood of Tiberias; but in loose stones also on the coasts of the *dead sea*, as well as here at the lake Genazereth. They cut mill-stones out of it in this place, which are sent by water from Acra to Egypt. I saw an incredible quantity of them at Damiata.

3. The spring which comes from the mountain, is in diameter equal to that of a man's arm, and there is one only.

4. The water is so hot, that the hand may be put into it without scalding, but it cannot be kept there long; consequently it is not boiling hot, but the next degree to it.

5. It has a strong sulphureous smell.

6. It tastes bitter, and somewhat like common salt.

7. The sediment deposed by the water is black, as thick as paste, smells strong of sulphur, and is covered with two skins or cuticles, of which that beneath is of a fine dark green colour, and the uppermost of a light rusty colour; at the mouth of the outlet, where the water formed little cascades over the stones, the first mentioned cuticle alone was found, and so much resembled a conferva, that one might easily have taken this, that belongs to the mineral kingdom, for a vegetable production; but nearer the river, where the water stood still,

one

one might see both skins, the yellow uppermost, and under it the green. There was a miserable house with seats for bathing, built close by it; but it was not kept in repair, as no body here makes any use of these gifts of nature.

## XII. The DEAD SEA.

1. The soil is a crumbly clay, impregnated with salt, and greatly resembles that of Egypt.
2. Quartz, to which adhered a crust of salt.
3. Nodules of clay, which are round and compact. These I saw in the clay near the coast.
4. Schistus. Slate resembling flint, scattered here and there on the banks.
5. Perpendicular layers of a lamellated brown clay, in the common clay on the banks. Is this imperfect slate?
6. No rush or reed.
7. No plants near the shore. A stinking plant with a labiated flower, at some distance; and a plant of a salt taste, in the plain.
8. The *Asphaltes* is gathered by the Arabs in considerable quantities every autumn on the shore, where it is thrown. It is carried to Damiata, and there sold for dying wool.
9. Shell fish were common on the shore.
10. The Arabs say, there are no fish in this sea; however, I doubt the truth of this, as there are shell fish.
11. No navigation.
12. The neighbouring mountains are composed of a soft calcareous stone, and appear to be formed by this sea, which has gradually decreased.
13. The slate seen in the mountains has been Asphaltes, now changed into slate.

14. The hardness of the remote mountains.

15. The Asphaltes appears like the balsam of mummies (Balsam. mumiarum), and is the same substance; has there ever been a lake in Egypt impregnated with this matter?

16. The petrefactions on the opposite shore are the same now as those in the dry lakes of Egypt.

17. *Poma-sodomitica*. Mad apples, are the fruit of Solanum Melongena.

PLANTS,

# PLANTS, ANIMALS, &c.

### Mentioned in the SCRIPTURES.

CUCUMIS melo. Melon. Arab. Kaun.
Cucurbita citrullus. Water melon. Arab. Battech. Syriacis jabbas.
Cucumis sativus. Cucumbers. Arab. chiar.
Cucurbita lagenaria. Gourd. Arab. charrak.
Brassica sativa. Cabbage. Arab. krump. Syriac. malfuf.
Cucumis colocynthis. Bitter apple. Arab. Handal.
Momordica balsamina. Male balsam apple. Balsamita.
Momordica elaterium. Spirting cucumber. By the Syrians called adjur el hemar, *i. e.* Asses cucumber. These names may be compared with the Hebrew, to explain the scriptures, where mention is made of the cucumbers of Egypt.

Luke xvii. ver. 6. συκαμίνος. Christ certainly meant the Sycamore of the Ancients, and Pharaoh's fig-tree of the Egyptians, which the Arabians call *Guimez*, when he pointed to a large tree, which he said the disciples might, by faith, remove into the sea; for such there are now in Judæa and Galilee, where Christ then was, see ver. 11. of the same chapter. Luther, therefore, translated it very badly in calling it a mulberry-tree, which is neither congruent with scripture nor natural history.

Luke

Luke xix. ver. 4. συκομουρία. The tree on which little Zachæus climbed near Jericho, to see Christ pass. The Greek text shews it was a sycamore; therefore the Roman Catholicks, Greeks and Armenians are led into an error, when they visit the holy places, for they are shewn a tree of a different genus, and contend that it was on one of those Zachæus climbed. This is a-kin to the prunus, (plumb-tree) and has oval leaves, &c. an Eleagnus? (wild olive?) it grows in the plains near the ruins of Jericho; from this fruit, the Arabs extract an oil, which they sell to travellers, who keep it amongst their other holy things, and pretend it possesses a singular virtue in curing wounds, for which reason, they call it the *Oil of Zachæus*, attributing its virtue to the stay Zachæus made on the tree. Of the stone of the fruit, which is of an oval form, with four ridges, and almost the size of a walnut, the Latin monks make beads, which they send to Europe as being of great value. I have before observed, that Luther interpreted this passage very badly, when he called the tree a mulberry-tree; for the mulberry-tree is not, at present, found growing naturally in the territory of the town of Jericho, where the affair happened, and much less is it cultivated there at this time, as it scarcely ever grew in Judæa, very little in Galilee, but in abundance in Syria and Mount Libanon: neither did I see the Sycamore growing near Jericho, but it is probable it grew there formerly, being to this day found in Judæa, and was once doubtless very common, as it is mentioned so often in the Scriptures.

*Poma sodomitica*, or mad apples, are the fruit of Solanum Melongena Linnæi, by other authors called

called mala infana; thefe I found in plenty about Jericho, in the vales near Jordan, not far from the Dead Sea. It is true, they are fometimes filled with a duft, yet this is not always the cafe, but only when the fruit is attacked by an infect (*tenthredo*) which turns all the infide into duft, leaving the fkin only entire, and of a beautiful colour.

Nux Behen. Balfamum Aaraonis.

The oil of behen, which emits no fcent or fmell at all, is very proper for preparing odoriferous ointments and balfams. On this account it is much ufed by the inhabitants of the Eaft, who lay flowers of jeffamine, narciffus, &c. in this oil, and thus make an odoriferous ointment, which thofe who love perfumes apply to the head, nofe and beard. And this is undoubtedly that with which Aaron, as is faid in the Scriptures, ufed to anoint the head, and David fo much praifed on account of its agreeable fcent.

This tree grows in Mount Sinai and Upper Egypt. The Arabians call it feftuck el Ban.

Rhamnus fpina Chrifti. The Egyptian buckthorn.
Œnoplia fpinofa, Cafpar Bauhin. 477.
Nabca *Paliurus athenæi*, Alpin. Ægypt. 16. 19.

The Naba or Nabka of the Arabians.

In all probability this is the tree which afforded the crown of thorns put on the head of Chrift; it grows very common in the Eaft. This plant was very fit for the purpofe, for it has many fmall and

and sharp spines, which are well adapted to give pain; the crown might be easily made of these soft, round, and pliant branches, and what in my opinion seems to be the greatest proof, is, that the leaves much resemble those of ivy, as they are of a very deep green. Perhaps the enemies of Christ, would have a plant somewhat resembling that, with which emperors and generals were used to be crowned, that there might be calumny even in the punishment.

Spinæ Biblicæ. Of **Thorns** mentioned in the Scriptures.

We know very few of the Thorns which are mentioned in the Scriptures. The rest-harrow, (Ononis spinosa) that most pernicious and prickly plant, covers entire fields and plains in Egypt and Palestine. I make no doubt, but this is referred to in some parts of the holy Scripture; I shall leave Philologists to determine which of the Thorns there mentioned it is. The Arabians, at present in Egypt, call it *akol*. This is, perhaps, that which Moses means when he curses the earth; it grows in great plenty, promiscuously with the large thistles, in the uncultivated parts of Egypt.

Labrusca. Of the wild **Grapes** of the Scriptures.

Isaiah in chap. v. ver. 4. sayeth: *What could have been done more to my vineyard, that I have not done in it; wherefore when I looked that it should bring forth grapes, brought it forth wild grapes?* I am inclined to believe, that the Prophet here means the hoary nightshade (Solanum incanum) because it is common in Egypt, Palestine, and the East, and the Arabian name agrees well with it.

The Arabs call it *aneb el dib*, i. e. *wolf-grapes*. The Prophet could not have found a plant more opposite to the vine than this, for it grows much in the vineyards, and is very pernicious to them, wherefore they root it out; it likewise resembles a vine by its shrubby stalk.

## Of the Onions of the Israelites.

**Allium cepa, Onion;** by the Arabs called Basal. That this was one of the species of Onions, for which the Israelites longed, we may guess by the quantity to this day used in Egypt, and by their goodness there; whoever has tasted Onions in Egypt, must allow, that none can be had better in any part in the universe: here they are sweet, in other countries they are nauseous and strong; here they are soft, whereas in the North and other parts they are hard, and the coats so compact, that they are hard of digestion. Hence they cannot in any place be eaten with less prejudice, and more satisfaction, than in Egypt. The just longing of the Israelites teaches us, that they were introduced into the kitchen, about the time they left Egypt. They eat them roasted, cut into four pieces, with some bits of roasted meat, which the Turks, in Egypt, call *kebab*; and with this dish they are so delighted, that I have heard them wish they might enjoy it in Paradise. They likewise make a soup of them in Egypt, cutting the Onions in small pieces; this I think one of the best dishes I ever eat.

*Allium sativum.* Linnæi. Garlick.

Is by the Arabians called Tum. This is also much used; but I am inclined to think, it was not known to the Israelites, as it does not grow in Egypt,

Egypt, but is brought hither from the islands in Archipelago.

*Allium porrum.* Linnæi. Leeks. **Karrat** of the Arabians.

This was **certainly one** of those desired **by the Children of Israel**, as it has been cultivated from the **earliest** times to the present in Egypt. The seasons for this, are the winter and spring months: the inhabitants are very fond of it, eating it raw as sauce for their roast meat; the poor people eat **it raw with bread, especially for breakfast,** using the earth for a table, and would **scarcely** exchange **their leeks** and a bit of bread **for a** royal dinner.

Leo. The Lion. The Arabs call this Animal Sabbe.

This is not met with in **Syria or Palestine**; but in great numbers at Babylon, now Bagdad). It is not an inhabitant of Egypt, unless it be on the confines of Lybia, coming from the inland parts of Africa. How is this consistent with the Bible, where the Lion is mentioned as an animal common **to Palestine and Syria, especially in the history of Sampson? Where** did **the fight between** Sampson and **the lion happen?**

Locustæ Johannis. St. John's Locusts.

Of these I have already treated.

Petra Mosis.

The Rock which Moses **broke** by a miracle, Exod. xvii. **6.** and **out of which** he made the tables

tables for the Ten Commandments, was a *faxum micaceo fpatofum particulis quartzofis paucioribus*, in plain terms, a granite, of which Mount *Horeb*, where the miracle happened, confifts, as does Mount *Sinai*, where the tables were formed. Mofes had learned the ufe of this ftone, for infcribing letters and figures, from the Egyptians, as in Egypt hieroglyphick obelifks are made of the fame ftone, and are miracles of art.

WHEN the Arabians intend to defcribe a beauty, they make ufe of feveral fimilitudes. They compare her face to the moon, &c. &c. Amongft others, the moft remarkable and common expreffion of this kind is, when they compare the eyes of a beauty to the eyes of a rock goat, (Capra cervicapra, Linnæi) which is a common animal in Syria and Egypt. I think this comparifon remarkable, becaufe Solomon in his Canticles ufes comparifons, which are taken from the fame animal; let us compare the Hebrew text to explain his meaning. We have therefore no reafon to doubt, but that the *Doe* of Solomon was this Rock goat. The beauty of the animal, its being common in the countries where Solomon wrote his books, and finally, the cuftom, which has continued to this day, and is the fame with that of Solomon, are all circumftances which help to confirm us in this opinion.

# MATERIA MEDICA.

### The Description of the true Balsam of Mecca.

IT is of a yellow colour, and pellucid. It has a most fragrant smell, which is resinous, balsamick, and very agreeable. It is very tenacious or glutinous, sticking to the fingers, and may be drawn into long threads. It scarcely ever becomes fluid or liquid by the heat of the sun in Natolia.

I HAVE seen it at a Turkish surgeon's, who had it immediately from Mecca, described it, and was informed of its virtues, which are: first, that it is the best *stomachick* they know, if taken to three grains, to strengthen a weak stomach; secondly, that it is a most excellent and capital remedy for curing wounds; for if a few drops of it are applied to the fresh wound, it cures it in a very short time.

### An Experiment to know whether the *Balsam* of *Mecca* be true and not adulterated.

A DROP of the Balsam is dropt into a glass of clear and fresh spring water; if this drop remains in one place on the surface of the water, the Balsam is of little value; but if it instantly extends itself like a skin or pellicle, over the whole surface, and with a hair, silk or thread, this skin may be taken off the water, which must afterwards be as clear

clear as at first, it is a sign that the Balsam is of the best kind, and not adulterated. It is admitted, even by the Turks, that it is very difficult to find Balsam which will stand this proof; for the true Balsam of Mecca is scarcely to be found any where but in the possession of the Turkish Emperor and the grandees of the kingdom, who get it as a valuable present from some traveller who hath been at Mecca. In order to make sure of getting this valuable drug unadulterated, it is necessary either by friendship or money, at the time the caravan goes to Mecca, to gain the interest of a Turk, who will procure it genuine from the first hand, and then we may be assured of its goodness, and that it possesses the excellent virtues, which the innumerable experiments made by the inhabitants of the East confirm.

The 20th of June, I went round the city of Cairo to enquire for Balsam of Mecca, with an intention to buy some, if I could get any that was good. I saw the manner in which an Italian merchant, who had been thirty years at Cairo, tried it, it was as follows: He dropped some drops of the Balsam into a little China cup, filled with clear cold water; if these immediately extended themselves in a skin, and this skin was even and clear, and entirely free from bubbles, he pronounced the Balsam good; but if it was some time before they spread over the water, and the skin was dirty, and had several bubbles or air bladders, it was a sure sign that the Balsam was adulterated and mixed with other things. If the skin can be gathered and wound up on a little straw, without breaking or leaving any oil on the water, it was likewise good; and on the contrary, if the skin cannot be gathered, but breaks into several

several pieces, and leaves on the water some oily colour, red particles, we may safely conclude, that the Balsam is adulterated. I saw experiments made, both of the true and adulterated, and found them well grounded. The bubbles in the first experiment, and the breaking or dividing of the skin in the second, are owing to the extraneous particles with which the Balsam has been adulterated. The drugs used to adulterate the Balsam, or to encrease it in bulk, but diminish its virtues, are oil of (*Sesamum*) oily grain, which is extracted in large quantities in Egypt; Cyprus turpentine and the fat of ostriches; these are not all mixed with it at one time, but according to the convenience of the seller; and in this manner, almost all the Balsam exposed for sale is adulterated, even in the place whence it is first brought.

NONE of those who have wrote on the Balsam of Mecca, have been acquainted with the place whence it is brought. Every body knows, that it comes from Mecca, and I believe imagine, that it grows somewhere near that place. We have even travels and histories informing us of the gardens round Mecca, in which this tree is planted and carefully cultivated, of the prerogative the Turkish Emperor enjoys, to preserve the best for himself, of the guard the Turks constantly keep that none of the trees may be carried thence. This story has been hitherto believed just as it was represented by the first relator, who told us this, that he might not be thought intirely ignorant of the matter. It would be worth while to make a journey to the place where this tree grows, in order to obtain a true history of it; but this cannot be done by a Christian; we must therefore trust to the informations we can get from such as are permitted to see those places, and believe the most credible of them. I have asked creditable persons, who had been in Mecca, concerning this affair, and in particular, an Aga of the Castle at Rosetta, and a Scheck in Cairo; the former in the presence of Mr. Chabert, a French merchant in Rosetta, and the latter through Mr. Le Grand, the French Interpreter in Cairo. They both gave me a very different account of the place where the Balsam-tree grows, from that which I had read before in books. They assured me, that the Balsam-tree is as little known at Mecca, as in Egypt and Turkey, and that not a drop of Balsam is gathered within many miles of Mecca. The place whence the Balsam is brought, lies many day's journey from Mecca, and in Petrea Arabia. There the trees grow in the mountains, and are possessed as a valuable treasure by certain Arabian families. The Arabians carry the Balsam to Mecca, and there sell it during the time the Caravan from Egypt and Turkey tarries there; by the Caravan it is carried to Damascus and Cairo, thence through all Turkey, and farther if possible, but this is scarcely credible, as very little of the genuine Balsam comes to Mecca. The Turkish Emperor enjoys no privileges, by which he may reserve the best for himself; the Arabians are an independant and free people, they sell their commodity to whom they please. The Sultan orders some considerable man at Mecca, as the first Scheck, or some other, to buy a certain quantity of it yearly on his account, and therefore is sure to have it good. I have been assured, by those who have been in Arabia and seen the tree, that its leaves resemble those of *Myrtle*, but are a little larger. By the informations which I could obtain, I have

reason

reason to believe, that Dr. Linnæus rightly guessed that the tree is a *Pistacia*, or nearest a-kin to it, and therefore closely allied to the *Mastich* and *Turpentine* trees *.

MASTIX, by the modern Greeks called μαστιχα; comes in large quantities from *Scio*, and is much used by the Turks; for the wives of the Turks in particular, the Sultan's and Grandees's, chew it constantly, to keep their teeth white and clean, and their breath sweet.

## Olibanum. Frankincense.

THIS is collected in both the Arabia's, whence it is brought to Giedda, which is the harbour of Mecca, thence over the Red Sea to Suez, a harbour in Egypt, and so to Cairo in considerable quantities; it is likewise brought from Mecca over land, by the Caravan. When it is brought over, it is so full of small stones of Spar and Mica, that 150 lb. will not yield above from 50 to 70 lb. of clean and pure Frankincense. The greatest part is carried to Marseilles, whence it is by the Dutch carried to Muscovy where the greatest part of it is used in making the Russian leather; a large quantity is likewise burnt by the Muscovites and Roman Catholics in their churches. It differs greatly both in price and goodness, 110 lb. selling from 9 to 23 Piasters, (each Piaster at 60 Medins) according to the goodness of it. The best is in tears, of a fragrant smell, pellucid, and of a yellowish

---

* Professor Linnæus in a letter dated Upsala, Feb. 12th, 1765, to John Ellis Esq; F. R. S. says, that the late Dr. Forskohl sent him a specimen of the Balsam of Mecca tree, by which it appears to be a species of Amyris. N. B. Several species of this genus grow in Jamaica.

white

white colour, brittle and easily pulverized; of this **very little is to** be found in large quantities in the common Frankincense, and is not to be separated **from it,** unless **it be** particularly desired for the Apothecaries shops.

### An Example of the nutritive Virtue of Gum Arabic.

THE Abyssinians make a journey to Cairo every year, to sell the products of their country: *Slaves, Gold, Elephants,* **Drugs,** *Monkeys, Parrots,* &c. They must travel over **terrible desarts,** and their journey depends as much on the weather as a **voyage at** sea, consequently they know as little **as a seaman how** long they must be on the journey, **and the necessaries** of life may chance to fail them, **when the journey lasts** too long. This happened **to the** Abyssinian Caravan in the year **1750,** their provisions being consumed, when they had still two months to **travel;** necessity obliges us often **to use things for food** before unheard or unthought **of;** this happened in the case in question; they **were** obliged **to** search for something amongst their merchandize, wherewith they might support life in this extremity, and found nothing more proper than Gum Arabic, of which they had carried a considerable quantity with them. This served to **support** above 1000 persons **for two months.**

GUM Arabic is gelatinous, and undoubtedly contains some nourishing particles. But here we may ask, Whether this food did not make these poor people very costive? It must in all probability have had this effect, but of this I could not learn any circumstances. I know however, that the Caravan

van arrived safe at Cairo, without any great loss of people either by hunger or diseases.

OPIUM. We are told that the Turks formerly consumed large quantities of this drug, at present it is used by very few, and scarcely by any, except those who strictly follow the laws of Mahomed, and therefore abstain from wine, and all other spirituous liquors. But there are very few at this time who observe them so strictly, especially amongst the vulgar; perhaps there were formerly more, and then it is possible Opium was more frequently used; such as now make use of Opium have a trembling of the nerves, are sleepy, and become very weak, therefore the Turks, who see this, with great reason, leave off a custom so evidently destructive.

### Cassia Fistula.
*The manner of preparing it in Egypt.*

THE Pods are collected before they are quite ripe, and carried into a very close room in which has been previously prepared a bed of palm leaves and straw six inches thick, on this they lay the Pods in a heap. The door is then closely shut, and the next day they sprinkle water on the heap, which is repeated the day following; thus they lay heaped for forty days, 'till they become black. Others dig a hole in the ground to put them in, but this method is much inferior to the former.

### Scammonium. Scammony.

THE best Scammony in the world is brought from *Marasch*, the residence of a Bashaw, about four days journey from Aleppo, near the confines of of Armenia. It is thence brought to Aleppo in small skins, and by the merchants sent to London and Marseilles. It was formerly, to be had very good from Mount Carmel by way of Acra, but at present, scarcely any comes from that place, as the Arabian inhabitants of the mountain have neglected to gather it, being more addicted to plunder than labour. I have seen the *Convolvulus*, from which it is taken, grow wild in the vales between Nazareth and Mount Carmel.

### Schœnanthus Officinalis. Camel's Hay.

This grows plentifully in the deserts of both the Arabias; it is gathered near *Limbo*, a port in Arabia Petrea, and exported to Egypt. The Venetians buy it in Egypt, as it enters the composition of the Venice treacle. This was undoubtedly one of the precious, aromatic and sweet plants which Queen Sheba gave to Solomon, being to this day much esteemed by the Arabians for its sweet smell. They call it Helsi Meccavi, and Idhir Mecchi.

### Senna.

All the *Senna* grows wild in upper Egypt. It is gathered by the Bedovines or Arabian Peasants, who sell it to their Scheick or Headman. When he has collected a large quantity he carries it to Cairo, where he sells it to a particular Person, who rents the privilege of selling this drug to the Europeans, from the corps of Janissaries at Cairo, who dispose of it to the best advantage. At present Ibraim Kiæfa, the powerful Governor and Usurper over Egypt, has assumed this privilege, and rented it to two Jews, who were likewise

farmers

farmers of the customs. Of these the Europeans buy yearly as much as they want. But it is not every European that can buy, nor can any nation purchase what quantity it thinks proper. They are obliged to make three lots, one for *Marseilles*, another for *Leghorn*, and a third for *Venice*, and each lot is to be purchased by one merchant. Senna therefore is a commodity which, next to Nutmeg and Cinnamon, of which the Dutch are the sole possessors, is more monopolized than any other. The Egyptians may also set what value they please on this drug, as it is wanted in all parts of the world, and grows no where so good as here. They send to Marseilles yearly 600 Boats, each containing 10 Quintals, each Quintal at 20 Sequins, more or less; a Sequin consists of 1100 Medins.

## Myrobalani Officinales.

THE writers on Materia Medica know very little of the Myrobalans, which are but little used at present, and should not obtain a place in the shops. But they are still in use with the Egyptians and Arabians, who drink the decoction of all the Myrobalans as a purge, especially in Upper Egypt. This medicine operates as a corroborant as well as a cathartic, and might therefore answer very well as a succedaneum for rhubarb, when this last cannot be had; but it is of no value as long as we can have rhubarb. The Arabian Physicians first introduced the Myrobalans, which at present are only used by them and their countrymen. *Botanists* know still less of this fruit, which grows in India near Malabar, and on the confines of Bengal; whence it is brought with other simples to Mecca, and over the Red Sea to Cairo. A tree of Myrobalans was seen at *Farschut*, a town in Upper Egypt, subject to an Arabian Prince, by Jeremias Kerner, a Silesian (Missionary from the Society to propogate Christian Knowledge) who asserts, that all the Myrobalans are taken from the same tree, but do not ripen at one time; and says, that the inhabitants are very careful to distinguish one from the other, and gather the ripe ones, without mixing or confounding them with the others, giving them different names according to their qualities, *Chabeli*, *Asphar Bellili*, *Emblili*, *Hendi*, *Chejri*. I ordered a person to bring me one of these trees from Upper Egypt, but I could not get it before I left Egypt.

## Spica Celtica. The Celtic Spiknard.

The Spiknard is much more used by the People of Inner Africa, Abyssinia, and Æthiopia, than by us; and in such quantities, that there are yearly 60 tons imported by way of Venice into Egypt from Germany, each ton is by the Æthiopian merchants bought for near 100 rixdollars. They make an ointment of it, which they use to keep the skin soft in their scorching climate, and to make it shine, for in this they think consists its greatest beauty.

## Mumia Mineralis.

This is a bituminous, shining, brittle, black, and almost inodorous mass, which is brought from Persia. It is excessively dear, for one dram of it costs from 2 to 4 and 5 Sequins in Egypt, according to its scarcity and goodness; it is much dearer than Amber, wherefore the Grandees of Egypt and Turkey preserve it among their other rarities;

rarities; these are: Amber, the true Bezoar stone, the horn of the Rhinoceros, particularly vessels made of it, out of which they drink water; all these are with them of the same value, as precious stones and jewels, and they preserve them as carefully. The **Ambergris** (*ambra grisea*) they offer to the Goddess of Beauty, whom these people venerate to the highest degree; the Bezoar stone and Rhinoceros horn, are both used as alexipharmics, sudorifics, and against poison, for which reason they preserve them as their tutelar Gods, against that kind of Death, to which the Grandees are so much subject, and therefore live in constant fear. But this Mumia Mineralis, they say, is a great vulnerary. If experience confirms the accounts the Egyptians give of it, it is certainly the greatest remedy hitherto known for curing wounds. They make an ointment of the Mumia Mineralis pulverized and mixed with sweet oil; break the leg of a hen, anoint it with this ointment and tie it up, if the Mummy is genuine, the leg is cured within three hours; and this is the method they use to try whether the Mummy is good; but if the leg is not cured within the time mentioned, they reject it as of no value. They say, that the leg of a man is cured within twenty four hours, if this remedy is applied. I have myself seen and described the Mummy, but have not been an eye-witness of its efficacy, as it is very dear and scarce: but several surgeons in Cairo asserted the truth of it, and told me, they had seen and admired the experiment; these were men of probity and veracity. It is certainly a species of *bitumen*, but I am not able to say, whether it is any of those hitherto known, if not the first in Linnæis's system of nature,

ture, which is the same as the Naphta of authors, hardened by the heat of the sun. The Egyptians call it, *Mumia Mineralis,* from the exact resemblance it bears to the mass, which is taken out of the skull of the Mummies in Egypt.

### Unguentum Mumiæ. Ointment of Mumy.

THE Egyptians make an unguentum potabile, or liquid ointment of Mumy, by mixing the powder of Mumy with butter, which they call *Manteg,* this they take inwardly when they are wounded. A credible person in Alexandria assured me, that he saw a Moor perfectly cured in a short time, without having used or applied any other medicine, of a wound in the side, between the ribs, made with a knife, which had pierced the musculos intercostales; this man immediately drank a dose of this ointment, about ℔ij, and likewise anointed the wound with some of it. The Egyptians use it also frequently for their cattle, camels, asses, sheep, oxen, &c. &c. both inwardly and outwardly, for wounds, fractures, against witchcraft, which they believe can hurt their cattle, and almost in all diseases with which their cattle are afflicted.

### The method of making Sal Ammoniac in Egypt.

Sal Ammoniac is made from the soot arising from the burnt dung of four-footed animals, that feed only on vegetables, and of human excrements.

THIS dung is collected in the four first months of the year, when all their cattle, such as oxen, cows, buffaloes, camels, sheep, goats, horses and asses, feed on fresh spring grass, which in Egypt, is a kind of trefoil or clover: for when they are obliged to feed their cattle on hay, and their camels on bruised date kernels, their excrements are not fit for this purpose; but when they feed on grass, the poor people of Egypt are very careful in collecting the dung quite fresh, and for that purpose follow the cattle all day long; if it is too moist, they mix it with chaff, stubble, short straw, or dust, and make it up in the form of cakes; then they lay it on a wall to dry, till it is fit to be burnt.

For want of wood, which none but the rich in Egypt can afford to buy, they burn this dung through the whole country, and sell a vast quantity of soot to the salt-makers. If the country wanted this dung for manure, it would be bad œconomy; but as nature has provided Egypt with manure of a quite different nature, viz. the mud deposited by the Nile when it overflows the country, the inhabitants are much to be commended for applying the dung to another use.

The excrements of the camel are not found at all preferable to any other, and its urine is never used for this purpose, although generally reported so by authors.

The salt workers pretend, that the human excrements, and those of goats and sheep, are preferable to any other. In the months of March and April only they make the salt.

The village *Giza*, which is situated at a small distance from Cairo, is the only place near that city where they make this salt. There is no manufactory of it in Cairo; but there are numbers in the island *Delta*.

A person who possesses a village, in which there is a salt manufactory, lets his peasants work it, for there is no great art in it. Those who work at it are miserable wretches; as indeed are all the common people in Egypt. The soot, and every thing else requisite for making the salt, is weighed to them, and they are obliged to deliver salt in proportion, by which they cannot wrong their masters of an ounce. I shall now describe the method of making it, which, though it is very simple, has puzzled many chemists. I doubt not but chemists may invent some better method, for this is very simple. They build an oblong oven, about as long again as broad, of brick and moist dung; of such a size, that the outside, or flat part of the top of the arch, may hold fifty glass vessels, ten in length and five in breadth, each vessel having a cavity left for it in the brick work of the arch. These glass vessels are globular, with a neck an inch long, and two inches wide. They are of various sizes, in different salt works, containing from a gallon to two gallons; but in general, are but eighteen inches diameter. They coat each vessel over with a fine clay, (which they find in the Nile) and afterwards with straw; they then fill them two-thirds full of soot, and put them into their holes on the top of the oven.

They make the fire gentle at first, using the above-mentioned dried dung for the fuel; they increase the heat gradually, till they bring it to the highest degree, which the workmen call hell-fire, and continue it so for three days and three nights together. When the heat is come to its due degree, the smoke shews itself, with a sourish smell, that is not unpleasant; and in a little time, the salt sticks to the glasses, and covers the whole aperture. The salt continues subliming till the above time is expired; then they break the glasses, and

and take out the salt, just in the same form, and of the same substance, as it is sent over all Europe.

At each salt-work they have a glass furnace, to melt the old glasses and make new ones.

The ingredients for the fine works, which are made in France and Germany, of Papier Machée, as snuff-boxes, heads for canes, &c.

℞ *Ichtyocollæ* lbij.  *Ol. Lib.* lbiv.
 *Minii rubri* ℨij.  *Terræ Umbræ* ℨiv.
 *Lithargyrii aurei* ℨiij.  *Vitriol. alb.* ℨiv.
 *Cerussa* ℨiss.  *Colophonii* ℨiij.
 *Electri* ℨviij.  *Spirit. Therebinth* lbj.
 *Terræ Tripolitanæ* lbj.

# MEDICA.

### Of Diseases, and their Remedies.

1. Pestis. The Plague.
2. Febris damiatæ. The Fever of Damiata.
3. Synocha. Fevers.
4. Tertiana. The Ague.
5. Cephalalgia. The Head ach.
6. Colica. The Cholick.
7. Calculus. The Gravel.
8. Asthma. Asthma.
9. Hysteria. Hysterics.
10. Imaginatio. Of the force of Imagination.
11. Tænia. The Tape worm.
12. Ophthalmia. Diseases of the eyes.
13. Siphilis. The Venereal disease.
14. Herpes Aleppica.
15. Hernia. Ruptures.
16. Sterilitas. Barrenness.
17. Puerperia. Of Child-bearing.
18. Excreta.

### 1. Pestis. The Plague.

I HAD a conversation with a practitioner in physick at Smyrna, and was solicitous to know whether he had made any observations on this distemper, in a place where it often rages. He answered me, that neither he nor his collegues knew any thing of it, as they are closely confined, and kept from all communication with those afflicted

flicted with the Plague. For no Physician can succour these wretches, unless he will shut himself out from all company, and perhaps afterwards be condemned to shut himself up in his house for forty days, and perform quarantine.

He had, however, an opportunity privately to visit a patient afflicted with the plague, and observed that his eyes watered (*lacrymatio oculorum*) and his tongue was covered with white pustules.

The famous Count *Bonnevall*, discovered a powder against the Plague, which had a surprising effect; and he proved, that scarce 10 of 100 died, of those who used this powder. I have been informed, that there is a French surgeon, now in Constantinople, who knows how to prepare this powder.

2. Febris *maligna Damiatæ singularis*. The Fever of Damiata.

This rages during the winter, but more in the spring, with a quick and high pulse, great heat, violent thirst, dry and clammy tongue, inflamed eyes; it ends in two or four days, with a red tumor and stupor on one side, but particularly the arm, foot and leg on that side swelled, are very red and painful; before this crisis, they perceive some serum to fluctuate within the skull, towards the under part of the os frontis. This crisis is not always a good omen, the patient often dying when it comes on. If the patient escapes death, yet the swelling of the limbs and stupor of the side often remain. The Arabians call it *Nyssham*, which signifies *fluxio calida* (warm fluxion) to distinguish it from the *apoplexy*, which they call Nysl-bred, which signifies *fluxio frigida* (cold fluxion.)

3. Synocha,

### 3. Synocha. Fevers.

They pound shell-fish (*cochlea*) both shell and flesh, making a cataplasm of them, which they lay on the sole of the foot; this serves for a vesicatory, and draws a blister on the sole. It is the only remedy the Greeks at Athens, Salonica, &c. use in violent fevers; and they apply it with success in the height of the disease. This they use in all fevers as a domestick medicine.

### 4. Tertiana. Ague.

A sympathetick cure for the Ague, which the Greeks, in the island Morea, prescribe.

When the patient begins to shake, he goes and leans against a peach-tree, until the fit or paroxysm is over; by this, they say, he loses his Ague, but the tree dies away. This was told me by a person who lived a long time on Morea, and saw it performed, as the disorder is common to all the inhabitants of this Island.

Take an egg, roast it in ashes till it becomes quite hard, sprinkle it all over with pepper, and eat it at once. A Swedish merchant in Smyrna was by this cured of an Ague, which never returned again.

### 5. Cephalalgia. A domestick cure, used by the Arabians, for the *Head ach*.

In a violent Head ach they shave the head, and with a knife cut several holes before the crown of the head (futura coronalis); the blood which runs out they stroke forwards with a sharp edged piece of of wood, letting it then run as long as they think proper, or until the patient's pain is mitigated. They cut the holes in such a manner as not to touch any vein, but only in the skin or fleshy part, so far resembling a scarification.

6. *Colicæ* Medicina. A Cure for the Cholic.

TAKE the *snuff* of a *candle*, and *German soap*, mix them well, and make pills. This in the Levant is found to be a sure remedy against the Cholic.

MAKE pills of pitch (bitumen vulgare) of the size of a pea, of which, three or four are to be taken, when the fit or paroxysm comes on. This is said to be a sovereign remedy against the wind Cholic in Tartary, which I learned from a Man in Smyrna, who had long lived amongst the Tartars.

*Colica flatulenta.* Gravidarum *Pessus.*

TAKE of powdered nutmeg, two grains; sweet oil, what quantity you please.

MAKE a tent of cotten, moisten it with the above mixture, and apply it. The patient must sit in warm water, almost up to her middle, for an hour, before the Pessus is applied. I saw a midwife at Cairo, with this remedy, cure a woman six months gone with child, of a Colica flatulenta, which the patient had erroneously taken for a sign of future or instant abortion; but the midwife prudently judged it to be the aforesaid distemper.

THE women in Egypt frequently use Pessaria; but in Europe they are scarcely ever used, tho' I doubt

doubt not but they might be of service. A people, however, so much given to lust as the Egyptians, often make a bad use of them. I was informed by physicians, apothecaries and priests, to whom they confessed it on their death-beds, that they often use them to help conception and to cause abortion and barrenness. But I was not informed of what substance, and in what manner they were made, nor did I think it worth my while to enquire.

A cure the Arabians have for their Horses, when they are troubled with Gripings (Colica sive Iliaca.)

They give the Gall of Bears powdered and mixed with coffee to the Horse; this is a most powerful remedy against this distemper, to which the Arabian Horses are subject. This Gall is very scarce with the Arabians, therefore they pay dear for it when they can get it, and preserve it as a valuable treasure to use it on this occasion; one cannot offer an Arab a more welcome present, than a bit of genuine Bear's Gall, which they know very well, and cannot be imposed on with the Gall of other animals.

7. Calculus. The Gravel.

The inhabitants of the East use the dried leaves of almonds infused in water to cure the Gravel.

8. Asthma.

Take a sea gull, chop it in pieces, boil it in water to make a strong broth, and drink it at once.

This domestick remedy I learned in Smyrna, where it is said to be used in the most desperate Asthmas.

### 9. Hysteria. Hystericks.

Fill a date with the powder of *mastich*, after taking out the stone; close it again, and lay it on coals to roast. The patient is to place herself over the coals, and draw the smoak of it, which is of an agreeable smell, up her nose; when the date leaves off smoking, or when the *mastich* is melted and mixed with the juice of the date, the patient eats it. This is to be done under the paroxysm, which I am told will certainly be obviated.

*Another*: Lay the eggs of the sepia octopodia the cuttle fish with eight claws on coals, and draw the smoke of it up your mouth and nose. Both these methods are used in the Levant.

### 10. Imaginationis *stratagema*.

A man afflicted with the hypochondriac disease, and of a very disturbed mind, continually complained of something in his throat which almost suffocated him. I endeavoured to cure him by stratagem. I ordered a hen to be killed, and an egg to be taken out; I then prescribed for the Patient a light vomit, persuading him that it would bring up what troubled him. While he was vomiting, I ordered the egg to be privately conveyed into the pot, and when the vomit had ceased operating, I shewed him the egg amongst what he had brought up; he was overjoyed, declaring

claring he felt it no more, nor did he afterwards complain of it.

## 11. Tænia. The Tape-worm.

The Tape-worm, which has of late years engaged the attention of many great Physicians, is a plague, from which the inhabitants of Egypt are not exempted, and which, in this country, affords opportunities enough for a Physician to enquire into its nature, of which we know very little. Mr. Foumace, surgeon to the French nation, at Cairo, was the first who told me this plague was very common in Egypt, and shewed me three pieces of a Tape-worm, which he had, at various times, forced out of a woman: one of them was forty, the other about fifteen, and the third ten French *pique*; it was near half an inch broad. After I had got this information, I used my best endeavours to be better informed, and to collect what observations I could get from him, and every body else who practised physic here, relative to a subject of so much importance. I here commucate them as they were related to me. The Tape-worm is so common, that Mr. Foumace, who has practised physick here for several years, believes two-thirds of the inhabitants of Cairo to be troubled with them. The Jews, and the common people of Egypt, are most afflicted with this disorder; many of the Coptites are also tormented with them, but not many of the Turks. I did not fail asking the Practitioners of Cairo, why the people in this country are more tormented with them than in other places, and why some sorts of the people here, are more subject to them than others? But I got no satisfactory answers. They

all

all agreed that the diet was the principal cause, but this was nothing new to me; however, I am of opinion, that the miserable food of the poor people, and particularly the nourishment they take great part of the year from melons, cucumbers, and all other kinds of ground fruit, deserve some attention. One told me, that the Jews are troubled with worms, because they eat so many sweet things; and the women in particular, eat more sweet meets, confections, pruins, &c. than other food. It is the general opinion, that sweet things nourish at least, if not occasion, worms in children. The Turks live here as well as in other places on good and well dressed victuals. Rice and flesh are their chief food. They likewise eat much fish, but the poor cannot buy them. The fish of the Nile do not perhaps contribute towards breeding worms, though we have reason to believe, that the fish of other rivers do. I made diligent enquiry with respect to the *Signs*, by which we may judge, whether any one has the Tape-worm or not; and was informed, that the surest method is to examine the stomach and eyes, viz. when a blue ring is seen under the eyes, and when the stomach swells round the navel; but I was told there is never occasion to search for more than one sign, and this is the surest, viz. the Vermes cucurbitini (Gourd worms.) As soon as he knew that the patient voided Gourd-worms, he never hesitated to prescribe medicines against the Tape-worm, and he never remembered to have been disappointed in his conjectures. It is very easy to know here whether a patient has Gourd-worms, five persons out of ten, and perhaps more, void them when they go to stool, some in considerable numbers, and almost all without attending to it, except when they

they afk the advice of a Phyfician, upon the vermins tormenting them, and he enquires whether they perceived them. They have no medicine in Egypt againft worms; nor do they ever require a Phyfician to prefcribe any thing for them. Even they who know they harbour them, and are tormented with all the inconveniences they are wont to caufe, require only a remedy for the fymptoms, *e. g.* gripes, head-ach, vomitings, but never fay any thing of the caufe, which is generally to be attributed to worms. They cannot conceive that the infignificant Gourd-worms, which they void with fo much eafe, can occafion a difeafe, and they never dream of the true caufe, I mean the Tapeworm; for which reafon they are greatly terrified when a Phyfician expels one from them. A Phyfician muft therefore know in what manner to prefcribe againft the real caufe, and not attend to what the patient fays of his fymptoms. I never was acquainted with more than one remedy prefcribed for the worms, by thofe who practifed phyfic in Cairo with judgment and applaufe, but this always fucceeded fo well, that they had no occafion to fearch for another. This is *Petroleum* given inwardly. Mr. Des Barats, M. D. of the Faculty of Paris, and Phyfician to the Conful at Cairo, communicated this remedy to me. Both he, and the aforefaid Mr. Foumace, have feen a confiderable number in Cairo cured by Petroleum, and the worm Mr. Foumace fhewed me, was expelled by it: they give it for three days fucceffively, for which purpofe they chufe the three laft days of the moon's laft quarter. When they have given it for three days, they try whether they can expel any of the worm which they fuppofe to be killed; if this does not fucceed, they wait till the next decreafe crease of the moon, and repeat the same course. Cairo, July 1, 1751.

Ophthalmia Ægyptiorum.   Diseases of the Eyes.

No Diseases are more common in Ægypt than those that affect the Eyes, especially in Cairo, where the greatest part of the inhabitants are afflicted with (Ophthalmia and Psorothalmia) sore and watry Eyes. More than one cause may be given for this endemic disorder. The excessive heat added to the incredible quantity of fine dust, which flies about the air of this dry country, is sufficient to make the diseases of the Eye more frequent in Egypt, than any where else, and perhaps in some places this alone may be the cause. But I am fully persuaded, that it is not the only thing that occasions this disorder in the city of Cairo. I have there observed one more remarkable. The inhabitants, especially those that live near the canal, have under their houses a sink or deep pit, that answers for a necessary-house, for the reception of all kinds of filth and excrements. From this sink there is a drain that leads into the canal which runs through the city, and is never opened but, in order to clear it out, once a year, and that at the time when the heat is most violent, and the canal has scarcely any thing in it but the fœtid mire left by the Nile: and to this filth and ordure I ascribe the cause of sore Eyes to the People in Cairo, for whilst these putrid substances are shut up in the pit they insensibly throw off some noxious particles, which become more perceptible when they are emitted into the canal, and unite their poison with the circumambient air. To confirm my opinion, I need only use the argument, which induced

the

the learned Ramazzin to write his treatise de Morbis Artificum, to which I refer the reader.

I have seen one example of this, which was more remarkable than all the others; a European forty years of age had been in Cairo three years, and was every year attacked with sore and inflamed Eyes, just at the time when the stench was greatest in the canal, on the side of which he lived. He attributed his Disease to his situation, as it went away as soon as the cause was removed, namely, when the water at the rising of the Nile flowed into the canal. Cairo, June 27 1750.

13. Siphilis. An example of *venereal* Ulcers, being cured in Egypt with *Tar-water*.

A man forty years of age had venereal Ulcers on his forehead, nose, chin, and in his throat, which had occasioned a hoarseness, &c. An English Nobleman, who was travelling in Egypt, saw this wretch, and immediately perceived the cause of his condition. He knew that *Tar-water* had been used with success in England in such cases, and therefore desired the English Consul, Mr. Barton, to try whether he could by the same means cure him of his Distemper. He procured Swedish Tar, from a Swedish Ship at Alexandria, prepared *Tar-water*, and ordered the patient to drink about a pint and a half a day. In a month the swellings in his throat began to abate, and he recovered his voice. By degrees the Ulcers in his face were cured, and when I saw him him, which was three months after he had begun to drink *Tar-water*, there only remained an Ulcer on his nose, and this was also beginning to mend.

Cairo, July 6th, 1750.

14. Herpes

## 14. Herpes *Aleppina*.

(1.) CHILDREN and women never escape this Disease. (2.) Very few men, who come from other parts to Aleppo, escape it; the inhabitants say there is scarcely one in a thousand. (3.) If any escape it, they are those who have black hair (of a melancholy temper,) according to the observations made by the inhabitants. (4.) It commonly lasts for six months, but there are examples of its continuing a year and more. (5.) It often affects the cheeks of the Ladies, and then does more damage by going off, than by staying, for it destroys their beauty by leaving a scar. (6.) It is very inconstant with regard to the place it occupies in men, sometimes affecting the cheeks, shoulders, nose, and even the glans penis. (7.) Nobody could yet discover the cause of this Disease; the inhabitants commonly ascribe it to the water. (8.) The inhabitants apply no medicines for it, but leave it to nature.

MR. JUSTI, secretary to the Swedish Consul, told me, that an Armenian servant in the Swedish Factory had the *Aleppo Mark*. I was desirous of being informed by the servant of the circumstances of this Disease, he related to me what follows: All who are either born at Aleppo, or come thither from other places, are attacked with a Disease, which has the following symptoms and effects; some part of the body, sometimes several, often ten or twelve, is affected with a sore or rather efflorescence, which is red, somewhat elevated, without heat or pain, and the patient scarcely knows that he has it. There appear neither *Vesicles* nor pimples. This continues a longer or a shorter time, and

and terminates with a scab (eschara), without having suppurated. When this falls off, it leaves an ugly and deep scar, which the people in the Levant call the *Aleppo Mark*; all who have dwelt in the city bear it, and perceive also more inconvenience after the Disease, than while it is on them, especially those who bear the marks of it in the face. But there are some who bear a much more unfortunate mark of this Disease, viz. those who become blind, when the sore affects the eyes. This servant had three scars, one on each cheek, pretty deep, of an irregular figure, and resembling much the scars which remain after burnt sores. They who have once got over the Disease, are never after affected with it, and they are seldom in the town many days before it attacks them. The inhabitants of the town and travellers ascribe the cause to the water; I asked the servant, whether he ever perceived any singular qualities in the water which is used at Aleppo, for meat and drink? but he knew of nothing, except that the water is brought into the town by aqueducts from a little inland river, and that it neither tastes nor smells different from other water, only a little warm.

Smyrna, December 30, 1749.

## 15. Hernia. Ruptures.

I HAVE been told by some persons in Syria, who had undergone the cauterium scroti in Ruptures themselves, and been perfectly cured.

## 16. Sterilitas. Barrenness.

THE man and woman are to drink a tea cup full of clove water before they go to bed. This is a sovereign remedy in Egypt in these cases, and I have been told, that women, who had been barren for many years, have conceived, by using this simple medicine. A midwife, who told me this, said, that she had often prescribed it with success.

Cairo, December 26th, 1750.

### 17. Puerperia.

I THIS day procured the following informations, concerning the birth of children, amongst the inhabitants of the East. (1.) There are both Turkish and Greek midwives here, who have learned their art by experience, without being taught by any body. (2.) The women here have good times, and we seldom hear of difficult labours in child-birth, much less of women dying in labour, especially amongst the Turks. (3.) When the child is born, they cut the string of the navel, as with us, and apply cauterium actuale, or a red hot iron to it. (4.) The head of the child is sprinkled over with the powder of gallnuts and nutmeg mixed together; this forms a crust on the head, which they leave on till it falls off itself; this usually happens within ten or twelve days. (5.) The mother or nurse is very solicitous to bend the arms and legs of the child. They bend, for example, the left leg backwards over the loins, and take the right arm and lay it over the back, so as to meet the foot, and in the same manner the other leg and arm. To facilitate this, they anoint the joints with sweet oil: I have been assured by some women, that this is the best remedy to silence children when they cry, and that the child by a natural instinct requires this to be done to it. May not this be the reason, why the eastern people are so much more active than the Europeans? The

Greeks

Greeks chriften their children immediately after their birth, or within a few days at leaft, dipping them in warm water, and in this refpect they are much wifer than their brethren the Ruffians, who dip them into rivers in the coldeft winter. The Jews circumcife their children on the 8th day, which feems to be a difficult and dangerous operation at that age. But the Turks are wifer, for they defer this great ceremony in their religion, until their fons have attained the 8th year of their age.

A Turk in Egypt had by feveral wives forty children, of which none lived. (2.) A Bey, who was murdered at Cairo about fifteen years ago, had at his death feventy feven women in his Haram, all with child. (3.) Children got in Egypt by foreign parents feldom live, whether they come of Franks or Levantines; we therefore fee few Turkifh children, tho' the militia or army of Egypt confifts of Turks who take women flaves from Georgia, Circaffia, Ruffia, and other places. The reafon of it may in great meafure be attributed to the curfed cuftom of deftroying the fœtus, as foon as they perceive they have conceived, in order to preferve the love of their hufbands, and exclude their rivals. (4.) However, a Turk in Cairo had by eight wives; within ten years, eighty children, all living, of which I knew feveral.

18. In Damiata, the Neceffary-houfe is in the Kitchen, which is very fingular. We fhall fcarcely find fuch a difgreeable cuftom in any place. In the other towns, of Egypt, this place is always in the dwelling-houfe, but not in the room where the victuals are dreffed.

# COMMERCE.

1. The Riches of Egypt.
2. The Trade.
3. The Trade of the French.
4. The Trade of Aleppo.
5. The Trade of Damiata.
6. The Trade of Persia.
7. The Weights of Egypt.
8. The Dress or Cloathing of the Turks.
9. Cotton.
10. Coffee.
11. Incense.
12. To give Wine an agreeable Flavour.

### 1. The Riches of Egypt.

THEY assure me, that Egypt pays 1000 purses a day to the Revenue, yet but a small part of this reaches the Sultan. The greatest part of it goes to the Beys in Cairo, who govern the country, and 4000 men only can be draughted from hence in time of war. Abdulha Bashaw, was by the Sultan sent to Egypt as Bashaw during my stay at Cairo; at his arrival he desired the Government to pay 200,000 ducats into his privy purse, instead of the moneys he had a right to levy hereafter; these were without further deliberation given him within a few hours. He likewise desired Ibraim Kiaja to give him 5000 ducats, which was also complied with: these sums, laid on one table, shew that Egypt does not want for money. *Ibrahim Kiaja*, who in my time was Usurper of Egypt, gave the present Bashaw, some days after his arrival, a grand entertainment, at which he and his brother Rodoau Kiaja, who was the other Usurper, waited at table. After dinner, he gave the Bashaw presents to the amount of 30,000 ducats, which consisted of horses with and without furniture, stuffs from India, diamonds and coined gold. An Usurper, possessed of the chief power over Egypt, might make such a present without losing by it, but he who received it, viz. the Bashaw, must certainly have been much grieved to find himself loaded with presents from a person, whose feigned respect was intended to shew him his power. They are not the most agreeable presents, which we are obliged, for certain reasons of state, to receive from those we would rather wish to see in a condition, in which it would be out of their power to make them.

## 2. Of Gain in Trade.

If we can procure a commodity from the first hand, and sell it ourselves without a rival for consumption, we certainly may gain as much as we please. The largest sum is given to the planter or manufacturer, the merchant gains the profit, and the purchaser suffers the loss. This has been the foundation of riches in England and Holland. The French have endeavoured to follow their example in Egypt, but they have always been obliged to leave a share of the profit to their teachers. A Frenchman buys coffee at Mecca from the first hand, he carries it to Marseilles,

and

and there sells it to the Dutch, Genoese and Swiss, by which he gains a little. These last sell it to the Germans, Swedes, Russians, &c. and gain a little; the Frenchman might likewise have had this profit, if he had himself carried it to those places where the Dutch, &c. sell it.

3. The French in *Cairo*, where they have eight merchants houses, sell annually to the Turks in Egypt 5 or 600 bales of cloth, each bale at 500 ducats Sermahabub. They diligently remark what colour the people like best, of this they send a sample to France, and order cloth suitable to the taste of the people. The cloth which the French export to the Levant, is not of the same kind with that they manufacture for themselves, the last being strong, thick, close and good, but that which they export to the Levant though very fine, yet it is thin, and soon wears out. They sell greatest part of it at the Beiram of the Turks, for then every one who can afford it must have a new suit of cloaths. The Grandees and rich people in Egypt at that time cloth their servants, which are often 5 or 600 in number, and this requires much cloth. The English, who have only one house here, have but a small share of this profit, as their cloths are much better, and consequently dearer, but the inhabitants prefer that which is cheapest and makes a fine appearance, and care not much about the goodness, provided it lasts one year. The French merchants received this day goods from France by way of Alexandria, to the value of 600,000 livres; these came in a ship from Marseilles, which was the richest that had come to Egypt in the memory of man; it had besides on board a quantity of goods for the French merchants in Alexandria and Rosette. The lading consisted

consisted only of cloaths and cochineal. Cairo, June 19th, 1750.

4. In *Aleppo*, which is the prettiest town in the Turkish empire, there are nine French and eight English houses. There are more English here, than in any other place in the Levant; they trade to Persia and India. When Persia is at peace, they can gain 300 per cent. on their broad cloaths. For these the market is as good in Persia, as it is for the French in Turkey; because the country is colder, and requires a thicker manufacture than the thin and wretched French cloths; it depends also on the different sentiments of the two nations. The Turks admire a brilliant colour and splendid appearance; the Persians are a wiser people and know the value of goods. The English, dispose of 8 or 900 bales of cloth every year at Aleppo, and the French the same quantity. They get in return Silk, Drugs and *Testic*. The silk comes from Persia, and is much valued in England.

5. The Trade of Damiata.

They export large quantities of Flax every year to Venice, Leghorn, and some to Marseilles. They make linen here, and sell it to great advantage, to France and Italy for lining, and where course linen is required; but most of it goes to Syria, Greece, Constantinople, and other places in Turkey; to each of these are every year exported 100 bales, each bale six feet in length, and four in breadth and height, being valued from 3 to 500 piaster. All Egyptian linen is coarse, and much of the same fineness with the ten or twelve-penny Irish linen, but with this difference, that the Egyptian is thin, and the Irish close, and in this respect, I imagine the former to be stronger than the latter, which is confirmed by experience, and allowed by the rules of mechanics. The antients talk much of the linen of Egypt, and many of our learned men imagine it was so fine and precious, that we have even lost the art, and cannot make it so good. They have been induced to think so, by the commendations the Greeks lavished on the Egyptian linens. They had good reason for doing it, for they had no flax themselves, and were unacquainted with the art of weaving. But were we to compare a piece of Holland linen with the linen in which the Mumies were laid, and which is of the oldest and best manufacture in Egypt, we should find that the fine linen of Egypt is very coarse in comparison to what is now made. The Egyptian linen was fine and sought after by kings and princes, when Egypt was the only country that cultivated Flax, and knew to use it.

Hides and Rice are the other considerable commodities which Damiata affords. Through this town goes all the silk which is used in Egypt, it is brought from Syria and Cyprus in considerable quantities.

6. The Persian trade has, since the reign of Thomas Kouly Kan, being utterly ruined. The English and Dutch who were at Ispahan had enough to do to save their lives, and were obliged to leave their goods and houses to be plundered, when the town was several times sacked by the troops of the competitors for the crown. There came formerly from Persia to Aleppo 1000 bales of the best silk, which the Franks sent to Europe, who in return sent to Persia a quantity of cloth and other European goods. This trade is at present entirely

tirely at a stand. There came also formerly to Smyrna several rich Caravans from Persia, which are not to be seen now, nor do they continue to trade to Persia, by way of Bassora; and all this, because this kingdom, formerly one of the most powerful in the East, is now entirely ruined, partly by the tyranny of Thomas Kouly Kan, and partly by the factions which after his death contended for the Crown.

### 7. The Weights of Egypt.

A *Cantar* of *Cairo*, one of the greatest Weights in Egypt, commonly contains 105 *Rotteli*, which make 38 Turkish *Oke*. They have a singular custom at Cairo, viz. each commodity is sold by its own weight, different from all others, so that a Cantar of coffee is different from a Cantar of myrrh or incense. There is also for every commodity a different manner of counting money; a piaster paid for incense contains sixty medins, when paid for another commodity it contains perhaps forty, &c.

### 8. Cloaths.

The Turks, even the poorest of them, must absolutely, have new Cloaths at their *Beiram*, which succeeds the Ramazan. By this the Europeans, but especially the French, who deal in Cloaths, become considerable gainers. It is very expensive to those who hold great offices, and consequently keep a number of slaves and servants; for these they must also cloath at this time. They reckon that a Grandee in Cairo can't cloath his servants for less than 20,000 ducats at the Beiram.

9. Cot-

# COMMERCE.   401

9. COTTON is the chief produce of Cyprus. This is the best and most valuable of any in the Levant, and much in request amongst the French and Venetians. Cyprus produced formerly 6000 Cantars of Cotton, which was sold in the year 1751, at 170 piasters a Cantar; at other times it commonly sells at 150 piasters a Cantar; but the scarcity which was for several years together occasioned by great droughts and locusts, and add to this the want of people, owing to the tyranny of the Turks, have made this and other products of Cyprus very dear and scarce.

### 10. Coffee.

THERE are yearly brought 36,000 bales of Coffee from Mocka to Egypt, each bale selling for sixty piasters. A Cantar of Coffee is sold at Cairo for eighteen Mahbub, each Mahbub consists of 110 Medins.

### 11. *Incense* (L'Encens, Incenso)

SELLS according to its goodness, from nine to twenty-three piasters, at sixty medins each, per Cantar, consisting of 110 rottoli.

### 12. A Method of giving Wine a fine Flavour.

PLUCK the *flowers* of the vine, when they are just come forth and in full blossom, dry them in the shade, but by no means in the sun or a strong heat; powder and preserve them. Take what quantity you please of this powder, tye it up in linen, and hang it in the cask, when the new Wine begins to ferment. Nothing is more natural,

ral, and nothing more efficacious in giving Wine a high flavour, than this powder. The quintessence of the virtues of a plant lies in the flowers. By drying them flowly, the evaporating subtle particles are concentrated, and they may be preserved a long time without losing their virtue. When the Wine ferments, it acts on these fine particles, and the motion thereby occasioned is sufficient to mix them with the Wine, which by these means, contains all the virtues of the grape and flower. I know that the Greek Bishop in Smyrna, from whom I learned this method, had a Wine of no fine Flavour, made of grapes which grow at *Urla*, a place near Smyrna; but by this method he gave it a smell and Flavour far surpassing any of the same Wine not thus prepared. I know not whether this has ever been tried in other places, yet I make not the least doubt but that it would be attended with equal good success, in any place where vines are planted, as nature is always the same, and never varies.

# Dr. HASSELQUIST's LETTERS,

To Professor

# CHARLES LINNÆUS,

Knight of the Polar Star, and first Physician to the King.

Smyrna, Dec. 16, 1749.

I NEVER undertook a task so agreeable as the present, when I have the honour to write to you from so distant a part of the world, to assure you of my highest regard and esteem.

THE many favours you have conferred on me, and the care you took to forward my journey, give me hopes that you will with pleasure condescend to receive a detail of what has happened to me from my departure to this day, and which I shall now have the honour to give you.

I CAME to Smyrna the 27th of last month, after a voyage of sixteen weeks. The sea agreed very well with me, though it is not without its inconveniencies; but by being cautious, and thro' the blessing of the Almighty, I have bore all without receiving any hurt, and am in as good a state of health at present, as I ever have been in my life. I have never been sick either at home or abroad; I am only sorry that a boisterous sea took from me all opportunities of seeing many of the wonderful works of nature. A fish, which
some-

sometimes we caught with our hook, or small birds driven by the winds to seek shelter with us, were all I had to satisfy my curiosity, and employ my time, in describing and reducing them to their proper tribe. The latter, viz. wag-tails, buntings, sparrows, larks, visited us oftener than we desired; as they never foreboded good. They began their visits in the Baltic, and continued them to the Archipelago, and as often as a little bird came on board us, we were always sure of hard weather. These little creatures are as forward at sea as on shore to take refuge with men. I should imagine, our Divines ought not to be ignorant of this propensity in them, as it very well explains the reason why Noah's dove, which was of the same tribe, was so faithful as to return to the ark, rather than keep out at sea, or live in a world destitute of men.

I HAVE always taken care to get hold of some of these travellers, and have described about thirty of them; some of which I have seen in Sweden, others not. I had them all preserved; but lost them by an unlucky accident.

IT was entertaining to see, when a lark intended to come and visit us, which however never happened, unless we were near some shore, that it had the same action at sea as on land, shooting down, and rising again perpendicularly; but it was ill-adapted to its nature, as there were no green fields whereon it might rest: this bird is not calculated to rest on the sea, therefore the greatest part of them perished in the waves; a few only, and those almost dead reaching us. I had a great inclination to see the Peteril, but not one appeared, though there were frequent opportunities. I also asked our old seamen, who for many years frequented the

the Spanish and Mediterranean seas, whether they had ever seen such a bird; but they answered in the negative. I have reason to believe, that it only appears in the great ocean near both the Indies, and especially the western. I have only been on the island Milo in the Archipelago, which is one of the worst; it was besides in the autumn, and I had no opportunity of searching for plants; yet I collected some as I went up to the town, which was in the middle of November, viz. autumnal dandelion, (*Leontodon autumnale*) Nerium oleander, which was already in seed. Mastich tree (*Pistacia Lentiscus*) an Anemone, which was in blossom, with variegated blue and white flowers. In the town, the date tree was in blossom, the flowers were brought on the table with the desert, at a place where I dined, to regale us with their agreeable odour. Majoram was kept in a pot, and given me as a rarity.

*A black Game*, (Tetrao urogallus) was shot there in a palm tree. I could never have imagined, that this northern bird was to be met with so far to the south, if I had not seen it myself. Woodcocks were also to be seen there, and I have since seen them here; they have their winter quarters so far to the south, but in the summer they quit this country.

I could not get many fishes on my voyage, though they please me most. I have described a *Scomber*, which Artedius hath not amongst his species, and I cannot find that he mentions it amongst his Genera. I got a *Sparus* at Milo, which I likewise believe to be a nondescript.

I enjoy the entire good-will and friendship of our more than good Consul Mr. Rydelius, where I board without expence. I am treated very politely

politely by the French Consul, Mr. Peysonel, the Dutch Count Hochpied, and some Greeks of condition; Mr. Peysonel is a very learned man, and affords me much pleasure.

The college of Physicians of this town which consists of five Doctors, all Greeks, who have studied in Italy, shew me much complaisance, and have called me several times to their consultations. This is a place, where I can do much in natural History, if the long journey I have to make, and my little money, will allow me to tarry here a few months. The sea affords fishes and variety of other animals. Wild fowl are in greater plenty here than in other places, and are daily brought to market from the country and sea. The hills, dales and plains, will be rich in flowers when the season once approaches; and I can never have a better opportunity of looking round me in a foreign country than I have here. Our Consul's Interpreters, Janissaries and horses are at my service, whenever I please; and besides, I live in a house, to which they daily bring fish and wild fowl.

The time I have been here has particularly afforded me an opportunity of seeing the kinds of fish and shell-fish the Greeks use in their Lent. I believe no people make so much use of shell fish, and other sea animals, as the Greeks do. I have seen them eat ten different sorts of shell-fish, (lobsters, crabs, prawns and shrimps are not included here, being ranked by Linnæus under the class of insects) when with us oysters only are eaten. Amongst others they sell here a Sepia (Cuttle fish,) which by them is called ὀκταπόδια; it has only eight tentacula, all of equal length; the whole animal is a foot long, and thick in proportion. Of this the Greeks have related me an anecdote, which I think remarkable:

remarkable: the Pinna muricata, or great Silk muscle, is here found in the bottom of the sea in large quantities, being a foot long: the ὀκτωπόδια, or cuttle fish with eight rays, watches the opportunity, when the muscle opens her shell, to creep in it, and devour her; but a little crab, which has scarcely any shell, or has at least only a very thin one, lodges constantly in this shell-fish; she pays a good rent, by saving the life of her landlady, for she keeps a constant look out through the aperture of the shell, and on seeing the enemy approach, she begins to stir, when the πίνα (for so the Greeks call the shell) shuts up her house, and the rapacious animal is excluded. I saw this shell-fish first at the island of Milo, and found such a little crab in all I opened: I wondered not a little what was her business there; but when I came here, I was first informed of it by the Secretary of our Consul, Mr. Justi, a curious and ingenious man, who has travelled much, and lived long in this place. This was afterwards confirmed by several Greeks, who daily catch and eat both these animals. I have sufficiently described these three animals, with the fish and birds I have seen to this day, and likewise preserve them all, some dried, others in spirits of wine. I have the honour to transmit a description of a *Coote* (Fulica), the others shall follow, as soon as I can copy them, and my journal.

As to what relates to the continuing of my journey to Palestine, I had at first an intention of going to Constantinople, and thence to Syria; but believe I shall alter my mind, and go directly hence, for many reasons. Here the opportunities of getting vessels are more frequent, the voyage is shorter: I have also heard, that in a short time there will be a good opportunity of going in company

pany with the Armenian Patriarch from Jerusalem, who is here at present. The journey I have still to make requires more money than I imagined, if I accomplish the purpose I intended. I think it would be a great pity, that a matter of such consequence, which has so far been pursued, should be dropped for want of money. I will answer for it, that with a little addition of money, and the assistance of the Almighty, the natural History of Palestine, and the adjacent places, shall be as well known, as that of any country, except Sweden. If my money would permit, I could take a servant with me from this place, who might be my Interpreter, and without one, I shall lose many fair opportunities of informations, in places where they don't speak so many European languages as in Smyrna; but there are besides other necessary expences in those places, without which I cannot advance a step.

I HOPE to have a fine collection of living and dead natural curiosities, by the time I intend to return home. Mr. Rydelius, our Consul, hath promised me some living pheasants, of incomparable beauty, from the borders of Persia: a kind of patridges called Francolins, which are not described in the Systema Naturæ, some turtle doves, and a Pelican preserved; I know a method of getting a living rock goat, besides a number of known and unknown fishes, birds and plants, which I have already got, and shall hereafter collect.

Smyrna, January 29, 1750.

I WAS this moment informed of a vessel's going to Europe, and therefore must not omit the opportunity of writing to you.

I AM

I am only sorry, that time will not permit me to make such expedition as I could wish in forwarding to you all the observations and descriptions I have made in Natural History to this time. But they shall speedily be transmitted.

*Francolins* and *Poulle de Montagnes* are new birds, which I apprehend have not been described, and are of the genus *Tetrao*; the first was drawn by Tournefort, in his travels, but badly. I have a kind of Blackbird which sings exceeding well, is black and grey, and comes from the islands in the Archipelago; it is often sold for fifty piasters at Constantinople. I have a living Turtle-dove, of a very rare sort, which came from Abyssinia in Africa, and is as white as chalk. I have the *Pelican* stuffed. I have seen all our Swedish sea fowl here. Mr. Rydelius is very desirous of procuring birds, and has lately taken measures to get some Ostriches and other rare birds from Egypt, all which he intends to send to Sweden. I have often seen, and have well described the Rock Goat. It is such a fine creature, that Solomon could not mean any other animal than this by the Doe, to which he compared his Bride in the Canticles. And they are found in abundance in the mountains of Syria and Palestine; but they are more like *Cervus Capreolus* in outward appearance, than a Goat. Canis aureus (Jackcal) is found in greater numbers here, than the inhabitants wish; I intend soon to go out and shoot one, and shall then make a compleat description of it.

I have botanized here several times this winter, and never lost my labour. I shall without delay have the honour to transmit my whole collection of plants and descriptions; in the mean time, I send one inclosed, which I imagine to be new; at least, I cannot range it under any genus in Syngenesia, Monogamia, though it belongs to the order. I have completely described and sufficiently dried it.

I HAVE not omitted to search for proofs of the sea's diminution; and I have found some, which are I think very evident; I shall do myself the honour of transmitting them the first opportunity to the Royal Academy of Sciences. For five days past, the cold in Smyrna has been unusually severe. The Florentine thermometer points to 68. The ice has been so thick at the sides of the harbour, that the Dutch have skaited on it. The oldest people in the town do not remember such severe weather to have lasted so long at any time before. If the winter in Upsala, is in proportion as severe as this, God alone can save Upsala garden.

BEING accustomed to Swedish winters, I should not mind this, if I had but a Swedish stove. I am obliged to sit at a miserable coal fire to write this, and never was so cold in Sweden, as in the miserable architecture of this country. I know not yet how soon the Patriarch, in whose company I expect to travel to Jerusalem, sets out; but believe, I shall remain here another month.

Smyrna, February 9, 1750.

I JOYFULLY embrace every opportunity I have of writing to you, and think myself happy, whenever I can fulfil this my duty.

I HAD the honour of transmitting a plant to you some days ago, which I know not, the description now follows; together with one of a *Sepia* (Cuttle fish.) If any mistakes have crept in to my descriptions, I request your favourable correction, as they are made by a young beginner. I have first learned,

learned, during my travels, to describe well the productions of nature; I improve every day, and if I can only in time arrive at a small share in the learning and ingenuity of my great master, I will not exchange it for the art of the greatest Painter. No natural curiosities are so difficult to describe, as shells and corallines, which are here found in great plenty, and I by no means pass them over. I possess in you a friend, who kindly and wisely corrects my errors. I have now a fine bundle of descriptions; I shall send them over, as soon as I can copy them.

THE inclosed, I request, you will deliver to Dr. Rosén and Dr. Bæck, the King's Physicians. I have given the former an account of the present state of Physic in Smyrna; the latter of an endemical disease in Aleppo; the copy of these I shall have the honour of transmitting to you soon. In this manner I intend to pay my respects to my Patrons.

Smyrna, April 6.

I STILL continue in the place, from which I have several times had the honour of writing to you. I have tarried here longer than I intended, for want of a proper opportunity; but I do not repent of my stay, on account of the opportunity I have had of living during a fine spring, at a place so rich in natural curiosities, as this neighbourhood of Natolia is. Each day brings to my knowledge new things in Botany, and this has been the case for a month past; if I had several to assist me, we should all have enough to do.

SOME time ago, I made a journey in Natolia to the town of Magnesia, eight leagues from hence. I botanized there on the mount Sypilus of the ancients, one of the higheſt in Aſia, which is covered with ſnow all the year. I ſhall have the honour of giving an account of the plants I found there, when I ſend the bulk of my collection.

I found alſo inſects there, which had never been before diſturbed. I daily collect numbers of them; and it is remarkable, that many of them are mentioned in the Fauna Suecica, but ſome are peculiar to this country. I have the honour of tranſmitting a little fly, which I took yeſterday in the fruit of a fig-tree; it lies incloſed in the germen of the female fig, which it has eaten up. Whether this is the inſect that ſerves afterwards to impregnate the fruit, I cannot yet determine. Before I quit this place, I ſhall endeavour to acquire a clear idea of the fig-tree's inſects; this muſt be a Cynips, and the fig its Galla; I have completely deſcribed it.

I have diverted myſelf for ſome time with the *Chamæleon* and *Turtles*, to ſee their qualities, when I had them alive in my chamber. I ſhall in time publiſh the obſervations I made on them. I wiſh I had ſome of the latter in Upſala to ornament your garden; it is very eaſy to get them home alive; I ſhall endeavour to accompliſh it. It is very amuſing to ſee how they make love. I have got a quantity of the *Cornucopiæ*, the rare graſs, which you were pleaſed to recommend ſo much to me, to ſearch for round Smyrna; I have likewiſe deſcribed it; and incloſed, ſend you ſome ſpecimens. I ſhall gather the ſeeds when they are ripe, and ſend them to the Academical Garden, which I hope will be the firſt that gets this fine plant.

This ſhort account how I have employed my time, is all I can have the honour to impart to you at preſent. I ſhall not omit to give you a larger

larger collection of my observations before my departure hence.

I am now determined to leave this place next ascension-day, and go from hence in a French ship to Alexandria in Egypt, there I intend to obtain what information I can in a short time, and so go over to Palæstine.

Smyrna, April 28.

I AM now at the point of leaving this place, from whence I have had frequent agreeable opportunities of writing to you. I have got a Turkish pass, and expect every day an opportunity to continue my journey in some vessel, which in all appearance will be first to Egypt, by way of Cyprus to Alexandria and Cairo, whence I intend, with the help of God, to go to the place of my destination, Palæstine. I hope these places, in a promising time of the year, will afford me sufficient opportunities for observations in Natural History, which I wish in time to lay before you. I shall esteem myself happy, if there should be any amongst them worth your attention, and shall have gained the greatest reward I can expect from my poor endeavours.

Flora begins now in this country to put on her best attire, fine varieties of *Anemones* adorn the plains: *Hyacinths* grow near the roads: *Ranunculus* of a large and fine variety is common in the vineyards: the *Almond-tree* blossoms on the bare branches, and gives the hills an elegant appearance, where they are mixt with the ever-green olive-trees. I often wish, that these were as common in Sweden as Fumitory and Treacle mustard are here, with several others, which I find are natives of Natolia as well as Sweden.

The following observations about the fig-tree I have acquired here, and now shall have the honour of communicating them to you, as I got them.

The possessors of fig-trees are very sollicitous, that the much-talked-of fly shall pierce the fig, and unless this is done, they are persuaded they shall have no fruit.

Another insect persecutes this and kills it, to the loss of the possessors; this they hinder by smearing a paint on the tree, just beneath the branches; this consists of common red paint and water, which the pernicious insect dares not to pass. I have in all places seen many such rings painted on the tree; but cannot know the insects, as the season of the year permitted me not to search for it, perhaps it is a pismire.

Those, who cultivate fig-trees, take the black figs (thus they call Capricus), and fasten them on a thread in the form of a necklace, which they hang on the fruit-bearing trees, and believe it to contribute towards producing good and great plenty of fruit.

The fig-tree is subject to a scurf (λέπρα Græc. hod.) I saw plenty of this scurf yesterday, and found it to consist of a quantity of insects cells placed on the bark of the branches, of the size of a pea, the top of them depressed, and a little pointed in the middle, of a very brittle substance, being easily rubbed to dust between the fingers; they consist of two membranes, of which the inward is brown, and the outward greyish, there are always three placed together, so as to form a triangle. They were dry and dead on all the trees

when

when I saw them, nor could I find either living or dead insects in any of them; however, I despair not of finding, at a proper time of the year, the insects which make them.

The Caprificus is planted in quantities round gardens for hedges; I suppose, no Swedish gardener will venture to plant these trees for the same use; but by the fine hedges which ivy makes round the badly laid out gardens of this town, I am persuaded it would serve for the same purpose, if we had it in sufficient quantities. The descriptions, which I made to this time of quadrupeds, birds, amphibia and plants, amount to about 500 species, which are all completely described; to which I may add as many observations on various subjects in Natural History. I shall have the honour of submitting to your favourable judgment, as many of them as I can copy off, before my departure. I send one inclosed; I know not whether this bird is described or not. The subsidence of the sea is so evident in this place, that it can scarcely be easier demonstrated in any other place, that the sea yearly decreases. In the inclosed letter, to Secretary Elvius, I have spoke my mind freely and clearly on this subject, but some things I have reserved to myself, which I wish in time to relate to you in person; and until then shall say no more on that subject.

May the Supreme Being let us see the time, when our country may acquire honour and benefit from those things, which foreigners have passed over on their travels, in which, as well as in almost every thing else, we have been the last; but God be praised! we hope not the worst in the world.

Alexandria,

Alexandria, May 18, 1750.

I HAVE now the honour to write to you, from a different part of the world, than I have hitherto done. I came hither the 13th of this month, after I had tarried in Natolia above five months.

In the few days I have been in Egypt, even in the most barren places that I have seen, I find that this fine country can afford an infinity of curious subjects in Natural History, to employ my time in the three several kingdoms of Nature. The four days I have looked round me, give me reason to hope much.

The first thing I did after my arrival was, to see the *Date-tree*, the ornament and a great part of the riches of this country. It had already blossomed, but I had, nevertheless, the pleasure of seeing how the Arabs assist its fecundation, and by that means secure to themselves a plentiful harvest of a vegetable, which was so important to them, and known to them, many centuries before any Botanist dreamed of the difference of sexes in vegetables. The Gardener informed me of this, before I had time to enquire, and would shew me, as a very curious thing, the male and female of the Date or Palm-trees; nor could he conceive how I, a Frank, lately arrived, could know it before; for, says he, all who have yet come from Europe to see this country, have regarded his relation either as a fable or a miracle. The Arab, seeing me inclined to be further informed, accompanied me and my French interpreter to a Palm-tree, which was very full of young fruit, and had by him been wedded or fecundated with the male, when both were in blossom. This the Arabs do in the following manner: when the *spadix*,

*dix*, has *female flowers*, that comes out of its *spatha*, they search on a tree that has *male flowers*, which they know by experience, for a *spadix*, which has not yet burfted out of its *spatha*: this they open, take out the *spadix*, and cut it lengthways in several pieces, but take care not to hurt the flowers. A piece of this *spadix*, with *male flowers*, they put lengthways between the small branches of the *spadix* which hath *female flowers*, and then lay the leaf of a Palm over the branches. In this situation, I yet saw the greatest part of the *spadices* which bore their young fruit; but the *male flowers* which were put between were withered. The Arab besides gave me the following anecdotes: First, unless they, in this manner, wed and fecundate the Date-tree, it bears no fruit. Secondly, they always take the precaution to preserve some unopened *spathæ* with *male flowers*, from one year to another, to be applied for this purpose, in case the *male flowers* should miscarry or suffer damage. Thirdly, if they permit the *spadix* of the *male flowers* to burst or come out, it becomes useless for fecundation: it must have its *maidenhead*, (these were the words of the Arab) which is lost in the same moment the blossoms burst out of their case. Therefore the person, who cultivates Date-trees, must be careful to hit the right time of assisting their fecundation, which is almost the only article in their cultivation. Thirdly, on opening the *spatha*, he finds all the *male flowers* full of a liquid, which resembles the finest dew; it is of a sweet and pleasant taste, resembling much the taste of fresh Dates; but much more refined and aromatick: this was likewise confirmed by my interpreter, who hath lived thirty-two years in Egypt, and therefore had opportuni-

ties

ties enough of tasting both the nectar of the blossoms, and the fresh Dates.

Thus much have I learned of this wonderful work of Nature, in a country, where it may be seen every year. I shall have the honour to give a relation of the use, and divers other qualities of the Date-tree, at some other opportunity. I hope in time to be able to give you a complete history of this Palm. I wish I was as sure of an opportunity of seeing all the Palm tribe.

The other plants I saw in this neighbourhood, are Egyptian Acacia, (Mimosa nilotica) Chaste-tree, (Vitex agnus castus) Palma Christi, several sorts of Goose-foot, (Chenopodium) and Fig-marigold, (Mesembryanthemum.) I never saw a species of Goose-foot in Natolia, where otherwise every thing grew; but I have seen very little in Egypt yet. Alexandria is the worst part of it, and is only a port for shipping off the riches of Egypt, Arabia and Abyssinia. Please God, I shall soon see Rosette, the garden of this kingdom; and the Nile, the repository of its natural curiosities. In Cairo, I shall endeavour to get some fragments of the Natural History of Arabia and Egypt. I have great hopes of learning the history of the Balsam of Mecca; I have already got a number of informations from the Mecca travellers, and only wait to get a little shrub of it from a Turk, at the end of the year, if possible, or at least a branch, and perhaps blossoms, for which I have already taken proper measures. There is a possibility of getting the plant, which yields the Myrrh, by the caravan from Ethiopia to Cairo; but it requires time, and some expences; I shall do all in my power. If it is possible, I shall make a tour to Upper Egypt; but of this I can say nothing

nothing for certain, before I come to Cairo. Please God, I shall see Palæstine, which is my chief business, next Autumn, and perhaps remain there to the Spring following, that I may see the two principal seasons of the year, viz. Autumn and Spring, when every thing is in blossom.

I REQUEST you will please to honour me with a letter before that time, and inform me, whether you would have me enquire after any thing in particular, and whether Dr. Celsius knows any thing in particular, which he would have me look after. Though I search after every thing, yet I may by such informations have an opportunity of clearing up some things, which, without them, I might perhaps pass over.

I REQUEST you will please to ask Dr. Celsius, whether the writers on Scripture plants have ever thought what vegetable David refers to in Psalm i. ver. 3. under the name of the Tree of the Righteous. David attributes qualities to this tree, which plainly shew, that he means some particular vegetable. And these qualities are such, that they cannot be attributed to any, but the *Nerium* (oleander) which grows in abundance in this country. One word about St. John's Locusts, which have puzzled the learned so much. They, who deny insects to have been the food of this holy man, urge, that this insect is an uncustomary and unnatural food; but they would soon be convinced of the contrary, if they would travel hither to Egypt, Arabia or Syria, and take a meal with the Arabs; roasted Locusts, are at this time eaten by the Arabians, at the proper season, when they can procure them; so that in all probability, this dish has been used in the time of St. John. Ancient customs are not here subject to many changes. The victuals of St. John are

not

not believed unnatural here; and as I was once speaking to a judicious Greek Priest about this affair, and told him that the learned in Europe were of different opinions, whether St. John in the desart, eat a kind of bird, or a plant, asking him which of these opinions he thought the true one? He answered with a laugh, that both were alike erroneous. Their church had never taken this food to be any other, than what is expressed in the Testament, nor did he know any thing to contradict it.

I HAVE the honour to send here inclosed the fly called Panorpa Coa, which I took on the island Meteline in the Archipelago; I have never seen this species in Sweden, and know not whether it is Swedish, if it is, it was unnecessary to send it so far.

LIKEWISE the measure (28 feet,) containing the thickness of the Plane-tree, which is a prodigy in our father's kingdom, I mean Stanchio, the town in which Hippocrates was born. This tree has forty-seven branches, each a fathom thick, supported by stone pillars, and covers a very large terrace, shades several houses of various sizes, being above twenty in number; I imagine, in seeing it, to have beheld the largest, oldest, and most remarkable inhabitant of the vegetable kingdom. All the observations and collections I made in Natolia, I have left in Smyrna, in the house of Consul Rydelius. I shall have the honour to send you copies of a great number of them, which I have taken with me in notes, as fast as I can write them. I am alone, and if I had only one to assist me in writing, I should do twice as much; *but how shall we get bread in the wilderness?*

A CERTAIN affair has happened to me, of which this opportunity will not permit me to speak, which

which will make my journey to Egypt easy and not expensive; but in Syria and Palæstine, I cannot avoid expence. Consul Rydelius, whose goodness I can never enough commend, has taken upon him to furnish me with money.

### Cairo, September, 1750.

SINCE my last, I have seen more of Egypt, and had an opportunity of acquiring some knowledge of a country, which is certainly one of the most remarkable on our globe. You will find by the inclosed list, what I have done in Natural History. I could have increased it with a larger number; but I would only mention the principal subjects, and such as I had time to finish as well as I possibly could upon a journey and destitute of Books, which are sometimes necessary to refer to. I shall add a few descriptions, and have attained my wishes, if you approve of them. The account how to prepare Sal armoniac, I intend for the Royal Society, having composed it on the spot, where Sal armoniac is made. I hope it will not be unacceptable, as it is the first account which, as far as I know, has been written at large and distinctly on the spot, and by an eye-witness. I send it open to you, desiring you will please to read it over, and afterwards seal it, and send it to the Royal Academy of Sciences.

I have not put down in my list, the *Pyramids* of Egypt, nor the *Mumies* and their sepulchres; but I ought not to pass over in silence my having seen them, which is sufficient. I cannot detain you longer with these things, without following the common track of every voyager, who never forgets to speak largely about the width, depth, height and breadth of these things, which now scarcely

scarcely deserve the least attention of a traveller, after having been seen by so many thousands. But I esteem myself happy in having seen something else in Egypt, which alone certainly deserves a voyage to this country, I mean the flowing of the *Nile*, which may with reason be called a wonder of nature, assisted by art. But the most surprising thing of all, is, that the fields of Egypt owe to our northern mountains their fertility, and of course the country its felicity. This is a matter which is certainly known to our natural Philosophers, as it is allowed by all the Wisemen of Egypt, who have it from their masters through many generations. They say, that the water, which every year encreases the Nile, rises from the earth towards the North Pole, is changed into clouds, and thus travels, when these have a proper wind, over Europe and Africa, as far as the Montes Lunæ in Ethiopia, where it falls down in rains, runs in abundancy from the rocks of the mountains, and is gathered in the Nile, which hath its fountain there, and below its fall is by channels led over all Egypt, according to the wise conceptions of the ancient Egyptians. This is the opinion of those of the Egyptians, who believe themselves to have some knowledge of nature, of which some are yet to be found here, descended from the Arabian school. I have thought this account worthy of relating, just as I received it, and will leave others to search, whether any useful information can be got hence, in a thing beyond the plan of my enquiries.

I shall rather pursue that which comes under my own sphere, and speak of what *Botanists* may expect from Egypt towards the increase and improvement of that art. Of this I have now an idea entirely different from that which Alpinus gave me me in Sweden. This Author made me believe, that I should find a botanical magazine in Egypt, but this is not the case. Egypt has very few indigenous plants. The greatest part of those to be seen here, and which are noticed by Alpinus, are cultivated by art; for this reason we find here a *Flora œconomica*, which is without doubt one of the richest under the sun. The quantity of corn, *wheat*, *barley*, *beans* and *peas*, the abundance of *rice*, the superfluity of *flax*, which this country yearly produceth, are evidences of this; besides the quantity of *indigo*, *safflower*, *dates*, *cassia*, and *senna*, with which the country enriches its possessors. The situation of the country and seasons is such, as will not permit many spontaneous plants to come forth, of which I hope to give you my observations more circumstantially another time.

I have gathered the flowers and seeds of every thing planted here, and described and collected every thing I found wild. What pleaseth me most of any thing I have found here in the vegetable kingdom, is, the knowledge I have got of the *Date-tree*, and scripture *sycamore*, two plants, which alone might deserve a Botanist's journey to Egypt. With respect to the former, I have with tolerable ease collected every thing that was necessary; but the latter has given me more trouble. This is a tree which in its fructification, manner of growing, living and dying, is doubtless one of the most singular in the vegetable kingdom. I have opened, not hundreds, but thousands of its figs (Receptacula) before I could get an idea of its fructification; I have however at length acquired some insight with respect to it: it has hermaphrodite and male flower cups distinct one from the other, as the common fig; but the latter dif-

fer

fer much from this. An insect called *Cynips* hath its dwelling and works in the male flower cups, but whether it ever enters the hermaphrodite cups, and whether it contributes any thing towards its fecundation, I have much reason to doubt; I shall however make some farther enquiry with respect to this. It is also singular in this plant, that the male cups are useful, and may be eaten; but the hermaphrodites serve for no use, just the reverse of the common fig: I shall, please God, send a cutting of this tree to Upsala garden next year, together with plaintain, Christ's thorn, &c.

I would speak of the Plantain-tree or *Musa*, the queen of plants, but it commands me to be silent, as it has had the good fortune to be completely described by the greatest master. I will however mention an odd story, which is taken for granted by the Egyptian gardeners: they say, that it can be produced by planting the kernel of a *Date* in the root of *Colocasia*, and that this was its first origin; a singular history of creation. I asked them, whether they ever made trial, as they so obstinately defended the truth of it; but they answered no, and that it was not worth while, as the plant grows so freely without culture; *et fabulosa juvant*. About this time we daily eat ripe Dates. I wish it were possible to get some baskets of them to Upsala, as I with joy could send them. In Europe, we seem to envy the felicity of the people who enjoy these fruits. I confess they are good to taste once or twice; but though I have got over the age when such things please most, yet I would gladly give two bushels of Dates for half a bushel of good Swedish apples, and am persuaded, I should find thousands in Egypt ready to make the same exchange. *Apples* are scarce here; they are brought hither

hither from mount Sinai, where the Grecian Monks have delightful orchards full of the finest apple and pear-trees, whence without doubt the finest varieties we have in Europe were first brought.

According to all appearance, I shall remain in Egypt all the winter, though I could wish to leave this land of slavery as soon as possible. It is very disagreeable to travel in Egypt. This country is governed by rebels who have been slaves; it may therefore be easily imagined, what order and police is kept up here; a Christian can scarcely be more despised, and worse treated in any place than this. I think no affront can be more grating, than that a Christian is not permitted to ride on any creature but an ass; and to encrease the affront, must alight from his ass when he meets one, who was perhaps a few days before a robber, but for his skill in murdering, is made commander in a place over a number of rebellious soldiers. This is our case daily, and to avoid all the trouble to which we are exposed, we must live as it were in a kind of civil arrest, keeping within our chambers, and when we intend to go out in the town or country, commit ourselves to the hands of soldiers, who conduct us with staffs and pikes through their villainous brethren. So that to travel to Cairo, and live there for some time, is like doing penance for crimes. I am however, always in a merry humour, and the singular life of Cairo gives me frequent opportunities for various pleasant reflections, which pass the time away.

It is possible I may this winter, have an opportunity of travelling to Upper Egypt, in company with some English gentlemen, who are expected hither. If it happens, I am sure it will amply reward my labour.

I INTEND next spring to see first Palæstine, then Syria, mount Lebanon, and other remarkable places; I hope to perform this tour with greater ease, in a country where the Franks are more regarded, and are at more liberty. I wish I had been empowered to purchase Arabian manuscripts for our library, as the most curious are to be had here at a reasonable rate. Other nations have got enough from hence; through the acquaintance I have made with some learned Arabians, I have got some on Physic and Natural History. I could with much ease serve our Library in this affair, if I were desired and supplied wherewith to do it. I remain, &c.

A LIST of the Observations which Dr. Hasselquist made, and had already finished, and were by him designed for Professor Linnæus.

1. Observations and remarks on the Tape-worm in Egypt.
2. The cause of the Egyptians *diseases of the eyes*.
3. The description of a kind of eruption or scab at the flowing of the Nile.
4. Of the balsam of Mecca, its country, the method of knowing it, with its uses in the East, its adulteration, and a description of the tree.
5. The use of the *Mumies* for physic in Egypt.
6. An unexpected use of *Gum arabic*, when it for the space of two months supported several thousand souls.
7. The preparation of *Sal armoniac* in Egypt, sent to the Royal Academy of Sciences.
8. The preparation of *Cassia fistula*.
9. The use of locusts for food in Egypt.

10. The use of the *Date-tree* in the œconomy of the Egyptians.

11. How *Indigo* is manufactured in Egypt.

12. The cultivation of *Safflower* in Egypt.

13. The cultivation of *Rice* in Egypt.

14. *Mimosa* (*Arabis Lebbeck.*) Egyptian Acacia described, and sent to the Royal Academy of Sciences at Upsala.

15. The Natural History of the scripture sycamore.

17. Two new species of goose-foot (Chenopodium) in Egypt.

18. A description of the Christ thorn by the Arabs, called *Nabca*.

19. *Chenna*, and its use for dying yellow.

21. A few *Stones* of a singular kind.

22. A description of all the *Petrefactions* in the Egyptian Pyramids.

23. The *Strata* of the *earth* in Egypt.

25. Two species of Bees described.

26. *Pharaon*, an animal (Ichneumon) which goes in the houses like cats, and every thing curious relating to it.

27. A species of *Rats*, which have a head like a hare, a snout like a hog; a body like a rat, tail like a lion; can never touch the ground with their fore feet, but hop like grashoppers, and live in the mountains between Egypt and Arabia. The whole description of this very wonderful creature is sent to the Royal Academy of Sciences at Upsala.

28. *Camelo pardalis*, the camel deer, which has scarce been seen by any other except Bellonius, with its whole description, sent to the Royal Academy of Sciences.

29. A *Parrot*, the prettiest of its kind.

30. A little *Dotteril* from Alexandria.

31. The ostrich and its tribe, with the snipes.

32. *Casuarius*, a very small kind of ostrich from Damiata.

33. A *Pigeon*, with straight and erect feathers on its back.

34. A curious *Turtle-dove*, common in Egypt.

38. Four sorts of *Serpents*, well distinguished by their Scuta abdominalia amongst these are the *Cerastes alpini*, or the true *Aspis* and *Jaculus* or Serpens Evæ, which have never been described before.

40. Two *Lizards* described in Egypt.

41. The *Lizard Gecko*, which through the feet emits a dangerous poison.

43. The description of the sucking fish and *Sardaigne*.

55. Twelve *Fishes* from the Nile, making as many new genus's.

56. The *Dermestes* which consumes dates.

57. *Cerambyx niloticus*. The capricorn beetle of Egypt.

58. A butterfly, from the subterranean passages at Alexandria.

60. Two singular new genus's of *Insects*.

75. Fifteen new species of *Insects*.

76. The *Cancer cursor* of *Bellonius*, or a crab, which runs on the shore.

77. The *Pismires*, which run in the sand near the Egyptian Pyramids.

78. The little *Pismire*, which keeps in the houses at Cairo, and is one of the seven plagues of Pharaoh.

79. An *African scorpion*.

THESE and much more Mr. Hasselquist has already amply described in Egypt.

December,

December, 29, 1750.

THE 6th of last October was one of my happiest days, as I on that day received both your letters, one dated the 27th of February, the other the 20th of April, and both forwarded to me by Consul Rydelius.

I at the same time received Counsellor Carleson's bill for 130 ducats in specie, which were sent me to the Levant. These were agreeable tidings, especially as the Counsellor was pleased to add, that more might be got. None in Sweden knows better than Mr. Carleson, how expensive it is to live in the Levant, even for those, who will live most sparingly, to do which I use my best endeavours. My long stay in Egypt has cost me money enough; but I should never have dared to tarry here so long, if I had not found other means of supporting myself, than with the public money; an affair for which I am to thank fortune, as I got by it an opportunity of accomplishing my purpose, which was to inform myself of the Natural History of this remarkable country. Perhaps I should never have come to Egypt, if I had not got this opportunity; at least, I could not have lived here all the seasons of the year, without which little could have been done here, in regard to the objects of my enquiries. Next to your kind care, I with profound respect acknowledge myself indebted to the most reverend Archbishop's, the Faculties of Divinity and Philosophy, Counsellor Carleson's, and to the other gentlemen's bounty, who contributed to defray the expences of this journey. Wherefore I most earnestly request, that you will please to present them my most humble thanks, and assure them, that I shall have nothing more at heart, than to show to the world, how much free gifts from Swedes can contribute to the encreafe of Science.

The news you were pleafed to favour me with, from the botanical world, were as many refreshments to me in a country, which inftead of Euphorbus's, Mefues and Avicennas, is filled with a number of Fortune-tellers, and ftrolling quacks, and where, inftead of the Alexandrian Library, one fees millions of murdering fabres and pikes: a country, in which a traveller has need of all the comfort he can get. I lament the death of the Librarian Mr. Norrelius; I had feveral conferences with this learned man before my departure, about the animals mentioned in the fcriptures, in which he had great knowledge: I wifh I could have continued them to him after my return, when I hope to have fome knowledge in that matter as a Natural Hiftorian. The great age of Doctor Celfius puts me in fear, that I fhall likewife lofe the advantage I wifh to have, at my return, to fubmit to this great man's judgment, the obfervations I have made on the fcripture plants.

I hope that my defcriptions of, and obfervations on, the *Cornucopiæ* (horn of plenty grafs) *Panorpa Coa* Cervus *Camelopardalis*, (camel deer,) *Mus Jaculus* (jumping moufe), &c. &c. which I had the honour to fend you from time to time, partly from Smyrna, partly from Egypt, have come fafe to hand. The *Herpes aleppina*, the hiftory of which I fent to the King's Phyfician, Dr. Bæck, is a very remarkable endemical difeafe in Aleppo, and I believe not yet taken notice of by any Phyfician. The attention, which I know the Royal Academy of Sciences paid to the obfervations made in feveral places about the decreafe of the fea, hath encouraged me to fend my opinion of it to Secretary Elvius. I know not how far this able Mathematician is inclined to this system; but I am almost assured, that those who have seen the proofs of the decrease of the water, which I have observed on my travels, cannot avoid being confirmed in this remarkable hypothesis, which you and the late Professor Celsius laid before the public with observations. I have at present the honour to send you a collection, singular in its kind, like the country from which it is sent. It consists of *Serpents* and *Lizards*, terrible animals, and the proper native productions of Egypt; which can only please those who study and know Nature. I have not forgot with what care you bid me get some knowledge of the *Hæmorrhois, Dipsas, Aspis, Seps,* &c. of the ancients, of which we know nothing; but lament, that notwithstanding all the pains I took, to get some information about these terrible animals of the ancients, I have not succeeded with more than Seps and Aspis, which according to the information I got, are one and the same serpent. The account is this: on the island of Cyprus, there is a serpent by the modern Greeks called ἀσπις, it is short, seldom above a foot long, but of an disproportioned thickness, sometimes as thick as a man's arm. The poison of this is the most terrible of any known in the East. When a man is bit by it he falls into a slumber, by degrees changed into profound sleep, which within twenty four hours becomes eternal, without any violent symptoms or other signs of death, than that the pulse grows weak by degrees, and the whole body becomes of a blackish yellow colour in a moment, and within the next twenty four hours, rots as if affected with a gangrene.

A a 4 Do

Do not we then find in one and the same serpent, the qualities of two of the Ancients? I mean *Aspis*, which killed so easy; and *Seps*, which killed in a very short time, with the like terrible symptoms, and effects as this does to this day.

Have not the Ancients, who never gave complete descriptions of those curiosities in Nature, of which they might have left us any account, and in which the name, characters, or descriptions are either omitted, or made and given in such a manner, as rather to confound the Reader, than to instruct him? Have they not perhaps, I say, given two names to one animal, because it had two different qualities? Examples of this kind are not wanting.

It is very possible, that the *Seps* of Lucan is the same as the *Aspis* of Horace; both have informed us of their effects; but neither of them has given us any description. I therefore conceive it is laudable to endeavour, by the informations which Natural History affords us, to explain their meaning, as they do not always express their thoughts so clearly as to be comprehended by their Readers.

I have the honour to send three descriptions of the serpents I found in Egypt: the first is the viper of Egypt. If this has been completely described before, the viper of the shops would be known; if not, this famous viper has to this day been unknown. I have always been of the opinion that our common viper (*Coluber vulgaris* Fn. suec.) was the same with the viper of the shops; but I changed my opinion, as soon as I saw how much the viper, from which the Venetians carry over all that is required in the shops, differs in number of scutæ and squamæ, head and tail, and appearance from that which is found with us. The true *viperæ officinalis*, I suppose, is scarcely met with in Italy,

as

as it has from time immemorial been carried from Egypt to Venice, from whence its preparations are sent all over Europe.

The second is a horned viper (*Coluber Cerastes.*) I have found two serpents with horns in Egypt of different genus's, as the one is a snake, (*Anguis*) and the other a viper (*Coluber.*) As different as they are with regard to their genus, so different are they also with respect to their horns; those of the former, are two large teeth, which bore through the cranium, so that their basis serves for teeth, and the upper pointed parts of them for horns; Whereas those of the latter are only two sharp points fastened to the head.

I shall not absolutely determine which of these Alpinus means by the name of Cerastes, of which he has given a bad figure, and a worse description. I am apt to believe, that he has them both under one name, as they both have horns. It was in this manner, that in former times they thought it sufficient to represent natural beings, by giving a figure without any description, to draw in a striking manner, what would excite the curiosity of the common people; for example, a *serpent with horns*; so that no attention was paid to the wise institutes of nature, before our Linnæus taught us to open our eyes in beholding and distinguishing her with clearness and precision. The third is the before mentioned *anguis dentibus molaribus cranium perforantibus.*

I have found a considerable number of *Lizards*, the other branch of this terrible tribe; but most of them were known before, except some few small ones, which I found in the burning sand in the desart: there is no place wherein some kind of living creature is not appointed to dwell. That which

which I have the honour to send I have preferred to the rest, as it is the only one I know, of which has hitherto been used, but was nevertheless unknown both to Naturalists and Physicians.

This lizard is the true *Scink*, which is found in plenty in the mountains between Arabia and Egypt, it is caught in great numbers by the Egyptian peasants, dried and sold to the Venetians in Cairo, who export a large quantity of it over to Europe. I had this alive, as well as every thing else which I have hitherto described.

I have likewise preserved every thing hitherto by me described, partly in spirits of wine, partly stuffed, with which I intend to increase the natural collection at Upsala, if God permits me to return home. At the beginning of next year, I intend to send some things over to you, viz. The seeds *Beben Nux*, *Cassia Sopher*, and several others, amongst the rest a stuffed ostrich.

Before I leave Egypt, I likewise intend to send to Upsala garden some trees, as *Alhenna*, scripture *Sycamore*, the buckthorn, of which the crown of Christ was made, Cassia fistula, the Plantain tree, &c. They shall be sent by way of Leghorn, to Stocholm, addressed to Mr. Grill. If it be possible, I shall shortly make a journey to mount *Sinai*. I have already been on the way to it, but was kept back by the excursions of the Arabians. If the scheme, which I have in view, turns out well, I hope to attain my wishes and see this famous place with safety.

I shall after that begin my journey early in the spring for Palæstine, and take such measures, that I may be on mount *Lebanon* in the most suitable season of the year. After that, no place in the Levant remains, which I want to see, except
Con-

Constantinople, from which city I could wish to return again to my native country.

### Cairo, February 18, 1751.

AT the same time, I have the honour to write to you by way of Leghorn, I send addressed to Mr. Grill, a small collection of natural curiosities, of which I have here enclosed a list.

### Seeds of

Cassia fistula from lower Egypt.
Cassia, (Arab. Keschta) from Arabia.
Cassia, (Ar. Sopher) from Upper Egypt.
Nux Behen from Upper Egypt and Sinai.
Cordia Sebesten from Upper Egypt.
Rhamnus, (Ar. Nabk) from Lower Egypt.
Cucumis (Ar. Abdellavi) from Cairo.
Mimosa nilotica. The true Acacia.
Lawsonia spinosa. Alhenna.
Preserved Dates in two large vessels covered with leather.
The Male flower of the Date.
The Web (Tela) covering the basis of the leaves,

### Stones.

*Silex*, a Flint which is opake, and variegated from the deserts of Egypt.
—— semipellucid with a variegated strata. Onyx?
—— semipellucid and unicolor (of one colour) from the deserts of Arabia.
*Melon*, from mount Carmel.
*Argilla*, a sandy clay, which is yearly deposited by the Nile.

### Animals.

Animals.

A Vulture with a naked head, described.
*Ostracion*, a fish with a blown up belly, described.
*Papilio Sultanus*, the Sultan Butterfly.

Miscellaneous Things.

*Vessels made of clay*, hardened by the heat of the sun, for drinking cold liquors, from Mecca and Cairo.

*Opobalsamum genuinum*, or true balsam of Mecca *lbfs*; with Carolus Linnæus wrote in Arabian letters.

THEY are partly for your table, and partly for your Musæum. For the former I have destined two vessels of dates, which I have had prepared in such a manner that I hope they will keep. And I shall esteem myself happy, if you think the other small collections worthy a place in the latter.

I HAVE sent as many seeds, as I have myself been able to collect from the trees themselves. I wish they may come safe, for I see, that it is almost impossible to send trees alive from Egypt to Sweden. I have had all the rare trees here taken up, and planted in pots, in hopes of sending them to you, by way of Marseilles or Leghorn, but they die notwithstanding all imaginable care; what would then become of them during so long a voyage, their freight would be very expensive, for water is a dear commodity when bought of a sailor. The wonderful sycamore, the fructification of which has puzzled me more than any thing I have yet seen in Nature. This, I say, I hope will arrive at Upsala; I have two in readiness that promise well, which I intend to send by way of Marseilles, addressed to Mr. Grill.

I HAVE

I HAVE the honour to send you a description of the *Egyptian vulture,* a fish of the genus of *Ostracion* and a *Moth*; the first I have translated into Swedish from my Latin manuscript, to give it into the Royal Academy of Sciences. If you will favour Counsellor Carleson with the description of the fish, he will perhaps, as a curious gentleman, read it with pleasure.

I HAVE lately been employed in anatomizing a crocodile, of which I shall have the honour to give you an account.

THE parts of the Viscera, which I think deserve the greatest attention in a crocodile, are the *Vesicul. fellea* (Gall bladder) and *Pancreas.* The wise laws of the Creator, which lie concealed in all his works, that man may give himself the trouble to search for them, appear in a particular manner in the parts abovementioned.

IT is well known, that the crocodile is a carnivorous voracious animal, and I believe more so than any other rapacious animal whatever; it cannot chew, but must swallow every thing whole, for though it can open its jaws extremely wide, yet it cannot move them sideways. For such a diet, and this manner of eating, there was certainly occasion for strong menstrua to promote digestion: these it is supplied with, in proportion to its size, more amply than any other animal. A crocodile, which I opened, three foot and a half long, had a gall bladder as big as a hen's egg, which contained three ounces of gall, thick, of a fine emerald green colour, and more bitter than any thing I have yet had on my tongue. The *Pancreas* was five inches long and four broad, and all its plicæ or folds were filled with a yellowish and somewhat frothy liquid. Both appeared to me larger than those

those in an ox, but with respect to the other parts of these animals, they are not to be compared together. His gut, which is quite rigid or stiff, and composed of strong thick membranes, is so narrow, that a small goose-quill can scarcely enter it; it is also remarkable, that the Intestinum rectum is nearest to the pylorus, whereas in other animals it is close to the anus; the crocodile's rectum is filled with excrements, which return the same way they came in, the narrow gut serving only to convey the chyle.

I have now had the pleasure for a month together of seeing the method in which the Egyptians hatch chickens in ovens. Nothing can be more amusing to behold, or easy to perform than this operation, which the ancient Egyptians learned from the crocodile and ostrich. It is pleasant enough to see an oven full of eggs, from whence hop out in a moment many thousand new inhabitants into our world, without a midwife, and I had almost said without a mother; she has at least no concern in bringing them forth. This is so easy to perform, that I am persuaded, every old woman with us might do it in her stove, if she were told it was possible, and a few ounces of superstition was added. They might be done to great advantage with us, and afford in the large towns plenty of so agreeable a dish, as broth made with fowls is, especially if made in the Swedish manner. How much time and trouble does it take to have 6000 chickens hatched in the natural way? And these come forth in Egypt in a month's time, without any farther trouble, except that one person takes care to turn the eggs and heat the oven.

The taste of the fowls so hatched, does not quite equal that of those hatched in the natural way;

way; Art would gain too much on Nature, could it equal her in her perfections. It is reasonable, that the latter should always retain its precedence. The difference is, that the Egyptian fowls hatched in an oven are always more dry, and have not the juice, which gives that agreeable taste to those hatched in the natural way. This difference may likewise be partly owing to the manner in which they are fed, which, considering the number and cheapness of them here, cannot be so proper as in Europe. The Egyptian fowls are fed, as indeed are almost all their poultry, with beans, which are never given to any of these creatures with us, as we must feed them with good corn, if we expect a palatable dish.

They are however good in Egypt, and much better than I imagined, from accounts I had received of them in Europe, and what recommends them, is, the reasonable price, which is scarcely to be found in any other place. I have (besides what I observed in the bringing up of the young ones, myself) received a description of it from Achmia, a little town in Upper Egypt, which is the compleatest, if I am not mistaken, that has as yet been made public. I shall have the honour to communicate it to you at a proper time.

I forgot an observation, when I spoke of the crocodile, which I made for the service of our Divines. I serve them with pleasure, they are my patrons.

Job asks, chap. xli. ver. 1. Canst thou draw out the Leviathan with a hook? I conclude, he means the crocodile by that which happens daily, and without doubt happened at his time in the river Nile, viz. that this voracious animal, far from being drawn up with a hook, bites off, and
destroys

destroys all fishing tackle of this kind, which are thrown out in the river. I found in one that I opened, two hooks which it had swallowed, one sticking in his stomach, and the other in a part of the thick membrane which covers his palate.

How is it possible, that Job could by the Leviathan mean the Whale, as several have explained his term, and as has lately done a French Author, who, in his language, wrote the works of the six days; when we reflect on what Job and David have said of the works of the Creator? How, I say, could he speak of an animal, which never was seen in the place where he wrote, and at a time when he certainly could have no history of Greenland and Spitzbergen? Besides, the whole description of Job comes much nearer the crocodile than the whale, if we consider, that he wrote in a figurative oriental style.

I intend soon to depart from hence for Palæstine, and there enjoy the spring. I have been a sufficient time in Egypt, and thank God, have disposed well of my time in this remarkable country, which ought to be the dwelling of the Gods, if they could take a place amongst mortals; but is condemned, I know not by what turn of fortune, to harbour Egyptians. I beg you will favour me with a few lines, which I could get in Constantinople at our Envoys, Mr. Celsing's house, or in Smyrna, at Consul Rydelius's. I have frequent informations from the latter, of the most material affairs which happen in my native country; but I cannot expect any thing from him but politics: the learned are of more consequence to me, and of these I expect news from your goodness. I should be in particular pleased to hear who succeeded Dr. Wallerius, as Professor extraordinary in in the Faculty of Physicians, after he was appointed Professor of Chemistry. I conjecture, it is one of my companions.

Mr. Rydelius is also very curious, and what is most material, as it happens so seldom, his attention is to Natural History. This is plain from by his collection of birds, which is the best in the Levant, and will in a few days be encreased with divers rare birds from Æthiopia, Nubia, and Arabia; those I find here, I shall send alive to Smyrna, after I have kept them a long time with me, to learn and observe their nature and manner of living, and described them. Amongst these is the beautiful *Guiney hen*, which I have got from Abyssinia, a bird, greatly to be admired for the regular manner in which the feathers are marked, with its crest or comb on the head, and for its shrill creaking voice, which is so piercing, that I thought I felt it affecting me in my very brain, in the same manner, as certain harsh notes on some instruments, strung with wire. It would certainly be admired in Europe, if it had not the misfortune, like the Peacock, to be already common, especially in Malta and France. In time, some of them may come to Sweden, if fortune will favour their journey.

Cyprus, August 8, 1757.

I HAVE now the honour to write from Cyprus, where I arrived a few days ago, having travelled through Judea, part of Arabia Petrea, Samaria, Galilee and great part of Syria.

As there is a vessel going this day for Marseilles, I embrace the opportunity, of shewing my duty to you, by writing this letter, though I have no time to transmit any of my observations. I cannot, however, but mention the Quail of the Israelites;

Israelites; this is a new species of Tetrao, which I found at Jordan, and in the wilderness near the mountains of Arabia Petræa. This Quail, very much resembles the red partridge, but is not larger than a turtle dove. I expect, in a few days, to get a score of them alive, which were promised me by a person at Jerusalem, whither the Arabians carry many thousands to sell at Whitsuntide.

If Natural History can give any information in the interpretation of the Bible, this bird is certainly the same with the Quails of the Israelites, and they alone would deserve a journey to Jordan; for my part, I was so pleased with this discovery, as to forget myself, and almost lost my life, before I could get one of them into my possession.

I shall write more particularly and send to you several observations before I depart from Cyprus.

Smyrna, August 29, 1751.

AFTER I had returned from my travels thro' Egypt and Palæstine, I was in hopes to write to you by this time from Constantinople, to which place I had already began my journey from Syria; but Heaven, which has this year poured over that place all the plagues, which its wrath had in store, has for a time prevented my design of visiting that city.

For these three months past there has been a plague in Constantinople, which sometimes has taken off 10 or 12,000 souls a day: a fire which lasted for twenty four hours, and reduced to ashes many thousand houses, and amongst others, the Guard-house of the Janissaries: an earthquake, attended by a storm of hail, which destroyed, by common report, 40,000 boats, and killed a number

ber of the rowers: an infurrection amongſt the foldiers, which threatens the fubverfion of the government, nor is famine wanting to complete their miferies. Thefe are fufficient reafons to deter a traveller from going thither; but as foon as I am informed, that the Almighty has withdrawn the rod, which he has extended over that city, I purpofe vifiting it, and feeing what natural curiofities this famous place, which is fituated between two feas, affords; and afterwards, pleafe God, I fhall think of returning home.

Inclosed, I have the honour to tranfmit you a defcription of the little Arabian Quail, which I found near Jordan. I imagine, this bird to be new, and not before defcribed. If the Writers on the fcripture can prove, that *Selaw* was a bird, they may be affured, that it was no other than this; but I have reafon to believe, that the food in queftion of the Ifraelites, was neither bird nor fifh, but rather infects, and moft probably locufts.

It is not in the leaſt probable, that *Selaw* was the flying fifh; how fhould the flying fifh, that fcarce lifts itfelf a few yards above the furface of the fea, and that only at fun-fet, come up into Arabia Petræa, and in fuch numbers, as to fupply the whole camp of the Ifraelites? If I fhould even perfuade myfelf, that the Mediteranean, at that time, came up to the walls of Jericho, which is now three days journey diftant, yet I could not give credit to it.

St. John's locufts, thofe fo often difputed locufts, come now at length in queftion. I have the honour to fend a collection of all the obfervations I could get relating to this affair, which I have

digefted

digested in order, to be inserted in the transactions of the Royal Academy of Sciences.

I shall leave Writers on the scriptures the liberty to make what they please of St. John's ἀκρίδες, calling them the Gemmæ or buds of different kinds of trees, according to the old Grecian Father Isiodorus Pelusiota; the fruit of the Crab-tree, according to some Interpreters; or birds, as some Calvinists imagined; but it is certain that this hypothesis is such, that Ælianus, Thucydides, Demosthenes or Aristotle, could never know their meaning. I am of opinion, that if any Interpreter of the scriptures should assert, that the ἀκρίδες of St. John are not locusts, and draw this conclusion, that *St. John did not eat locusts, because they have never been eaten by any nation*; he ought to make a pilgrimage to those places where they are eat at this day; I am persuaded he would not long remain an unbeliever in this matter.

Before I quit this subject of locusts, I will impart to you some observations I have made on these insects, which for several years have afforded so much matter for dispute in Europe, that it is become well worth our attention to set this affair in a clear light.

(1.) The grashopper or locust is not formed for travelling over the sea; I had an opportunity of observing this on my return from Cyprus to Smyrna. As we were becalmed for some days on the coast of Carmania, we daily got some grashoppers on board from the continent, and I then had the pleasure of seeing what miserable sailors these insects are. The locust has, like the lark, a quality from Nature, that it it cannot fly far, but must alight almost as soon as it rises. If they intend, I know not by what instinct, to fly over a sea

or

or river, they find their attempt succeed no better than the lark, of which I believe I have given you an instance before, which I observed on the Spanish coast, where I saw how miserably this bird perished, when it intended to come on board us. I saw the same happen to the locusts, and for one that came on board, 100 were certainly drowned, though we were but a pistol-shot from the shore. But better proofs of this are yearly seen at Smyrna, when they attempt to fly across the sea, after they over-run the country near it. We observe in the months of May and June, a number of these insects coming from the south, directing their course to the northern shore; they darken the sky like a thick cloud, but scarcely have they quitted the shore, before they, who a moment before ravaged and ruined the country, cover the surface of the sea with their dead bodies, which occasions a great nuisance to the Franks, who have their balconies near the harbour, on account of the stench which proceeds from such a number of dead insects, as they are by the winds driven close to the very houses. By what instinct do these creatures undertake this dangerous flight? Is it not the wise institution of the Creator, to destroy a dreadful plague to the country? Has the like destruction to the locusts been observed during their flight to Europe for several years past? Could they not by fright, or some other method, be turned from their dreadful course, to steer for some river, and by that means be obliged to destroy themselves, as they cannot be overcome by any other means?

(2.) But if locusts cannot fly over a sea of any extent, how could they come from the continent to Cyprus, which is entirely destroyed by Turks and locusts? Could they not at least come in vessels from the continent of Syria, having lain concealed during the voyage? But how then came they to Roslagia, as you were pleased to shew me before my departure from Upsala? Could it be done in any other manner but by ships from Dantzick, or some place adjacent, where they infested the country that summer? Would it not therefore be proper, that all masters of ships should be obliged to take care, lest they bring over such a destructive vermin? This ought to be done in the same strict manner, as is now practised to prevent the plague from spreading.

(3.) I know of no one Europe who has made sufficient observations, relating to the migration of locusts: of the place from whence they first set out, and of the course they take. I have had an opportunity of making the following in Asia and Africa.

The locusts, according to all appearance, seem to be directed by the same natural instinct as the Alpine rat (*Mus Lemmus, Lin.*) in a direct meridian line, by keeping nearly from south to north, as the other does from north to south, turning very little either to the east or west; they come from the desarts of Arabia, take their course over thro' Palæstine, Syria, Carmania, Natolia, go sometimes through Bythinia by Constantinople, and continue their journey through Poland, &c. as has happened in these latter years. They never turn from their course, for example, to the west, wherefore Egypt is not visited by them, though so near their usual track. The locusts therefore, are not to be reckoned amongst this country's plagues in our times, as they were when Moses lived there, tho' frogs, lice, cock-roaches, gnats, and all the vermin, which are mentioned amongst the

the plagues of Pharoah, torment the inhabitants and travellers in this country to this very day. Neither do they turn to the east, for I never heard that Mesopotamia, or the confines of the Euphrates, were ravaged by them. None but those countries of Asia which I mentioned, viz. Arabia, Palæstine, Syria, Carmania, and sometimes the sea coasts of Natolia, are infested with them yearly, either more or less.

I do not know whether the same generation of locusts which comes from Arabia can come to Europe, or whether it is the second or third generation. It might easily be known, if observations were made in two different places, when they are at either of them; and perhaps that would be to some purpose, as it might furnish means to destroy them, or at least, lessen their number.

The inhabitants of Asia, as well as Europe, sometimes take the field against locusts with all the dreadful apparatus of war.. The Bashaw of Tripoli in Syria, some years ago, raised 4000 soldiers against these insects, and ordered those to be hanged who refused to go. Thus a miserable insect, can put in motion an army of stubborn Turks, whom often an Ottoman Emperor with all his power cannot oblige to go farther than they chuse.

Smyrna, Sept. 13, 1751.

I Shall soon have the honour to send you a number of observations, which I made on the Natural History of the Bible, on my travels in Palæstine. I have been particularly sollicitous to search for the great designs which King Solomon executed here, especially those that contained any of the vegetable kingdom; whether I could find any traces of his vineyards or gardens, of which he speaks in the Scriptures; for to attempt to illustrate that kind of Botany, which Solomon understood, I think is the same as to look for the place where the Tower of Babylon stood; though it cannot be denied, but that Solomon knew much more of Natural History, considering the time and circumstances of the nation, over which he reigned, than any other of those times. But to leave his Botany, and return to his plantations; there is now not the least trace remaining of them; we can judge by certain circumstances, where one or other of his pleasure gardens was situated; thus have I found the situation of his vineyard in *Engedda*, in which he introduced vines from *Cyprus*, to which he compares his beauty, in his Canticles, ch. i. ver. 14. Here the Arabs have vineyards to this day, and sell the wine to the Christians; but the vines are now so degenerated, that they will not produce the rich Cyprus wine. It was not difficult for Solomon to get vines from Cyprus and plant them, but whence did he get the Rhenish vines, which he planted at Hebron, and which grow there to this day, affording a Rhenish wine, equal to any, that Europe produces, which I, and all the Franks who came to Jerusalem, took be real Rhenish wine; the Latin Monks, buy from the Arabs the small quantity, which they make yearly at Hebron. This kind of wine does not grow in any place of the East, nor in the Archipelago; perhaps this kind of grape has always grown wild in Palæstine, and was by Solomon transplanted into his garden. Might not the Europeans have got the first vines from hence, which they planted on the Rhine? This seems more probable, than that Solomon should have got his

his from Europe; it is also possible, that both have the same qualities, though the vines are of different origins.

Smyrna, Sept. 22, 1751.

IN my last, of the 13th instant, I promised to answer the questions, you were pleased to propose to me, in your letter dated the 11th of Dec. 1750. I shall now fulfil my duty, having answered some in my preceding letters.

I HAD no opportunity of seeing the Gall-nuts of the Tamarisk; I have, however, seen a little *Aphis*, that builds a nest between its leaves, but this I cannot take to be a Gall.

*Calaf*, is a little Willow, which never grows to a large tree; it has a strait trunk, with a smooth oval lancet-shaped leaf, deeply sawed on the edges. No tree in Egypt is more famous amongst the inhabitants, on account of the water that is distilled in the spring from its blossoms, which is much more used as a family medicine by the Egyptians, than treacle by our peasants. They are scarcely afflicted with any disease, but they use the water of Calaf. There are Apothecaries in Cairo, whose chief, and almost only employment, is to sell Calaf; for thus they likewise call the water. It is cooling, promotes perspiration, and is somewhat cordial, it therefore serves in the continual fevers, which are so common in Egypt, during the summer seasons. I suppose it to approach nearest in quality to the waters that are in Europe distilled from the blossoms of Cherries, Limes, and Acacias.

I HAVE got enough of the fruit of *Babobab*, though I could neither see the plant or flower, as it only grows in the remotest parts of Upper Egypt, where it has been introduced from the western parts of Africa.

I HERE

I HERE send inclosed, the flowers of Æschynomene Sesban (bastard sensitive plant) which is used for hedges round plantations, and affords an agreeable prospect.

*Absus*, is a Cassia. *Sopher*, is likewise a Cassia, of which I transmitted seeds, and in my last letter the description, together with that of the wild Marjoram or *Zatarbendi* of Alpinus.

*Kali* III, of Alpinus, must be a little fig marigold (Mesembryenthemum) common in Egypt; but it is somewhat difficult to clear up the names of Alpinus, especially all his *Kali*. I transmitted the seeds of the Alhenna, amongst my collection of last winter, and the seeds of the Plantain-tree, were in my last letter; and the Gall fly of the Scripture Sycamore, in my last but one. I have the jumping Mouse, in spirits of wine, and all the Egyptian fishes, of which I have some preserved and laid on paper, in the manner you taught me.

*Moses* and *Lichens* are scarce enough, though not entirely wanting in the East. The *Pyramids*, the oldest buildings in the world, have no *Lichenes crustacei*, which otherwise are the common marks of age; neither can they have them, for perhaps there never fell a drop of rain on them, without which, this kind of vegetable does not thrive. All the kinds are to be found on the old walls of Jerusalem; and out of the wall at Solomon's Well, there grows a little moss; may not this be his Hysop? It is, at least, as little, as the cedar is large, and therefore the other extremity.

IT is not long since I sent you the description of the Egyptian Water lily (Nymphæa).

I HAVE described the wonderful little Crab, the *Cancer cursor*; but who can conceive, why this little animal comes up in such large numbers out of the sea at sun-set, and runs on the shore; and why the *Dolphins* and *Flying-fish*, at the same time, lift themselves above the surface of the sea? It is probable, that each of them has some urgent reason, which, at present, we do not comprehend. As I was travelling from Tyre to Sidon, I followed the sea-shore for two hours about sun-set, and had constantly the pleasure to see this little crab run by hundreds to and from the sea. I caught several, in order to see whether I could find any thing about them to carry food, but found nothing. No creature can run so fast, in proportion, as this. The moment one sees it two or three yards from the sea, you observe it to turn back and return into it.

You were pleased to ask, how do the plants subsist in Egypt half a year without rain? This seems very odd to us in Europe, where we are used more to wet than dry weather; but what shall one think, when I say, that there are plants in Egypt, which have lived 600 years, and perhaps have not got 6 ounces of rain, in all that time, for nourishment; this may with reason be said of the old Sycamores round Cairo and in Upper Egypt, where perhaps, every second or third year, fall ten drops of rain. But if the Egyptian plants want rain, they do not therefore want water. The Nile, the wonderful Nile, singular in its kind, affords that, which heaven denied them. The country of Egypt is a river from the beginning of August to the latter end of October. A traveller coming to Egypt at this time, and being unacquainted with the true reason for the overflowing of the water, would immediately consider it as a miracle in Nature. He would imagine he beheld a sea; producing vegetables very different from Sar-

gazo,

gazo, Fucus's Reeds, Rushes, &c. He would imagine he beheld, springing from the bottom of the sea, Sycamores, Buckthorn, Acacia, Cassias, Willows, and Tamarisks, which form small woods or groves, above the surface of the water. This is the genuine appearance of Egypt, whilst it is overflown. Therefore the Egyptian plants, which consist chiefly of evergreen trees, are in no want of water, and art supplies those which are deprived of this benefit of Nature; for the Egyptians are very expert in hydraulics, and take great care to supply their gardens with water.

From this time, to the beginning of April, another season succeeds, the water is dried away, and the whole country is covered with slime or mud, deposited by the water, which makes Egypt a fruit-country. The husbandman then sows his corn with less sweat, and more assurance of a plentiful crop, than the Europeans; this work is done in the months of October and November; then come forth the spontaneous plants of Egypt, which are very few, some indeed come up with the corn, but their seeds must have been transported thither by the birds, as they are European. The trees then cast their leaves, that is to say, in the latter end of December and beginning of January, having young leaves ready, before all the old ones are fallen off; and, to forward this operation of Nature, few of the trees have buds (gemmæ); the Sycamore and Willows indeed have some, but with few and quite loose stipulæ. Nature did not imagine buds so necessary in the southern as in the northern countries; this occasions a great difference between them.

The Plantain and Date tree, the riches and ornament of Egypt, also at this time prepare to bring

bring forth their valuable fruit. After the latter has thrown off the lowermost old leaves, the new ones shoot out from the top, and at the same time the new *Spathæ* come forth in the months of December and January; at this period also, the branches of flowers of the Plantain-tree appear.

THIS season concludes with the harvest, in the month of April, and no signs are afterwards to be seen of Egypt's having stood under water the preceding year.

EGYPT is not absolutely destitute of rain in the months of November, December, January, February and March; but it must be particularly observed, that this does not extend farther than to the side nearer the Mediterranean sea; where it rains so hard some years, especially at Alexandria, Rosetta and Damiata, as to occasion very cold weather, to the great inconvenience of the inhabitants; it sometimes happens at Cairo, about this time, that a scattered cloud lets fall a few drops of rain in passing. This has been scarcely observed by any traveller, therefore they have no true idea of the Egyptian climate in Europe; some saying it rains there, others asserting the contrary, and both are in the right. After harvest, and with the month of May, begins a dreadful season in Egypt, a summer, which makes the earth resemble, in some respect, that of Norland in the months of January and February. Then the earth appears full of fissures, and, by the excessive heat, is brought into the same situation, that the severest frosts occasion with us, but with this difference, that the ruggedness of our frozen earth, is concealed by an useful and not disagreeable snow, whereas the parched earth of Egypt has no veil to hide its
misery,

misery, the sight of which every mortal dreads to behold.

EGYPT, two months before, well deserved a journey from the north and south pole. According to the accounts of some travellers, with whom I have conversed on the subject, and who had seen both the Indies, all Europe, the greatest part of Asia, and the accessible parts of Africa, there is not such a glorious prospect to be seen under the sun, as an Egyptian field, when the earth is in its verdure, and especially if it can be beheld at that same time and from the same place which I saw it, namely, the latter part of December, from the top of the highest Pyramid, where I was in company with some Englishmen, several of whom had travelled in the East, others in the West Indies, in Barbary, and in Europe.

EGYPT, which is so agreeable in our winter, is thus, to the highest degree, horrible in our summer. The birds desert it, and fly to more northern climes. The vegetable kingdom is in no better situation. The spontaneous plants are withered, and those they cultivate are removed; the Rest-harrow and Succory alone remain; of the former, these flower in the strongest heat, and amongst the latter, the banks of the Nile are covered with all kinds of Melons, Cucumbers, and oily grain (Sesamum) which ripens in the fields, where it is sown after the corn; and this, I presume, is the reason, that some travellers speak of two and three harvests in Egypt.

ALL Egypt however does not suffer alike from the heat of the summer. The rising grounds about Rosetta and Damiata are to be excepted, being at this time covered with Rice, which is planted in May, and harvested in October, to effect which,

the

the water is carried with much labour from the Nile. The inhabitants of these places have therefore the pleasure of beholding green fields, when the Egyptians see nothing but a parched earth; but they pay dear for their pleasure, for all the plagues of Pharaoh, frogs, flies, gnats, &c. which delight in putrid water and a moist earth, make their dwellings almost uninhabitable.

It is in this excessive hot weather, that we must admire the wisdom of God, who ordered that a quantity of *Dew* should fall in the evenings and mornings, and prevent the total destruction of the country.

This *Dew* is particularly serviceable to the trees, which would otherwise never be able to resist this heat; but with this assistance they thrive well, blossom and ripen their fruit. Therefore, the upper parts of the Egyptian trees, at one time of the year, do the office of roots, attracting nourishment by their absorbent vessels, the leaves, from the moist air; which the root, at other seasons of the year, draws from the damp earth. It is farther to be observed, that the dew falls at the same time, that the heavy clouds move from the north to south; and by the number of these, the Egyptians judge of the future affluence of the Nile. These darken the Heavens in the morning; but in the day it clears up, and the nights are as resplendent with as many stars, in the midst of summer, as the lightest and clearest winter nights in the north; this appearance of the skies in Egypt never changes, and has been, undoubtedly, a great inducement for the ancient Egyptians, and afterwards for the Egyptian Arabs, to study astronomy. I am surprized, that none of the European Academies of Sciences, have ever thought of supporting

porting an Astronomer in Cairo, which is favoured with the sereneſt horizon, a conſtant mild climate and clear ſky; and theſe would, I imagine, afford opportunities for eaſy and conſtant obſervations. He might, perhaps, have ſome trouble from the inhabitants, on account of their ſuperſtition, but even this, he might ſoon get over. He would find learned Arabs, powerful men, who love and ſtudy Aſtronomy in their manner, whoſe protection would defend him from the people, and the expence would not be very great.

The E N D.

www.ingramcontent.com/pod-product-compliance
Lightning Source LLC
Chambersburg PA
CBHW020105020526
44112CB00033B/937